PIETY VERSUS MORALISM

PIETY VERSUS MORALISM

THE PASSING OF THE NEW ENGLAND THEOLOGY

BY

JOSEPH HAROUTUNIAN

ARCHON BOOKS
Hamden, Connecticut
1964

Originally
STUDIES IN RELIGION AND CULTURE
American Religion Series IV

COPYRIGHT, 1932, BY HENRY HOLT AND COMPANY, INC.
REPRINTED 1964, IN AN UNALTERED AND UNABRIDGED EDITION
BY ARRANGEMENT WITH HOLT, RINEHART, AND WINSTON, INC.

LIBRARY OF CONGRESS CATALOG CARD NUMBER: 64-24715
PRINTED IN THE UNITED STATES OF AMERICA

To

MY PARENTS

ACKNOWLEDGMENTS

I wish to acknowledge my indebtedness to Professor Herbert W. Schneider of Columbia University for his constant and invaluable help in the preparation of this volume. To Professor William Walker Rockwell of Union Theological Seminary in New York City, I am indebted for his careful reading of the manuscript and many important suggestions. I must also express my appreciation of the facilities afforded by the Library of Union Theological Seminary. I am grateful to the several members of the Department of Philosophy, Columbia University, and those of the Department of the Philosophy of Religion, Union Theological Seminary, for their criticisms and advice which contributed to the improvement of this book.

It must be added that for deficiencies contained in this volume the author is solely responsible.

J. H.

New York, N. Y.
February, 1932.

CONTENTS

PRELUDE

THE decline of Calvinism is the belated rendering of the great cultural transformations which separate the modern world from the ancient and medieval. With the passing of the medieval culture passed the medieval mind, though its thought-patterns persisted long enough to annoy another culture. The ideas of a culture often survive their historic occasions, and become components of new structures; but they thereby change their minds.

In medieval society Christianity was a living religion. Of course, the Christianity of Christ has never been too much at home in this world. The kingdom of heaven is as yet in heaven, and mankind remains true to its Adamic origins. However, the outline of the Christian scheme of salvation, the attitudes and mentality which it represents, was accepted in the premodern periods of European history as a true and plausible account of things ultimate. There was a certain congruity between the medieval mind and the inherited Christian faith, a congruity which disappeared with the rise of modern culture.

The idea of the transcendent excellence and power of God, His government of the world and control of the destinies of men, which was essential to the Christian scheme of salvation, was congenial to the minds of men who lived in a society wherein distinctions of power and dignity, of authority and privilege, were well accepted facts. The longing of the medieval mind was for order and peace, and not for equality and progress. When the organic

conception of society was basic to political theory and
ideal, and the good of the community, often confused with
the good of those on top, was primary in considerations of
justice, no serious objection could be raised to the ways
of a deity who disposed of the fate of men according to
the scrutable and inscrutable dictates of His wisdom, towards ends which transcended the present or future bliss
of any given individual. The dependence of man on God,
for his life, preservation, and salvation, was an idea acceptable to men who preferred well-being to independence,
social regulation to self-love, security to prosperity.   In
ages when men were not quite so conscious of their excellences and happy moral state as the modern regard for
self-respect has taught the wise and the foolish to be, men
found it not hard to accept their need of salvation, and to
depend upon the grace of God for it; nor did they conceive it improbable that their moral, as well as physical, state should lead them to the gates of hell.   Therefore, the Christian scheme of salvation met the intellectual and moral approval of the times, and the institution
which protected it against contamination and neglect became a power in the world.

When one considers the stratification of medieval society into levels of privilege and dignity, the primacy of
the group as the object of rational benevolence, the principle of mutual obligation as definitive of economic or-
ganization, and the phenomena of undisciplined warfare,
it is not hard to see how the spiritual fruits of such a social
pattern in the affections of the people appear as humility,
gratitude, homage and reverence, the feelings of dependence and grace, of privilege and duty.

In such a cultural setting, the orthodox "scheme of

salvation" appears as a heavenly counterpart of daily experience, embodying the variations which reflection and imagination weave into the relatively colorless matrix of social relations. God, who created and owned and governed the whole world, was great and high as no earthly ruler could be, more powerful than any lord, more benevolent than any giver of gifts, more glorious than any king. If the vassal is a humbler being than his lord, how much more is man a being humbler than God! If the serf is ever indebted to his lord, how much more is man under an obligation to serve the Lord of heaven and earth, to rejoice and be grateful for the gracious mercies of God! A vassal can repay his lord, but how can he ever repay the Giver of life? It were impossible for man to be justified in the sight of God, were it not that the Son of God, in a way "very God," has offered Himself as the payment for man's debt to God. He redeemed men through the payment of their debt, He saved them by becoming their ransom price. He appeased the righteous wrath of the Deity, and procured forgiveness. As the lords saved their captive subordinates, so the Lord saved men from the bondage of the devil.

Theological imagination, when occupied in significant thinking, is the unfolding of genuine relationships. Reflection upon the wisdom, the power, the goodness, and the glory of God; upon God's relation to the events of life, and the manner of His government and influence; attempts at comprehensiveness and consistency,—produced theologies which were often formidable, and sometimes repellent. And yet they were normal to the life of the age, and as such they shared the general structure of the culture from which they emerged. To the medieval mind,

theology was philosophy: an attempt at a consistent and
intelligible statement of experience. It was organic with
the facts of life, a religious interpretation of normal human
relations. However, such a statement is almost a perversion of the truth. It is the secularized modern who must
speak of the "religious interpretation of life." The religious world of the medieval man was the world in which
he lived. It was one piece with his social and natural life.
Wherefore, medieval religion is stamped with a mark of
sincerity which may inspire the sympathetic modern to a
certain approbation; while, nevertheless, it defies imitation
and appropriation.

In the religion of Calvin, the Christian "scheme of salvation" was restated in its most rigorous form, that of
St. Augustine. Calvin's theology was a reclamation of
Christian truths which had become obscured by the
Church's worldly politics and patronage of the pagan
Renaissance. When regarded as a protest against Rome,
and not as representing the spirit of the modern age then
in the making, its true import and character become clear.
The union of Calvinism with the commercial forces of the
time was a wedlock of incompatibles, effected by their
common enmity to the established order. When the crises
of the struggles of medieval and modern forces had
passed, Calvinism started a long process of decline.

But in its early years, Calvinism gave men a significant
practical theology. It supplied the new society with a
church. It comforted men in their sufferings under perse-
cution. It gave them freedom to work out their earthly
salvation, while God was left to take care of election to
either heaven or hell. It made room for the new morality

of an acquisitive society, and allowed men to worship God on Sabbath and to serve Him by helping themselves. Thus it was that although the Calvinistic theology was not built upon the pattern of the new society, the use or misuse to which it was put by Calvinist moderns made it a social power.

The looseness of the union between the theology of Calvinism and the principles regulating the life of the new society led to its disruption and the emergence of a religion more in line with the spirit of the age. The troubles of Calvinism began in Geneva, and reappeared wherever commercialism had already molded the form of the life of a city or a people. The explanation of the decline of Calvinism is seen in the divorce of the modern everyday life of the middle classes from their ancient, Augustinian philosophy.

With the coming of science, the Renaissance humanism, the discovery of new lands and the growth of commercial enterprise, the middle-class Calvinists emerged into modern society. Independent merchants or farmers replaced the lord and his underlings. The riches of the world became the private property of individuals, who indulged in profitable exchange and erected vast machineries of credit and banking. Such men began to demand the protection of their *rights* as owners, freedom to accumulate wealth and to keep their rightful earnings. The end of government, in peace and in war, became to insure the rights and the "lawful liberties" of aggregates of free individuals, to enact laws and enforce them, so as to further the happiness and the prosperity of the people, especially the owners of things.

The quality of mind which grew out of such a social

pattern had for its dominant traits the principles of the freedom of individuals, their right to happiness, their right to seek their own ends, for their own success and prosperity, in so far as they did not impede others from being similarly occupied. The greatest happiness of the greatest number became a basic principle of social and economic theory, and the autonomy and intrinsic value of individuals, the foundation of social justice and public law.

The new society's conscience dictated its own commands. Prosperous merchants have to be thrifty, industrious, dogged, sober, dependable, and decently selfish. They have to recognize their own responsibility for their success and their failures, their own powers to earn and to control wealth, their innate endowments waiting for use and expansion. They have to realize that other men are similarly, perchance identically, constituted, wherefore they have a right to exercise their own powers and virtues, for their own success and prosperity. They have to respect others, to treat them as persons, or as ends unto themselves. In a word, they must be *moral*.

It is hard for the modern moral philosopher to appreciate that his "first principles" are not essential to the "nature of things." The categories of moral theory, as the modern understands them, the free-contracts of autonomous persons, conscious and dutiful reciprocity, and the like, have a quality or flavor peculiar to the moral consciousness of an individualistic and enterprising society.

The temper of modern religion, as disclosed in the writings of the English Deists and the champions of "liberal Christianity," is that of modern secular morality. That God is the "moral Governor" of the world, that the relationship between God and man should be of the nature of "personal relationship," that God has given man a "free-will," and thus made him a "moral agent," thereby restricting His private power; that He purposes nothing that is not conducive to the happiness of man; that men have an innate capacity for the good, that they have infinite possibilities for moral perfection, that they can and must co-operate with God to bring about the actualization of God's intended "moral kingdom"; that Jesus made human salvation possible through His revelation of the good life, that men ought to try to imitate Him; that sin consists in moral delinquency, and salvation, in the progressive achievement of a good life and the building up of moral personality, which is to be followed by the reward of the blessings of heaven, the abode of all good dead men;— the spirit of such religion is the spirit of modern morality, and not less secular for being a theory of things ultimate. It was a new Christianity which the modern world created, fundamentally alien to medieval Christianity, both Roman Catholic and Protestant. The Protestant Reformation, compared with the "rise of modern religious ideas," was a negligible theological performance.

When placed in such a setting, the judgment of Calvinism pronounced by William Ellery Channing rings with significance and persuasive power.

"Calvinism, we are persuaded, is giving place to better views. It has passed its meridian, and is sinking to rise no more. It has to contend with foes more powerful than theologians; with foes from whom it cannot shield itself in mystery and metaphysical subtleties,—we mean the progress of the human mind, and the progress of the spirit of the gospel. Society is going forward in intelligence and charity, and of course is leaving the theology of the sixteenth century behind it. We hail this revolution of opinions as a most auspicious event to the Christian cause."

Whatever the merits of this statement in regard to Calvinism in general, Channing was right in regarding the New England Calvinism of his day as a cultural anachronism. And there is much justice in making the social value of a theology the measure of its adequacy. The sociological approach to the problems of the intellect is plausible in so far as society determines the minds of its members almost completely. Reflection proceeds along lines of valuation growing out of social experience and uses conceptual instruments which fit the facts and the practices of a social group. A good citizen is one who has identified his spirit with the spirit of his city; and most men are good citizens. Most men achieve happiness by limiting their minds to the pattern of their social environment. "Philosophical" problems, matters dealing with permanent relations belonging to the texture of man's primeval experience, which lie hidden under the flux of cultures, are derided as theoretical and put aside as worthless for practical living, which they often are. What is meant by practical life is social life, and practice follows reasons other than "pure reason." Such is the power of social fact that it is common to men to consider their practical life as the measure of theoretical truth, and to construe the mind of their society as indicative of the more permanent natures of things.

It is harder for theologians than for philosophers to transcend social fact. A church which aims to serve multitudes follows the dictates of practical reason. It "reinterprets" its message continuously and proclaims a gospel which is of immediate social significance. It clothes things

temporal with the garb of eternity and transforms rela-
tives into absolutes. It assumes the function of inspiring
people to be useful men and helps the perpetuation of
group forces by appropriating their ends and enhancing
their progress. No church is free from such responsibility,
and few dare shirk it. There always are more priests
than prophets.

Having lost its social basis, Christianity tried to manu-
facture a modern equivalent. It absorbed the moralism
of the new age, and drenched its theology with humanism.
The consequence was a theology which succeeded merely
in becoming a "legalistic" and "dialectical" superstructure
in a practically alien world. Medieval theology could
have been saved only through a metaphorical and poetical
translation of its doctrines. The truths contained in it,
in so far as they transcended the peculiarities of medieval
culture and sank deep into the nature of things, could have
been saved through their assumption of an allegorical significance. For mystical language is relevant to those
depths of personal experience which defy expression
through the institutions of any given culture. The Calvinist moderns, through their appeal to "reason and common sense," failed to conserve and preach verities concerning man's place in nature which were not congenial to the
spirit of modern culture. For the reason of the new age
was in the service of its own peculiar passions, making
the reason of another age appear unreasonable. What was
rational to medieval society became "mystery" and "mysticism" to modern minds. Therefore, in repudiating
"mysticism" the Calvinists repudiated the only chance
they had of giving meaning to their theology. They in-

sisted on taking it literally. They thought they could make "science" out of it.

The consequences of the application of the categories of modern science and morality to Calvinistic theology were invariably disastrous. Metaphysical and unimaginative rationalism was in no position to vindicate the theology of a socially dead religion. Salvation became a good life to be followed by the happiness of heaven. Sin against God became metaphysical responsibility. Belief in human depravity came to rest upon a consummate (though empirically unverifiable) cynicism concerning the moral state of men, and regeneration became invisible. Predestination became *pre*destination, and election was no longer eternal but in time. The atonement of Christ was now a performance in high magic. The Holy Trinity, divine agency, the divine origin of the scriptures,—became standing *meta*physical puzzles. When believed as "facts," they were either meaningless or irrational. To render them intelligible was impossible. No matter how dialectical Calvinism became, it could not be made reasonable. Metaphysics breeds upon the remains of dead religion.

In the year 1729, when Jonathan Edwards became full pastor of the church at Northampton, Mass., New England religion had already undergone a long process of decline. The theocratic ideal of the first settlers was disappearing, Calvinistic theology had become largely a matter of formality, and worldliness had been growing among the people. Calvinistic Christianity was being buried under a heavy coating of political and economic facts which had little relevance to its theology. It was not being effectively disputed, nor was it being openly discarded. It was

simply being ignored as a matter of little consequence for
practical living, by men who said one thing and did another. New England was becoming involved in the ways
of the Old World, striving for commercial success, com-
peting for profits, tasting power and assuming rights,
ready to defend them legally or otherwise. The spirit of
European nationalism, capitalism, and rationalism, with
its apparatus of political and legal theory, was already
growing strong. The theocentric piety of Calvinism
seemed doomed.

Edwards revitalized religion for at least a part of New
England. For him religion was independent of the problems of social morality and civil government. He ignored
the social principles in the Calvinistic idea of theocracy,
and made Calvinistic piety a matter which concerned primarily the relation of the individual soul to God. Edwards put the theology of Calvinism upon the basis of
an empirical piety, and defended its doctrines philosophi-
cally and rationally. He reinterpreted Calvinism as a religious philosophy of nature, and reasserted its doctrines
in view of the facts of life as well as on scriptural foundations. Calvinistic theology was thus separated from its temporary social and political aspects, and restated as a religion
of permanent human significance.

The Edwardean Theology is a chapter in man's quest
for truth and the good life. It was a fresh attempt to
come into right relations with the world, to understand experience, and to govern life accordingly. It was inspired
by a piety induced by the course of events, and derived its
rational justification from insights into the logic of experience. It had a wisdom peculiar to its piety, which never-

theless is of permanent human appeal, because it typifies truths which belong to enduring structures of reality.

Thus Edwards gave New England Christianity a new and powerful impulse, which continued to be felt for almost a century. But the weakening of this impulse began immediately after he had done his work. His disciples and later champions lacked either his profound piety, or his intellectual vigor, or both. They reverted to governmental and legalistic conceptions of Calvinism, and under the influence of new political and humanitarian principles, modified Edwards' theology, subtly, variously, and greatly. This process culminated in the work of Nathaniel W. Taylor of Yale College, based upon a morality and philosophy profoundly other than those which motivated the theology of Edwards. After Taylor, the New England Theology adopted the style set by him, and became progressively "liberal."

As seen from the perspective of the theology of Edwards, the history of the New England Theology is the history of a degradation. It declined because its theocentric character, its supreme regard for the glory of God and His sovereignty over man, made it ill-fitted to give expression to the ideals of the eighteenth century New England and to meet its immediate social needs. The social and political forces of the time gave rise to principles which were either inimical or irrelevant to the spirit of the Edwardean theology.

The historians of the New England Theology have usually presented it as a minor chapter in the history of Christian theology. They have studied it from a strictly theological point of view, in the light of their own theological opinions, and have sought to criticize it by pointing out philosophical misconceptions and logical errors. The consequences of such treatments have been that the purport of the New England Theology has been misunderstood or overlooked, the causes of its passing have been misjudged, and its significance lost in doctrinal discussions and criticisms in terms of debatable philosophical issues. An important instance of this is Frank Hugh Foster's *A Genetic History of the New England Theology* (1907), the only comprehensive treatise written on the subject, and valuable as a guide to the major sources. It is an erudite and carefully prepared book. However, the author's own aggressive belief in a certain theory of the "freedom of the will," evidently suggested by N. W. Taylor and E. A. Park, has prevented him from doing justice to the Edwardean Theology. The Edwardean doctrines are presented in their relations to his psychology of the will, and criticized as inadequate or pernicious to the extent that they ignore or seem to vitiate this psychology. This is unfortunate, because the chief aim of the Edwardean Theology was not to formulate a theory of the will; it was inspired by a piety which sought to glorify God and His sovereignty over man. On the other hand, it asserted human responsibility, and sought to reconcile it with its theocentric piety. The task of holding fast to both divine sovereignty and the need of human effort was of course a delicate matter, and many Edwardeans were wrecked on the horns of the old dilemma. However, this difficulty was neither the only nor the chief cause of their ultimate failure to make their theology acceptable to their opponents. It was merely a symptom of profound and practically significant discrepancies between the Edwardean piety and social philosophy in the eighteenth century New England. To understand the passing of Edwardeanism, one must keep in sight the connections between things and ideas. He must be aware of those powerful cultural forces which often lead men to discard ideas which they may not have properly disproved.

It is hoped that, presenting the subject in such a light, the present essay will help toward a new understanding of Edwardeanism; and that it also will serve as an illustration of that perennial conflict between theocentric piety and humanitarian morality which is a problem to-day as it was in the eighteenth century.

There are stable and elemental realities underlying the pattern of any culture which survive its process and recur in others. When the superficial enthusiasms of an age subside, the human mind returns to a just view of its traits, and forgotten truths reappear to strike a balance. A culture can create a spirit, but it cannot always destroy it. A spirit may abdicate, and return to heaven; therefore people say that it is dead. But spirits never really die. When the world gets tired of the tyranny of new favorites, and cries for help, old ones return to shed new light, and there is progress. There are some spirits whom no amount of neglect will ever induce to leave the world. They belong to the "nature of things," the people's good sense. They often go into hiding, but they continue to annoy. People seldom give them a full ear, and always refuse to allow them a full triumph. However, in the long run, Nature has its own way; it either makes people wise, or it kills them.

Whereas the language of Calvinism is in disrepute, the elements of good sense in Calvinism must always remain wherever there is good sense. Piety is not dead. So long as men refuse to shut their eyes to the world, so long as they recognize their connection with and their dependence upon a world which supports them and often ignores their personal welfare, so long as they find happiness in self-denial and a love which grows out of wisdom, so long as their sense of the tragedy of life persists and can be transmuted into victory over the world,—there will be the essence of Calvinism. The optimism and the humanism of the nineteenth century have already lost their rational quality.

It is probable that a revival of the "tragic sense of life," together with the wisdom and sobriety which grow out of it, should be forthcoming. It is necessary that men rediscover the truths once signified by the doctrines of divine sovereignty and divine grace, of predestination and election, of depravity and regeneration. Pure spirits harbor no loyalty to names. It is men who love to exchange old names for new, for that gives them a sense of progress and makes them happy.

If the humanitarianism of Channing is modern, a post-modern mind is already in the making. Its spirit is as yet skeptical and "naturalistic." It believes itself to be in an alien world. In order to become religious, it must become reconciled with God.

PIETY VERSUS MORALISM

CHAPTER I

IMPIETY AND MORALS

"Alas! Alas! Are there not many and great Impieties to be found in our Land? Is not God Himself too much neglected, and our Loyalty to Him forgotten, and a bare Formality, without the Power of Religion, the Guise of many High Professors? Is not His most Dreadful and Sacred Name greatly Dishonoured . . . ? Is not His Holy Day Prophaned? And does not His House too much lye waste, by Multitudes forgetting the Assembling of themselves together; by a Contempt cast upon the plain Ordinances and Institution of Christ, to Remember Him in a Serious and Worthy Approach to His Holy Table?" [1]

This normal lament of every conscientious minister of the Gospel was uttered with unusual earnestness in New England during the eighteenth century. The zeal of the people to attend to the "religious duties" prescribed by the "instituted churches" was on the wane. The Puritan conception of the Church as the proper means of salvation was being forgotten by an increasing number of people. Many were successful in achieving respectability without the help of the churches and the ministry. The Rev. Solomon Stoddard, for example, sensed the increasing peril of such cultivated indifference to sin. He embraced the ecclesiastical expedients which his common sense dictated as necessary for an effective appeal to the respectable unregenerates. He had his heart set on the "pros-

3

perity of Zion." Consequently, he invited all those who
desired "moral improvement," together with a certain interest in regeneration, to the Lord's Table, which had been
reserved by tradition for the elect of God. With the opening of the century, he set forth his notorious *Doctrine of
Instituted Churches explained and proved from the Word
of God,*[2] the burden of the said doctrine being that "all
professors of the Christian Faith, as are of blameless conversation, and have knowledge to examine themselves and
discern the Lord's Body, are to be admitted to the Lord's
Supper." [3] All those who are good enough to be admitted
into the churches as members, are also good enough to
partake of the Lord's Supper; [4] and these are those who
comply with the "general moral rules," and are not "scandalous." [5] In answer to the criticism of the formidable
Increase Mather, Stoddard had to write an *Appeal to the
Learned, being a Vindication of the rights of Visible Saints
to the Lord's Supper, though they be destitute of a Saving
Work of God's Spirit on their Hearts.*[6]

The fact of the matter seems to have been that the problem confronting the churches of New England, at the beginning of the eighteenth century, was the failure of the
people to attend to "any duty of worship." Stoddard admitted that the people failed to support the churches "under the pretence of being in an unconverted state." But
he also knew that this was little more than mere pretense.
Church duties were becoming not privileges but burdens.
Whereas before it had been advantageous to be a church
member of "compleat standing" (for high social standing
and the franchise in Massachusetts had been limited to
such), this had now become a privilege of dubious value.
Therefore, many people were turning away from the

churches to attend to their worldly concerns, pretending
that they considered themselves unworthy of the privileges
of real saints. Stoddard was determined to make such
claims "inexcusable." "Sanctifying grace," he asserted,
"is not necessary to the lawful attending" of any duty of
worship.[7] All good men, that is, all who are not of any
scandalously immoral behaviour, may and should attend
the "instituted churches," and this is the way to prevent
"corruption."

Stoddard's way became popular, while the churches continued to profess their "Calvinism." Although the dangerous tendency of his views was sensed by the Mathers,
it was ignored by the majority of the ministers.[8] These
were too busy lamenting religious indifference, and vainly
exhorting people to declare the work of grace on their
souls, according to the doctrines inherited from their
fathers. The doctrines of divine sovereignty, original sin,
and justification by faith, were maintained as revealed
truths, and preached intermittently with sober and pedan-
tic exhortations to the people to behave like saints and
give God the glory. Calvinism was becoming merely a
body of doctrines, to be believed chiefly because taught
in the Holy Scriptures. Hence it became increasingly
necessary to preach the Calvinistic "Faith," which all
confessed but few took seriously. In the year 1723, *The
Confession of Faith, together with the Larger Catechism
. . . with a brief Summary of Christian Doctrine* was published in Boston.

Question. What is the Chief and highest End of Man?

Answer. Man's chief and highest End, is to glorify
God *a*, and fully to enjoy him forever *b*.

a Rom 11. 36. *I Cor* 10. 31. *b Psalm* 73. 24 *to the end.*
John 17. 21, 22, 23.

.   .   .   .

Q. What are the Personal Properties of the three Persons of the Godhead?

a. It is proper to the Father to beget the Son *m*, and to the Son to be begotten of the Father *n*, and to the Holy Ghost to proceed from the Father and the Son from all eternity *o*.

m Heb 1. 5, 6, 8. *n Joh* 1. 14, 18. *o Joh* 15. 26. *Gal* 4. 6.

And so on in perfect order, propriety, and formality.

In the year 1726, Samuel Willard, former president of Harvard College, published *A Compleat Body of Divinity, in Two Hundred and Fifty Expository Lectures on the Assembly's Shorter Catechism.* While in the same year, the more practically minded Cotton Mather collaborated in the preparation of a *Serious Address to those who unnecessarily frequent the Tavern; with a Letter* [by I. Mather] *in answer to the Question, "Whether it be lawful for a Church-member among us to be frequently in Taverns?"*

Neither the "compleat body of divinity" nor the "serious address" of the Mathers, neither the theological innovations of Solomon Stoddard nor the exhortations of William Cooper to the "young people" that they be "mindful of their sins," prevented their backsliding sons and grandsons from going from bad to worse.[9] In 1734, John White, "M.A. and Pastor of the first Church in Gloucester," a venerable ancient, uttered *New England's Lamentations under these three heads, The Decay of the Power of Godliness; The Danger of Arminian Principles; The Declining State of our Church-Order, Government and*

Discipline. The pamphlet was recommended by Peter Thacher, Thomas Prince, William Cooper, Joseph Sewall, and Thomas Foxcroft.

"We profess the *Faith* and *Order* of the *Gospel;* but does there want *Proof* as to the Decay of the Life of *Religion,* or the Power of Godliness? No; this is more sufficiently proved by the Contempt cast upon *Gospel Grace, Ministry,* and *Ordinances.* By the Unchristian contentions in *Towns, Churches,* and *Families,* by notorious Excesses in *lawful Liberties,* &c." [10]

" 'Tis grievous and vexatious, yea a resisting of the Holy Spirit, when God's Professing People violate the *Covenant* in any of its Branches; when they neglect or Superficially perform the Duties of the *Closet* and *Family.* And when they watch not over their Fellow-Members in Love. When they prophane the holy *Sabbath,* stifle *Convictions,* and act contrary to their pious *Resolutions, vow and don't pay. . . .* They are over-heated, and deeply engaged in their Affections, towards the Profits, Pleasures, and Preferments of the World." [11]

"O then! let the secure World, drowned in its sensual Pleasures, and sunk into a deep Sleep of carnal Security; that flatter themselves by saying, The evil Day is afar off; *awake out of Sleep:* and as you are hastening unto the coming day of God; O! look out sharp for this dreadful Day, *wherein the Heavens being on fire, shall be dissolved, and the Elements shall melt with fervent Heat: the Earth also and the Works therein shall be burnt up.*" [12]

"The methods to be taken to recover or maintain the Power of Godliness," suggested by White, were of the nature of closer civil and ecclesiastical vigilance, "diligence and zeal in plucking sinners out of the burning." [13] To this end it seemed imperative that the churches should be organized more adequately, and that the "Divine Authority of Ruling Elders" should be "vindicated." [14]

Of course, that kind of thing had been tried by Increase Mather and his son, Cotton Mather, and had proved to be quite futile.[15] Jonathan Edwards of Northampton had another remedy. To him Calvinistic piety was a living affair, and he would not mince words. He preached the sovereignty of God, the necessity of regeneration by the Holy Spirit, the lots of the saved and the damned, in terms which actually transformed many parts of complacent New England into congregations of awakened sinners. "The Spirit of God began extraordinarily to set in and wonderfully to work." [16] The Great Awakening began. The details of its complicated story are not relevant to our purpose. We shall be satisfied to indicate its contributions to the launching of "the New England Theology." These fall under two main heads.

First. The one grand matter of dispute which was perpetrated between those who sympathized with the workings of the Spirit during the upheaval and those who did not, was the nature of regeneration and true godliness. Men like Edwards and Bellamy, who had been active in bringing about the revivals, claimed that in spite of the many excesses, God had been undoubtedly working among the people,[17] and that many of the conversions were genuine. However, this party was composed mainly of common folk who had experienced these conversions, and believed themselves to have been saved from the torments of hell-fire. The majority of the clergy were openly opposed to "enthusiasm." It had shaken the very foundations of ecclesiastical dignity and control. The people complained that their ministers were not spiritual enough, that they preached in the "old way." [18] They had the temerity to bring suits against their pastors, and in many instances separated from their churches. They even went so far as to believe that they could be saved without the ministry and the "ordinances of the Gospel." To the clergy of the "instituted churches" this looked like nothing less than antinomianism.[19] And then, there were the itinerant preachers who went from one place to another, and supplemented the work of the resident ministers with their "enthusiastic" exhortations. This also was very unpleasant.[20] Hence, many of the clergy decided that the phenomena of the Awakening, far from being genuine cases of conversion, were mere matters of excessive physical commotion, and no "evidence of man's spiritual state." Thus the setting was prepared for the great controversies on the nature of regeneration and true godliness.

The second outcome of the Great Awakening was the opening of the way to the new, humane, and "liberal" ideas which were already creeping in from England.[21] The Awakening had been the fruit of Calvinistic preaching. The idea of the awful majesty of the sovereign God, lurid pictures of sinners at the point of being flung into hell, the necessity of complete regeneration, in many cases accompanied by convulsions,—had been the dominant notes of the preaching of the revivalists. Therefore, it was natural that people of sobriety and learning, especially the clergy, should have leaned towards views which negated such ideas. Heresy crept in unawares, and the movement away from Calvinism began its tortuous course. Arminianism had been the dreaded heresy, but now even respectable ministers became infected with Arianism, which was worse.

As early as 1736, Robert Breck was accused of holding that the good among the heathen shall be saved; [22] that men shall be saved if they only believe; [23] that moral living only is necessary for salvation; [24] that Christ did not die to satisfy God's justice; [25] that some portions of the Scriptures are not inspired.[26] The ministers who disapproved of Breck's opinions received a strong protest from people "around Boston." [27] In 1743, William Balch, pastor of the second church in Bradford, published *The Apostles St. Paul and St. James reconciled with respect to Faith and Works . . . preached in some neighbouring churches.* A council met at Bradford, and found him heretical. The first church at Gloucester supported Balch, and "Letters" were sent to the people of his church, with a view to eliminate their complaints.[28]

Balch had written:

"And is not this agreable, not only to the whole Current of the Scripture, but also to the best *Reason* of Mankind? which hath *ever* told them, that if they would *please* God, it must be by *doing well:* That if they would be acceptable in his Sight, it must be by an Imitation of him in his moral Perfections." [29]

His accusers were quick to see that, in spite of his vague conformity to the doctrines of orthodoxy, Balch was undermining the doctrines of justification by the imputed merit of Christ,[30] the efficacy of the Holy Spirit,[31] and human depravity.[32] He was understood to teach, "that man by nature is more inclined to virtue, than vice"; [33] "that morality is the height of Christianity." [34] Balch wrote a "vindication," which is subtle and difficult; but it is not hard to see that his opponents were not without reason to suspect that he cared much more for morality than for the religion and the doctrines of orthodox Calvinism.

Of all the liberals Jonathan Mayhew was the most outspoken and thoroughgoing. On reading his sermons one is confronted with new outlooks and thought-forms, new problems and solutions, which make the Calvinism of another day irrelevant and negligible. The mere title of his first publication tells almost the whole story of the mind of this new kind of Gospel-minister: *Seven Sermons upon the following subjects: viz.,* I. *The Difference Betwixt Truth and Falsehood, Right and Wrong;* II. *The Natural Abilities of Men for Discerning These Differences;* III. *The Right and Duty of Private Judgment;* IV. *Objections Answered;* V. *The Love of God;* VI. *The Love of Our Neighbour;* VII. *The First and Great Commandment, &c.* His biographer says that he was "shunned and censured as a heretic," which is hardly surprising.[35]

Mayhew carried on an extensive and prolonged correspondence with ministers in England, and received some of the books which had been revolutionizing English thought for almost a century.[36] He was influenced by Clarke on necessity and free-will,[37] by George Benson on liberty and charity,[38] by Samuel Butler on the nature of religious truth,[39] by Algernon Sydney, and most probably Milton and Locke, on the nature and end of civil government.[40] He soon developed a marked disdain for the culture of his country, and despised the doctors of theology who concocted doctrines and devised speculative systems.[41] As for himself, he had appropriated the humanitarian rationalism of eighteenth century England, and preached its principles with the confidence and power of a zealous reformer.

"To say that subjects in general, are not proper judges when their Governors oppress them and play the tyrant; and when they defend their rights, administer justice impartially, and promote the public welfare, is as great *treason* as ever man uttered; it is treason not against one single man, but the state, against the whole body politic;— 'tis treason against mankind,—'tis treason against common sense,—'tis treason against God." [42]

"The end of all civil government" is "the good of society." [43]

Mayhew had already caught the vision of "another Gt. Britain rising in America," a land of free Englishmen, a prosperous and happy nation.[44] It is remarkable' how secularized and humanized the thought of Mayhew had become. Society is a group of men who have come together to contribute to their mutual advantage. Civil government is vested with power and authority, by the people, to maintain peace and prosperity.[45] So long as a government serves this end, it is to be obeyed. When it fails to do this, it is to be resisted and overthrown. Mayhew was an intimate friend of Samuel Adams and James Otis, and was praised and quoted by both of them.[46]

It is only natural that this champion of the rights of men should have entertained humane and exalted ideas concerning them; [47] that he should have had their natural and moral capacities in full view; [48] that he should have considered it the grand duty of a man to be a worthy member of a happy society.[49] It is no less natural that love to God and love to our fellowmen should have constituted the essentials of his religious thought; that he should have thought of God as a benevolent Father, and of "the meek and lowly Jesus" as a friend of mankind, who "came into the world to save sinners," because God "is not willing that any should perish, but that all should come to repentence." [50] What did Mayhew care for the doctrines of Calvinism!

"It is greatly to be lamented, that this gracious gospel . . . should be perverted by many, and so restrained as to the number of those for whose salvation it was designed, so narrowed, so clogged with needless difficulties and unscriptural mysteries, by dark systems of divinity, produced in dark and corrupt ages, as to become rather an engine for disturbing truly pious and good Christians with doubts and fears, than to be an adequate relief to awakened sinners, by really manifesting the riches of God's goodness to a guilty world, in its proper extent, through Him that 'gave himself a ransom for all, to be testified in due time.' " [51]

Mayhew was too obviously heretical. He was so completely out of sympathy with the respectable theology of the age that he aroused little more than mere hostility. Down to 1761, when he published his more orthodox *Striving to enter in at the Strait Gate,* his opponents did not even take the trouble to enter into controversy with him. His significance, at this place, is that of a clear and extreme example of a type of minister which had already appeared, and was destined to transform, slowly and laboriously, the Puritan mind. Throughout the following studies of the decline of Calvinistic piety in New England, we shall recognize the workings of the spirit which had come to possess Mayhew with power and might.

The middle of the eighteenth century was full of portents of evil days for New England Calvinism. In England, Arminianism had already bored through the Calvinism of the Church, and the controversies of the time were but elaborate applications of the humanitarian rationalism which had been well established half a century since. In New England, Calvinism was too deep-rooted in the emotional and mental habits of the people to be overthrown at once and completely. Worldly pursuits did not prevent the churchgoer from holding fast to correct doctrine. The initial effect of the sentiments of the enlightened liberals on the Calvinists was to make them declare *heaven shut against Arminians, Antinomians,* etc.[52] President Clap of Yale College, as late as 1755, considered it sufficient to state the "doctrines received and established in the churches of New England," and to give a "specimen of the new scheme of religion beginning to prevail,"—so as to let the readers judge for themselves.[53]

However, the "new scheme of religion" could not be disqualified and set aside in such a summary manner. In spite of its inadequate interest in the glory of God, it was beginning to prey upon the minds of "giddy youth" and many of the orthodox, especially those who were disgusted with the performances of the Great Awakening. In 1757 began a series of controversies in which would-be Calvinists contended one against another; confusion and compromise, speculation and exaggeration, which were to prove fatal to Calvinism, became the order of the day. The new protestants directed their attacks upon those aspects of the Calvinistic scheme which seemed to be most obnoxious, or least consequential, or most disputable. The doctrines symbolizing Puritan piety began to fall, one after another, and the worst ones first.

CHAPTER II

GOD'S WICKED WORLD

"THE human faculties are capable of a real and clear understanding of the greatness, glory, and goodness of God, and of our dependence upon him, from the manifestations which God has made of himself to mankind, as being beyond all expression above that of the most excellent human friend or earthly object. And so we are capable of esteem and *love* to God, which shall be proportionable.

"These things may help us to form some judgment, how vastly the generality of mankind fall below their duty, with respect to love to God; yea, how far they are from coming half-way to that height of love which is agreeable to the rule of right. Surely if our esteem of God, desires after him, and delight in him, were such as become us, considering the things forementioned, they would exceed our regard to other things as the heavens are above the earth, and would swallow up all other affections like a deluge. But how far, how exceeding far, are the generality of the world from any appearance of being influenced and governed by such a degree of divine love as this!" [1]

Jonathan Edwards' high vision of the marvelous manifestations of God, his recognition of man's dependence upon God for his enjoyments and his accomplishments, his disinterested regard for things as they really are, and his acute sense of the profound disparity between the ca-

pacity of men to love God and their actual indifference to
Him,—convinced him of the sinfulness of mankind.

And it followed self-evidently that such universal sinfulness has its basis in "human nature." A sinful act is
the act of a sinful nature. Therefore, where there is sin,
there is sinful nature. That any man sins under any circumstance whatsoever proves that he is capable of sinning,
that he has a "propensity" to sin, which is a consequence
of his "inherent nature." [2] The character of any "creature" is exhibited in its actions, and hence, a moral judgment passed upon them is also passed upon its "nature."
Therefore, the universal failure of men to "love God,"
"to treat everything as it is, according to its nature," is the
consequence of the "innate depravity" of all men.

"It is agreeable to an established course and order of
nature, that since Adam, the head of mankind, the root
of that great tree with many branches springing from it,
was deprived of original righteousness, the branches
should come forth without it. Or if any dislike the word
nature, as used in this last case, and instead of it choose to
call it a *constitution*, or *established order* of successive
events, the alteration of the name will not in the least alter
the case of the present argument. Where the name,
nature, is allowed without dispute, no more is meant than
an established method and order of events, settled and
limited by divine wisdom." [3]

The processes of nature are not mere successions of
events, but sequences in which one event "springs" from
another and partakes of a common nature. Flowers and
fruits are not spontaneous, external appendages of
branches, but grow out of them and possess characteristics
peculiar to themselves. A man born of a given pair of

parents "inherits" their traits. Such continuities in nature are evidences of a "constitution or established order."

"Thus it appears, if we consider matters strictly, there is no such thing as any identity or oneness in created objects, existing at different times, but what depends upon *God's sovereign constitution.*" [4]

In this constitution, Adam, "the head of mankind," is representative of all men. Adam sinned, and so do all men. Mankind sinned in Adam because through the sin of Adam an order of succession was established whereby all men are "by nature" sinners. Therefore, all men sin because they are the children of Adam, *or*, because they are sinners, which is the same thing.

"Both guilt, or exposedness to punishment, and also depravity of heart, came upon Adam's posterity just as they came upon him, as much as if he and they had all co-existed, like a tree with many branches; allowing only the difference necessarily resulting from the place Adam stood in, as head or root of the whole." [5]

The calamities which befall mankind grow out of this established order, as punishment naturally follows upon sin. As the punishment of Adam was the consequence of his sin, so the punishment of all men is the consequence of their sins. If the "constituted oneness or identity of Adam and his posterity," makes all men partakers of his sin, the same identity exposes all men to the punishment with which Adam was threatened.[6] Thus, the woes of mankind are consequences of Adam's original sin, or, in other words, in this state of nature, men are born to sin and suffering. Afflictions are chastisements, and only secondarily are they means conducive to edification, coming "from the hand of a wise and good Father." [7]

Edwards' justification for such an account of the state of mankind was worthy of a confirmed empiricist.

"It appears that a *divine constitution* is what *makes truth*, in affairs of this nature." [8]

"It signifies nothing to exclaim against plain *fact*. Such is the *fact*, the most evident and acknowledged *fact*, with respect to the state of all mankind, without exception of one individual among all the natural descendants of Adam, as makes it apparent, that God actually deals with Adam and his posterity as *one*, in reference to his apostacy, and its infinitely terrible consequences." [9]

When certain facts contradict what one would reasonably expect, on the basis of ideas derived from other facts, one's duty is not to overlook or falsify the facts, but to "get over them," "either by finding out some solution, or by shutting our mouths, and acknowledging the weakness and scantiness of our understandings; as we must in other innumerable cases, where apparent and undeniable *fact*, in God's work of creation and providence, is attended with events and circumstances, the *manner* and *reason* of which are difficult to our understandings." [10] Edwards was well aware of the objections which had been raised to the doctrine of original sin, but he first of all insisted on the fact. Having established the empirical foundations of the doctrine, therefore, he answered the moral objections as best he could.

It was objected that the doctrine makes God the "Author of sin." To this Edwards replied:

"When God made Adam at first he implanted in him two kinds of principles. There was an *inferior* kind, which may be called *natural*, being the principle of mere human nature; such as self-love, with those natural appetites and

passions, which belong to the *nature of man,* in which his
love to his own liberty, honour, and pleasure, were exercised: These, when alone, and left to themselves, are what
the scriptures sometimes call *flesh.* Besides these were
superior principles, that were spiritual, holy, and divine,
summarily comprehended in divine love. . . . These
principles may, in some sense, be called *supernatural.*" [11]

"These superior principles were given to possess the
throne, and maintain an absolute dominion in the heart;
the other, to be wholly subordinate and subservient." [12]

Such was the Original Righteousness of Adam's nature.
The consequence of his sin was that these "superior principles" were lost to him, and he was left in a state of mere
nature.

It was objected that the transmission of the sin of Adam
to his descendants does not seem to be just. Edwards replied that men are punished not merely because they inherit the sin of Adam, but because they themselves are
sinners. The fact that a man's sinful choice is consequent
upon his nature does not make it any less sinful, nor any
less deserving of punishment, which is the consequence of
that sin.

"These confused inconsistent assertions concerning virtue and moral rectitude, arise from absurd notions in
vogue, concerning *freedom of will,* as if it consisted in the
will's *self-determining power,* supposed to be necessary
to moral agency, virtue and vice." [13]

Vice and virtue inhere in the character of a given voluntary action. Volitions are consequences of a person's motives and dispositions, which belong to his "nature."
Hence in a strict sense it is not true that Adam's sin is
transmitted to his descendants. Men sin because of their

"constituted oneness" with Adam, because they possess his sinful nature.

The seeming arbitrariness of the appointment of Adam as the "federal head" of mankind, the "covenant of God" with him, together with the "threatening and sentence," is an arbitrariness involved in the givenness of a *fact*. God's covenanting with Adam, as the representative of mankind, is the legal translation of the fact that all men are united to Adam under the "established order" of nature.[14] Hence, God's moral government is arbitrary only in the sense that the course of nature is arbitrary.

Not only is the doctrine of original sin descriptive of the facts of human experience, but it also is essential for an adequate appreciation of other truths comprised in the Christian "scheme of salvation."

"The representations of the redemption by Christ, everywhere in scripture, lead us to suppose, that *all* whom he came to redeem are *sinners;* that his salvation, as to the term *from which* (or the evil to be redeemed from) in *all*, is *sin*, and the deserved *punishment* of sin." [15]

"The truth of the doctrine of original sin is very clearly manifest from what the scripture says of that *change of state*, which it represents as necessary to an actual interest in the spiritual blessings of the Redeemer's kingdom." [16]

"This inward change, called *regeneration* and *circumcision of the heart*, which is wrought in *repentance* and *conversion*, is the same with that spiritual *resurrection* so often spoken of, and represented as *a dying unto sin, and a living unto righteousness*." [17]

The significance of the doctrine of original sin in the Calvinistic "scheme of salvation" is, therefore, all important, and for that very reason it needed to be distinguished from the popular conception of the imputation of Adam's sin to his descendants. Therefore, Edwards emphasized the distinction as follows:

"By original sin as the phrase has been most commonly used by divines, is meant the *innate sinful depravity of the heart*. But yet, when the *doctrine* of original sin is spoken of, it is vulgarly understood in that latitude, which includes not only the *depravity of nature*, but the *imputation* of Adam's first sin; or, in other words, the liableness or exposedness of Adam's posterity, in the divine judgment, to partake of the punishment of that sin." [18]

Edwards' scientific analysis and scrupulous logic were of no consequence, however, after the atmosphere of New England had become saturated with "enthusiasm." The Great Awakening had rendered this doctrine incredible to the humane and soberminded onlookers of its spectacular "enthusiasms." The dominant note of the evangelists had been the impending fall of the unregenerate into the pit of everlasting hell-fire. It rang far and wide, louder than ever before, that all those who were not moved with the experience of "saving grace" must, and might at any moment, go to hell. Even "tender infants" must suffer because of the sin of Adam. This is what the doctrine of original sin popularly came to mean and imply. Could it be true?

Samuel Webster of Salisbury, Mass., wrote a dialogue which bore the genial title, *Winter-Evening's Conversation upon the Doctrine of Original Sin . . . wherein the notion of our having sinned in Adam, and being on that account* ONLY *liable to eternal damnation, is proved to be unscriptural, irrational, and of dangerous tendency.* He presented the characters with the following problem:

"Whether we, and all Adam's posterity, are charged by God with this first sin of his, so that men, women and children, are exposed, by this alone, to the eternal damnation of hell." [19]

The answer is:

"How can you reconcile it to the *goodness, holiness* or *justice* of God, to make them (infants) heirs of hell, and send them into the world only to breathe and die, and then take them away to hell, or even send them to hell from their mother's womb before even they have seen the light of life? What! make them first to open their eyes in torments; and all this for a sin which certainly they had no hand in . . . a sin which, if it comes upon them at all, certainly is without any *fault* or *blame* on their parts. . . . And all this from the *holiest, justest* and *kindest* being in heaven and earth! Mayn't we venture to say 'tis impossible!" [20]

Since the infants under consideration were not in existence when Adam committed his heinous crime, they cannot have been implicated in his deed. Sin is a matter of conscious working against God. Babies who "breathe and die" cannot be accused of sin. A God who would send them to hell would fall below the standards of even a most commonplace morality. Every one is punished for his own sins, and for none other. The doctrine of original sin contradicted this obvious principle, therefore it was false. Our author does not mince words.

"*Sin* and *guilt* (so far as I can see) are *personal* matters, as much as *knowledge*. And I can as easily conceive of one man's *knowledge* being imputed to another, as of his sins being so: No imputation, in either case, can make the thing to *be* mine, which is not *mine*, any more than one *person* can be made, in the like way, another person." [21]

It is contrary to reason that Adam "should stand as a federal head or representative for all his posterity, so as that if he sinned, he and all his posterity should be condemned to hell fire for his first transgression." [22] Adam sinned *personally*, and he was punished *personally*.

Men are not "by nature children of wrath." It is absurd to claim that men and women come into this world endowed with a nature "odious" to God and "exposed to damnation." [23] Webster is constrained to admit that men suffer because of the folly of Adam; in fact, that men not only suffer but also sin. For this he offers no explanation. How "moral beings" who are not even "exposed to damnation" can indulge in sin and go to hell, is a question which he puts aside. Instead, he leans heavily on the "goodness of God."

"And as to the *goodness* of God, O good father of heaven and earth! What doleful apprehensions must they have of this thine excellency and glory, who can suppose that thou shouldst pronounce a sentence by which myriads of infants, as blameless as helpless, were consign'd to the blackness of darkness to be tormented with fire and brimstone forever! Is this consistent with infinite goodness, nay with any general character of goodness? Impossible!" [24]

"This seems but little more consistent with the lovely character of our *compassionate* heavenly father . . ." [25]

"Our compassionate heavenly father," with "the lovely character," was the new deity who was coming to dethrone the "Creator and Ruler of the universe." The conse-

quences of this heavenly *coup d'état* will be traced throughout this essay. At this point, it is sufficient to observe that
the conflict between Calvinism and the sentiments of the
new age can be epitomized as a conflict between the conceptions "Almighty God" and "our compassionate heavenly father." From the very first, theological change was
a process of substitution of new dogmas for old.

Webster was under no illusions concerning the significance of his humane sentiments. In denying original sin
and human depravity, he had struck at the roots of the
orthodox "scheme of salvation." Therefore, he urged his
readers to be tolerant, and that for two excellent reasons.
First, all the more intelligent Protestants are agreed on
the fundamentals of faith.

"These all agree in believing that there is One God,
infinite in wisdom, power, holiness . . . the maker, governor and judge of the world. They all believe the
difference between virtue and vice, good and evil. . . .
They believe in Jesus Christ, the glorious redeemer and
saviour of men, appointed by God. . . . They believe a
future state and a resurrection of the dead." [26]

Compared with these, the doctrine of original sin is
estimated to be "a very little thing," about which men
"can have charity for each other."

Secondly, considering that either side may be mistaken,
"if, therefore, neighbour, those who suppose your doctrine
an error can have charity for you, never think of breaking
with them, but live and love as brethren. If you dispute
do it with a Christian temper . . . for remember, 'the
greatest of these is charity.' " [27]

Webster's arguments, humane as they were, did not
carry conviction to theologians. The fact of human sin-

fulness calls for an explanation which shall be worthy of its oppressive importance. Webster had been too easy with it. Some one sympathetic with his views attempted to fortify his position by ascribing man's actual sinfulness to an "original disorder in the body," inherited from Adam, which "inclined the soul to evil." This body is not in itself sinful; it is simply "impaired in Adam." Sin is the result of the influence of the body on the soul, although neither of them is originally sinful.[28] Thus sinfulness is explained away, and the new deity is cleared from the charge of evil conspiracy. It was all very reasonable, and the Calvinists were aroused. These kindhearted gentlemen were questioning the very foundations of the accepted and respected theology of New England.

Peter Clark, pastor of the First Church in Danvers, answered Webster in *A Summer-Morning's Conversation*.[29] Five ministers commended it "to the diligent and prayerful perusal of God's people." It was a time of trouble.

"We apprehend, the prevailing of corrupt principles (as well as of corrupt practices), not duly testify'd against, is a ground of God's awful controversy with his people at this day, and a reason why he in his Providence is threatening to unchurch and disinherit us."[30]

Clark, no less than Webster, can appeal to the consciences of his readers. "This is a doctrine most disagreeable to the proud heart of man, as it tends to beat down that pharisaical conceit he is apt to entertain of the goodness of his nature."[31] As yet, New England was not sufficiently enlightened to ignore such an appeal. Clark is certain that "fact and experience, as well as the dictates of the Sacred Writ," put the doctrine of original sin upon an unquestionable basis.

"Original sin is plainly included in, and necessarily inferred from this universal apostacy. For that which affects not only some few *individuals*, but the whole *species*, must originate in some common cause or principle, that extends it's influence to the whole kind; and what can that be, but the Sin and Fall of our first parents from a State of Innocence?" [32]

To Clark's mind, "the course of natural generation" is sufficient to account for the constancy and universality of human sinfulness.[33]   Of course, "natural generation" does not need any apology.   But it leaves the main point at issue, namely, the imputation of Adam's sin to his descendants, unsettled.   Clark failed to make use of Edwards' concept of the *oneness* of mankind, in virtue of an "established order of nature," which oneness makes all men partakers of the sin of Adam, the representative man.   Here Clark was confused, and made the unfortunate distinction between the imputation of natural acts, which he rejected, and the imputation of moral acts, "in respect of their guilt," which he accepted.[34]   Having thus separated things which God has united from the beginning, divine constitution and divine covenant, he was left with no better basis for his belief in the imputation of one man's sin to another than that such imputation is recorded in the Book of Joshua, a basis which even a Calvinist could not take seriously.   Clark himself was suspicious of the truth of his doctrine, and admitted that, after all, belief in human depravity is far more essential than belief in the imputation of Adam's sin to mankind.   The pamphlet ends with a plea that we consider our littleness and stupidity concerning things divine. And this in the appendix:

"There are two things to be distinctly considered in original sin. One is, the corruption and vitious inclination of our nature. The other, the original of this corruption, or its derivation from the sin of Adam. This latter, we confess, is a matter of *faith;* being made known to us only in the Holy Scriptures. The former is a matter of sense and experience; yet not so fully manifested, as when the light of Scripture is brought to our hearts." [35]

Clark was obliged to concede nothing less than that the idea of the imputation of the sin of Adam to mankind is a matter of "faith," derived solely from the Scriptures, and with no support in sense and experience. The new idea of sin as a purely personal matter had made the doctrine of imputation of sin rationally indefensible. Therefore, nothing could be done but to appeal to Scripture and to faith. But since neither of these is a compelling vindication of the doctrine in question, human depravity had to be distinguished from the imputation of the sin of one man to another, and the latter relegated to a position of secondary, negligible importance.

Clark not only shared the moral principles of his opponent, but also his humane sentiments.

"But most of the said gentleman's arguments or objections against the derivation of Adam's sin to his posterity, are rather pathetick exclamations against the *damnation of infants,* or their suffering the torments of *hell-fire.* . . . A thing which few or none maintain; even tho' some may suppose them liable to eternal *death,* that is, an eternal privation of life; as they may be, and yet not suffer the torments of hell. . . . Secret things belong to God, but things revealed belong to us and to our children . . . and God has not tho't fit so far therein to gratify our curiosity, as to acquaint us with the method of his dealing with *infants in a future state.*" [36]

In fact, it is hoped that through Jesus Christ the infants are situated as well as possible. There is "no reason to conclude they suffer the eternal torments of hell." [37] The damnation of the conscious and mature sinner is justified on the basis of both Adam's sin *and* his own. Once more, the distinction between sinful nature and sinful act vitiated the empirical basis of the doctrine of original sin, although it saved the "innocent infants." Clark hesitates to accept the idea of the strictly personal character of sin, and yet, the thought of infants burning in hell forces him to admit that they merely have the "principle of sinfulness"; [38] which, of course, may not be sufficient to cause eternal damnation. In fact, this principle may be only the privation of the principle of goodness, without a positive character of its own; in which case, infants may die to "eternal death," but they will certainly have no place in hell.

It was this ill-concealed double-mindedness that brought forth the sharp and decisive rebuke of the broad-minded Dr. Charles Chauncy of Boston, *The opinion of one that has perused the* Summer-Morning's Conversation . . . *in two things principally;—First, that he has offered that, which has rendered impossible the doctrine of the imputation of Adam's guilt to his posterity, should be held true in the sense that it is held by Calvinists. Secondly, that tho' he pretends to be a friend to the Calvinistical doctrine of imputed guilt, he has deserted this doctrine, and given it up into the hands of his enemies, as it teaches the liable-*

ness of all mankind, without exception, to the torments of hell, on account of the first sin.[39]

Chauncy is clear and categorical. The damnation of all the unregenerate is a necessary inference from the doctrine of original sin. The infants, however poor, innocent, and helpless they may be, are predestined to hell-fire.[40] This is no secret to Calvinism. Eternal death for infants, or their possible salvation through an extraordinary intervention of Christ in heaven, are notions which are foreign to the Calvinistic scheme. Chauncy does not "blame this gentleman for hoping the best concerning the future state of infants." [41] But he insists that Clark has deserted true Calvinism. The five ministers who had endorsed Clark's pamphlets are charged with the same "mistake" "about the infants." [42]

The truth is that the opponents of Calvinism had succeeded in putting the doctrine in an obviously obnoxious light. They had removed it from its proper setting in the Calvinistic theology, and insisted on its significance in reference to the future state of "innocent infants." In such a light the doctrine was revolting, and therefore false. It contradicted the most elementary principles of justice and humaneness. To the eighteenth century moralist it was becoming increasingly evident that guilt is a personal matter, and that it is unjust to punish one for the guilt of another. The notion of "tender infants" being consigned to hell because of the guilt of a man who had lived several thousand years before, seemed to be sufficient proof that the doctrine of original sin was a huge lie. Even the Calvinists had become enlightened enough to feel the force of such an argument. Clark and the other five ministers accepted both Webster's logic and his sentiments. The outcome was a compromise which was as unstable as it was inconsistent, and the way was opened for further improvements.

The new standards of justice and equity made it impossible to accept the facts of life as revelations of the will of God. It was no longer possible to accept events as divine decrees unless they measured up to the ethical principles which had come to constitute the standards of righteous human intercourse, and to which even the Creator and the Ruler of the universe had to conform. Therefore, in order to show the wisdom and the goodness of God in governing the world as He actually does, it now became necessary to show that any given act of God is in some way conducive to the greater welfare of his "intelligent creation." Like the King in England, God had to justify His rule in and through His respect for the "natural rights" of His subjects. "Unlimited submission" to any sovereign power, not excluding the Almighty, was now definitely sinful. Sovereignty became permissible only when it was used for the comfort and the happiness of those on whom it was exercised.[43]

Joseph Bellamy, one of the brightest of the "New Lights," did not believe all this. Nevertheless, in the same year in which Edwards' book on *Original Sin* appeared, 1758, he presented the public with a vindication of the *Wisdom of God in the Permission of Sin*.[44] The question is: Why did God permit Adam to sin? He knew from the beginning that Adam would sin. If He had wished He could have prevented the sinful act of Adam which filled the world with sin and misery. And why did He not wish it? In answering this question, Bellamy does not set forth the principle of Edwards that facts describe the will of God and carry their own credentials of wisdom and justice. He is interested neither in "natural generation" nor in "God's sovereign constitution." He investigates into the consequences of the sin of Adam in the history of mankind, and attempts to demonstrate that "of all possible plans, this is the best." [45] Bellamy's thesis is clear. After copious illustrations from sacred history, he says:

"In all these instances of God's permitting sin, he had a view to the manifestation of himself. They gave him opportunities to act out his heart; and so to show what he was, and how he stood affected; and he intended, by his conduct, to set himself, that is, all his perfections, in a full, clear, strong point of light; that it might be known that he was the Lord, and that the whole earth might be filled with his glory." [46]

A detailed demonstration of God's wisdom in the permission of sin involves the description of the many virtues and benefits which are conditioned upon the various facts of sin and salvation. A swift perusal of the story of Joseph, his original pride, the wickedness of his brothers, his imprisonment, his promotion, the visit of his brothers, etc., culminating in the sojourn of Israel in Egypt,—supplied Bellamy with convincing evidence that in and through it all the wisdom and the goodness of God became manifest, and that the final outcome was to the benefit of the children of Israel. [47] Bellamy is well aware that the exodus of Israel from Egypt involved the hardening of the Pharaoh's heart, and his destruction in the Red Sea. For Pharaoh this was pure evil. And Bellamy makes no attempt to show that it was otherwise.

"He [God] designed to give a lively picture of himself, as of one infinitely too wise, great, and powerful, for feeble mortals to contend with; resolved to vindicate his own honour at all events, and revenge affronts offered his majesty, and carry on his own designs in spite of all opposition, that the Israelites might see it, and know it for their good . . . For he intended that these mighty works should never be forgotten among men, so long as the sun and moon should endure." [48]

This same principle applies to the story of Adam, and explains the reason and the purpose of God's permitting him to sin.

"A theatre being erected, proper to raise, in intelligent creatures, sublime and exalted thoughts of God, in the next place Man, a noble creature, an intelligent free agent, capable of moral action, and a proper subject of moral government, is formed by God, and placed upon the stage, as head of a numerous race, and made lord of this world." [49]

"Our first parents' design, in eating the forbidden fruit, was to make a surprising advance in knowledge and happiness . . . Deceived by Satan's lies, captivated by his temptation, the food also appearing pleasant to the eye, and good for food, they took and ate." [50]

"Satan's design was to bring dishonor upon God, ruin upon man, and then to lift up himself, exult, and triumph in his deed." [51]

"God's design in permitting Satan so far to succeed in this most hellish attempt, was, that he might take occasion to bring more honor to God, and to make the good part of creation more humble, holy, and happy." [52]

"I say, if God had become surety for all intelligences; if the only immutable being had, in such circumstances, undertaken, by his ever-watchful eye, and the constant influences of his spirit, to have rendered all intelligences immutably good . . . they would not have been in a capacity to have discerned the kindness scarce at all; much less to have been so thoroughly sensible of their absolute dependence upon God, and infinite obligations to him, as now, according to the present plan, the saved forever will be." [53]

There is a naïve and touching dignity to this Calvinistic evangelist's apology for God's government. Ruminating over the marvelous works of the Almighty, his thoughts move swiftly and with ease to the conclusion that all things have happened for the best. He is convinced that if human vision were sufficiently comprehensive and human insight sufficiently profound, men would appreciate the infinite wisdom and goodness of God in the permission of sin. One cannot resist the temptation to put it in his own words:

"As all God's works are uniform, so we may justly argue, from the wisdom and beauty of particular parts, to the wisdom and beauty of the whole. As God's nature is always the same, and as he always acts like himself, so therefore, his works are always harmonious and consistent. So that if we can see the wisdom of God in the permission of sin in some instances, we may justly argue to his wisdom in his whole grand scheme, yea, from the wisdom, glory, and beauty of particular parts, we may be rationally convinced that God's grand scheme is perfect in wisdom, glory, and beauty, although it be so incomprehensibly great, as to confound our understandings." [54]

Therefore, what do modesty and sobriety require of men, but that they should regard it as the best of all possible worlds? Human vituperations against divine government are merely expressions of the arrogant stupidity and the self-centeredness of those who indulge in them. "The creature has taken the throne, and the Creator is become his servant." [55] Bellamy was a genuine Calvinist. To him the fall of Adam, and the condemnation of mankind in him, were the beginning of that stupendous and glorious drama which preceded the redemption of the world by the Son of God and all the marvelous workings of the Spirit of God since then. This was the vision, so dear to the Calvinist, which the questionings and the objections of the time tended to obscure.

Nevertheless, Bellamy's vindication of the ways of God represents a significant deviation from the spirit of Edwards' work. Bellamy has accepted the challenge of the new age that God's permission of sin be justified on the basis of its conduciveness to greater human happiness. The new age wanted to know wherein God's permission of sin made this a better world than one without sin, and wherein it contributed to maximum human felicity. The end of Bellamy's present work is to answer this query, and to vindicate the ways of God in the sight of the mid-eighteenth century New Englander. He tried to show that divine government is not objectionable in the light of the then current standards of justice and goodness, and that it is ultimately conducive to the welfare of those governed.

This was a slightly perceptible, but very significant, departure from the perspective of Edwards. The thesis of Edwards' *God's last end in the creation of the world* is that the glory of God, and not the happiness of man, is the last end of creation. A clear view of the acts of God reveals, not that all things are designed for human happiness, but, that human happiness is conditioned upon the discovery that they are not so designed. It is not the utility of events for any limited purpose, but their reality as actuals and potentials, that defines their excellences. An adequate sense of proportion, such as that of God, would make it appear wrong that the happiness of individual human beings, nay, of whole nations and the whole of creation, at any given instant, should exhaust divine purposes or reveal the fullness of divine glory.[56]

Bellamy himself, with some inconsistency, insists that it is wrong to conceive human happiness as the measure of all things, "for if nothing was of importance but the creature's good, why was not that solely attended to?" [57] Moreover, for God,

"To have concerned himself only for his creatures' good, unsolicitous for the rights of the Godhead, in the very beginning of his reign, and when the first foundations of his everlasting kingdom were laying, had been to counteract his own nature, and his chief maxims of government. And indeed, as he is the Great Being, and in a sense, the only being, all the creation being nothing compared with him, yea, less than nothing, and vanity, so it was fit all intelligences should early be taught to view him in that light. And what method could be better suited to this end, than to let all the intelligent system know that their everlasting welfare was suspended on the condition of their paying supreme honor, and yielding constant obedience to this glorious Monarch of the universe . . . ?" [58]

But when Bellamy set himself to justify the ways of God in the sight of man, his Calvinism became confused and vitiated. He tried to save the honor of God by attributing the origin of sin to Satan or to Adam.[59] He apologized that man is a (free) moral agent, and that therefore the foreknowledge of God neither implicates Him in the sin of Adam nor does it make His punishing him unjust.[60]   The sinner is responsible to God, for he knows the law, and is free to comply with it, if he will.[61] "In the nature of things," God had to make man finite and fallible.[62]   In all this, the apologetic attitude is evident. Bellamy the Calvinist was losing his nerve.

Samuel Moody, M.A., was a thoroughly enlightened Christian, and could see nothing in Bellamy's pious contemplations but "doctrines" with "fatal and pernicious consequences." [63]   In a short and solid pamphlet, published in 1759, he set forth the faith of the new age with a clarity and precision which could not but have made his orthodox opponents writhe with pain.

"All that we can, I conceive, with safety and certainty affirm with regard to sin, is, that it is in the world;—that God is holy;—hates sin—cannot be the author of it; and therefore the creature must.   And is not this enough?" [64]

It is evident to Moody that there are many agents in this world who are responsible for the various happenings in it.   There is God, there are the angels, there is the devil, and there is man.   God and the good angels plan and will that which is good.   The devil and the bad angels are wholly bent to evil and unrighteousness.   Men may be bent to good or to evil.   God is in no way responsible for moral evil; He neither plans it, nor wills it, nor performs it.   God made a perfect world.   He created man upright, which proves that He meant this to be a sinless world.[65]   But some angels revolted against His righteous rule, and Adam ate of the forbidden fruit.   And thus it was that sin entered into the world.   Now that there is sin, God is bent upon overruling it, and turning it to good. [66]

It cannot be that God permitted sin for His own glory. The glory of God can be reflected in nothing less than perfect harmony and perfect happiness.[67] This world would have been a far better world if there were no evil in it.[68] There is nothing glorious about evil, and under no circumstance does it reflect or enhance the glory of God. Goodness, wisdom, and love, are sufficient manifestations of divine glory, and the supposed advantages to be derived from a view of His vindictive justice are greatly outweighed by the intrinsic ugliness of sin.[69]

"God is represented under the relation of a Father: and in what a delightful view must he appear, environ'd with all his numerous progeny; equally sharing in his unbounded munificence, and returning love, gratitude, praise, obedience? What a lovely endearing sight is it to see among men, a wise, tender, indulgent parent making happy a whole family of pious, dutiful children? Surely it can be no dishonour to the Father; no injury to the family, that they all are virtuous; all happy." [70]

This is what the heaven and the earth would have been like if the original plan of God had been accomplished, if men had not fallen into sinful ways. Then, all men would have been forever happy, and God would have been the happy and well contented Father of a happy and well contented progeny. Surely, Bellamy cannot claim that this is the best of all possible worlds! This world full of sin and misery!

Moody has no less than ten formidable objections against the "scheme" of Bellamy.[71] It makes God the author of sin; it presents the devil as really righteous and

busy doing the will of God; it makes the sin of Adam a
great deed of goodness, and the sinners more saintly than
saints; it dishonours God by limiting His wisdom, and supposing Him "unable to communicate the highest degrees
of possible happiness to his obedient and holy creatures,
without concerting a scheme for the extreme and eternal
misery of vast numbers of them." [72]   Such obviously erroneous views will only tend to increase "Deism and Infidelity." [73]

Such was the response Bellamy received from the humanitarian Christian of the day.   A best of all possible
worlds in which all men are not forever happy had become
a contradiction in terms.   It was now impossible that God
should seek to manifest His glory by "concerting a scheme
for the extreme and eternal misery of vast numbers" of
men.   God never ordains evil, moral evil, in any sense.
If there is evil in the world, it is because there are "agents"
besides God.   All this was very plain.

Bellamy offered a *Vindication* of "the God that made us
all." [74]   It is remarkable how incapable he was of grasping
the temper and the import of Moody's convictions.   "We
agree," he says, "that, if God had pleased, he could have
hindered the existence of sin, and caused misery to have
been forever unknown in his dominions." [75]   The truth is,
according to Moody, sin exists in spite of the plan and the
will of God, and it is not within God's power to prevent
it from happening; although, it is within His power, in
some instances, to overrule it.   Moody's God was good,
but He was not Almighty.

This is what Bellamy the Calvinist could not understand.   A God who could not and did not accomplish the
eternal purposes dictated by His wisdom and goodness was

to him unthinkable. Such a God, a being whose goodness
could be rendered ineffective by powers beyond his control, was not the God of this most God-intoxicated Calvinist. Therefore, perhaps the failure of Bellamy to understand Moody was inevitable, but it also was unfortunate; because it made his "vindication" very much beside the point. Moody did not question God's good intentions; he questioned and denied that God could in
every instance carry them out. Bellamy set out to show
that God intends that men should sin, *because* sin is a
means to greater good. This he could not demonstrate,
and Moody's objections remained unanswered. Moody's
logic was perfect. This world is imperfect, because all
men are not happy. God is good, and would have His
children forever happy. Therefore, God did not and does
not will or permit sin, and cannot always prevent it; an
easy and decisive solution for one who neither understood
nor cared for the piety of Bellamy.

The prosecutors of God had become many, and quite
vociferous. It was becoming increasingly difficult to see
why God should permit any sin at all.[76] Therefore,
Samuel Hopkins, the most formidable of the "Edwardeans," set himself to show that *sin, through divine interposition,* [is] *an advantage to the universe, and yet this is
no excuse for sin, or encouragement to it.*[77] In the preface
is the striking statement:

"If the sin and misery which take place in the world are
not for the general good of the universe, then they are
absolutely evil, or evil in every view and sense; and so
God's will to permit sin and misery is not wise and good,
and therefore, cannot be submitted to."

Hopkins' thesis is one more step in the humanization of

Calvinism. God permits sin because through divine intervention it is conducive to the good of the universe, and not
because it is a manifestation of the glory of God. The
glory of God has now become identical with the advantage of His creation. Heresies creep in unawares; Hopkins thought he was following in the footsteps of Edwards.
But in reality he had deserted his master.

And what does an "advantage to the universe consist
in"? Hopkins turns to Biblical history, much as Bellamy
had done; and thus, practically, the good of the universe
becomes the good of man. He cites the cases of Joseph,
Pharaoh, Jesus, and the Jews after Crucifixion, as instances
wherein God used sin as "occasion of great good." [78] As in
the case of Bellamy, he was really trying to show that God
overrules sin to the advantage of men. And he was no
more successful than Bellamy. Ultimately, he presented
no better argument for his contention than that God *can*,
and therefore *does*, overrule sin.[79] The standard recognition of human ignorance was thoroughly harmless, because
the real difficulty was not that his opponents did not know
how God intervenes to turn evil into good, but that they
were convinced that He sometimes does *not* intervene.
Assuming an implicit notion that God's supreme interest
must center in the "advantage" of man, the argument of
Hopkins could not carry conviction. Bellamy fell back
on his Calvinism, and denied vehemently that the glory of
God is identical with the happiness of man. Such re-
lapses in Hopkins are rare and half-hearted.[80] For him
the good of the universe, rather, the good of man, is the
last end for which God created the world.

This subtle repudiation of the spirit of Calvinism is seen
also in Hopkins' view of God's relation to sin. That God

merely "intervenes" to change evil into good implies that
facts which are considered evil arise from sources extraneous to the realm of divine government. Calvinists
had always been careful not to admit that God commits
sin, but since their God was the Ruler of His creation, they
had to insist that, in some sense, the facts of sin must be
related to the will and the eternal purposes of God. It
was a difficult position to uphold, but it was a rational
necessity, and they did their best to "get over" it.[81]   By
limiting God's relation to sin to one of intervention and
over-ruling, Hopkins had vitiated the sovereignty of God.
He was unconsciously doing what his opponents did, saving the goodness of God at the expense of His sovereign
power over His creation. In other words, he was unable
to admit that the facts of life reveal the manner in which
God governs the world.

The hidden timidity of Hopkins is still more evident in
his attitude to "decrees." "I am willing to leave the word
decree out of the question . . . as it is a word that is become hateful and frightful to many." [82]   However, "I
would ask whether any can possibly conceive God's permitting sin without determining to permit it? Surely God
determines to do all he does; therefore to say that God
did not determine to permit sin, is the same as to say he
did not permit sin. If, then, God has permitted sin, he
certainly has determined to permit it." [83]

Superficially, to decree sin, to determine to permit sin,
and merely to permit sin, are very much alike. However,
one will ask the question, Why has the word "decree" become "hateful and frightful"? The answer is, Because it
denotes an act of an arbitrary and sovereign Will, who dis-
poses according to His own supreme pleasure. It was this

that had become obnoxious. God had no more right to
make His own will His own rule of conduct than the king
in England had a right to impose his will on the colonists
in America, irrespective of their good and happiness. The
will of God and the will of the king were to be subservient
to the interests of their subjects. They both were sovereign only to serve ends which transcended their own
glory. The last end of the king was to seek the welfare
of his subjects; the last end of God was to seek the good of
the universe, and more especially, the good of His "intelligent creation." Therefore, although it was "hateful"
that God should "decree" sin, Hopkins tried to show that
it was quite permissible that He should determine to permit sin for the good of the universe. But, "there are
multitudes to whom sin is never the occasion of any good,
but it proves to them an infinite evil, even their eternal un-
doing." [84]

This was the real objection to God's permission of sin.
And Hopkins, in spite of his clever and tortuous dialectics,
was unable to answer it. No amount of sophistry could
convince the new age that all evil is conducive to some
greater good. Hopkins could not prove that God's last
end is the good of the universe, and much less could he
prove that it is the happiness of men. The new dogma
was that it *must* be. And since all men are not happy, the
unavoidable conclusion, in spite of Bellamy and Hopkins,
was that God is unable to accomplish His good purposes.
When men refused to make God's will their own, when,
on the contrary, they made their own ideals the standard
of excellence, the idea of the sovereign God was doomed.

CHAPTER III

REFORM WITHOUT REGENERATION

In Jonathan Edwards' own life being religious meant being possessed of a specific kind of vivid, dominating "affection," or, as we should say, emotion. From his childhood, the glory of God in the heavens and on the earth had moved him to delights which had come to be the dearest possessions of his heart. God, the Creator of all things, the inexhaustible Fountain of this vast and colorful realm of Being, aroused in him "affections" which he had come to consider as constitutive of the very essence of piety.

"All dependent existence whatsoever is in a constant flux, ever passing and returning; renewed every moment, as the colors of bodies are every moment renewed by the light that shines upon them; and all is constantly proceeding from God, as light from the sun." [1]

Therefore, a disinterested observation and appreciation of the perfections of God as manifested in the comings and the goings of events, a gracious regard for the manner in which God has ordained and operates the motions of things and the destinies of men, were for him the foundation of holiness. A loving conformity of the will to the will of God as revealed in the facts of existence and in the "economy of redemption," were, for Edwards, inseparable from any genuine experience of divine grace. The height of human excellence, "real sainthood," thus rested upon a relish of the heart for insight into the divine nature of Reality and a grasp of the perfect constitution wherewith God governs the world. To be sure, he had difficulty in accepting human sinfulness and human damnation as revelations of the glory of God; but finally, his piety triumphed, and these also, as *facts*, became objects of "holy affection" to him. Considered in their place in God's "scheme of salvation," they partook of the divine quality of "God's sovereign constitution." [2]

"It would be very strange, if any professing Christian should deny it to be possible, that there should be an excellency in divine things, which is so transcendent, and exceedingly different from what is in other things, that if it were seen, would evidently distinguish them. We cannot rationally doubt, but that things which are *divine*, that appertain to the Supreme Being, are vastly different from the things that are *human*. There is a God-like, high, glorious excellency in them, so distinguishing them from the things which are of men, that the difference is ineffable; and therefore such as if seen, will have a most convincing, satisfying influence upon any one, that they are *what they are, viz.* divine." [3]

This distinction between the divine and the human may be said to be the most fundamental and recurrent theme of Edwards' religious thought. Nothing struck him as more true to experience and essential to a right view of the Christian religion. The profound disparity between the "holy beauty" of God or that of the "real saint," and the human qualities common to all men as "natural" beings, was the fact by which he determined the validity and adequacy of any religious belief. His derivation of the doctrines of orthodox Christianity from this distinction is remarkably plausible and clear. Given the "relish" of Edwards for "holy beauty," his Calvinism followed as a matter of course.

"The same eye that discerns the transcendent beauty of holiness, necessarily therein sees the exceeding odiousness of sin . . . He now sees the dreadful pollution of his heart, and the desperate depravity of his nature, in a new manner; for his soul has now a sense given it to feel the pain of such a disease." [4]

It is now easy to understand why Edwards could take this religious affection to be nothing less than "supernatural." The natural affections, being qualitatively different from the sense of divine glory, do not and cannot produce it. The "natural man" may be a sensible and well-behaving person; he may follow the dictates of his conscience; he may even be affectionate toward his neighbors. But in all this he is guided merely by prudence and the natural affections, which are necessary for self-preservation. Human depravity does not consist in a lack of these qualities. Edwards does not deny that the natural man may be good. But he will not permit himself to lose sight of the fact that to be religious and to be moral are two different things. Morality is natural, religion is supernatural. The latter is based upon a "new principle," [5] derived, not from nature, but from God. The sense of the divine is produced by the Divine, through the operation of the indwelling Spirit of holiness, introducing a "new principle" and a new object of affection.

"Upon the whole, I think it is clearly manifest, that all truly gracious affections arise from the special and peculiar influences of the Spirit, working that *sensible effect* or *sensation* in the souls of the saints, which are entirely different from all that is possible a natural man should experience; different not only in degree and circumstances, but in its whole nature . . . and that which the power of man or devils is not sufficient to produce, or any thing of the same nature." [6]

It follows that the regeneration of the natural man into spiritual life can be accomplished only by the indwelling divine Spirit. For his salvation man is entirely dependent upon God. There is nothing that he can do to merit or bring about his salvation. A "mere" man, endowed with the common social and moral virtues, is totally ignorant of the spiritual life. He neither knows it, nor wants it, nor can attain it. Relish for religion is an evidence of regeneration and the presence of a new principle in the mind. It is a free gift of God to those upon whom it is bestowed. The doctrine that out of the body of mankind, God elects some unto salvation, and He forsakes the others to damnation, is founded upon the fact that some men love God and others do not. Regeneration, therefore, is a free act of the sovereign God, agreeable to His infinite wisdom and good pleasure.

Facts of a more practical character, however, awaited the attention of the clergymen of New England. By 1761, the Great Awakening was a thing of the past. "Three quarters of the Christian world" were unconverted, and neglected the gospel ordinances. The practical question was, therefore, no longer, what can be done to turn these to the path of godliness, but rather, what can be done to the path of godliness to make it acceptable to the churches?

In spite of their theology, the Calvinists of New Eng-

land never questioned the place of organized religion in
the Kingdom of God. From the very first, it was readily
recognized that the churches of the land constituted an
integral part of the "covenant of grace."   Salvation was
the work of the Holy Spirit.   And yet, it was seldom
questioned that the churches played an indispensable part
in the drama of human redemption. After all, nothing
was of more importance than that men should undergo
an adequate preparation for the world to come. The
clergy instructed the children of God in the first principles
of religion, inculcated the doctrines which were conducive
to the edification and the perseverance of the saints, expounded the Scriptures, and exhorted men to live the life
of righteousness as taught in the Word of God. No less
sacred were the administration of the Lord's Supper and
Holy Baptism. The former was the sign and seal of the
inner working of the Spirit of God, and the latter initiated
little sons of wrath into the visible body of God's elect.
Therefore, it was evident to all that there was an intimate
relationship between the functions of the churches and
the salvation of souls. In fact, the clergy seldom failed
to feel that if the many evils and sufferings which troubled
the land were to be eliminated, it was first necessary to
increase the power of the churches.

One of the more lasting effects of the Great Awakening
had been an exaggerated emphasis upon the immediate
working of the Spirit of God in the soul of the sinner. It
was preached loudly and persistently that God, and only
God, can save the sinner. In the heat and frenzy of the
movement the less striking and more methodical means
which God employs to bring men to Himself were often
ignored, and salvation became a matter of a sudden and

overpowering experience attributed to the Holy Spirit. In theory this was nothing new. But the importance of churchgoing, not to speak of church-membership, became a question. It became rather doubtful if organized religion was a necessary means of salvation. Churches were broken into parts and separated. Their ministers declaimed against each other, and charges of heresy and misdemeanor filled the air. The religious unity of New England, never very evident, was now disintegrating. The churches of God had become a house divided against itself, and were no longer felt to be indispensable either for good government or good conduct.[7] In short, the immediate operations of the Spirit were undermining the influence of the churches. Hence some of the clergy were seeking for a new gospel, more applicable to more church-members. The champion of such a gospel was Jonathan Mayhew.

His common sense mind sensed with certainty that decent and moral living is a matter of effort and achievement. If men are to attain the Christian life, they must *strive;* they must *strive to enter in at the strait gate.*[8] This gate is the "gate of eternal happiness." [9] Sinners who become awakened "to the sense of their sin," [10] who "earnestly desire salvation," [11] should strive on to eternal happiness. They should take "Jesus Christ for their guide, and heartily desire to know the truth as it is in him." [12] A man who strives to follow the example of Christ, is on his way to eternal life and happiness. Apart from this there are no absolute requirements for salvation; there are no specific errors of thought "respecting the way of life" which can be said to be "fatal." These are matters which God only knows.[13] Men are "fallible creatures," and God does not expect any more from them than what is within their power.[14] If they take Jesus Christ for their guide, and strive to imitate him, then, God is good, and He will not count their errors and failures against them. The Gospel *promises* salvation to all sinners who *strive*. If they do, God is just, and rewards them accordingly.

It was all very clear to Mayhew. The claim of Calvinism that regeneration is a free gift of God looked to him like pernicious error. Men must have a capacity to accept the Gospel, so that if they will, they can.[15] Calvinism, by minimizing the necessity of effort to will the good, discouraged men from striving. This, surely, was contrary to the interests of the sinners, and kept them away from the "gate."

If Mayhew had stopped here, he would have had no response from the Calvinists, except, perhaps, he would have confirmed his reputation as an Arminian, which would have settled the matter. But, he tried to make it clear that the mere striving of the sinner is no guarantee that he will be saved.[16] In fact, he declared that *some* divine influence is necessary for salvation, and that this is a gift of God.[17] He did not make it quite clear if this influence is absolutely necessary for salvation. If it is, of course, no amount of striving will get the sinner to the "gate," and salvation is a free gift of God. If it is not,— but Mayhew denied this possibility.[18] He even denied that the sinner can strive antecedently to "*any* influence or operation of the good spirit of God upon his heart." [19] This was good Calvinism, but his view of the nature of this "influence" revealed his real sentiments.

"God undoubtedly strives with the sinful, by his word,

his spirit, and the dispensations of his providence; awakening them to a sense of their guilt, misery and danger, antecedently to their striving, or doing anything tending to their salvation." [20]

God, as it were, puts before men His truth and His light, the vision of which tends to make them strive to be saved. Mayhew's account of the "influence" of the Spirit was, thus, a pious way of reiterating his basic notion, namely, that awakened sinners must strive to live in the light of Gospel truth. Of this he was absolutely certain, and he interpreted divine "influence" so as not to contradict its certainty.

He was no less careful not to give the impression that he believed in "salvation by works." Although the sinner must strive, and as a result, may be saved, this does not mean that he *merits* salvation because of his striving.[21] God has freely made salvation conditional upon striving, so that He *may* save him who strives. Having freely laid down this condition, God fulfills it, but not because He is bound by justice to do so. For a free gift does not bind one to an obligation. But again, this is clearly a half-hearted concession to the sentiments of his orthodox public. God has promised freely that He will save sinners if they strive, and He fulfills His promises. God does this freely and necessarily, not because man merits salvation, but because he fulfills the conditions thereof. Anyway, man must strive.

The main thesis of Mayhew's sermons could not but be obvious to his readers. That he covered and apparently modified it with pious statements on the operation of the Spirit and dependence upon God, was useful only in making it sufficiently orthodox to invite criticism and attack from the Calvinists. His views were just pious enough to make them dangerous. Moreover, since the publication of his *Seven Sermons*,[22] liberalism had made sufficient progress to invite genuine controversy. And the doctrine that sinners must strive, being attractive to liberal Calvinists as well as to the more radical liberals, started a heated dispute, in which one Calvinist turned against another, thus sharpening the line dividing those who would glorify God from those who would reform men. Samuel Hopkins took up the cause of the former.

He began boldly. A sinner is one who does not "sincerely and heartily" desire the spiritual blessings included in the "promises of the Gospel." [23] He will not strive to be saved, because the bias of his heart is such that he has no taste for a holy life. Mayhew assumes that the unregenerate can and do strive after holiness.[24] But in doing this he has raised their status too high, and made them regenerate.[25] In order that a man may desire the good, the bias of the heart for evil must be replaced by a bias for good. This takes place in and through regeneration. Therefore, any one who prefers holiness to sin is, by definition, regenerate.

Hopkins has no difficulty in understanding the text of Mayhew's sermons in his own way. "Strive," there, refers to the "exercises and labor of true Christians in their way to heaven," and not to the "unholy exercises and endeavors of those whose hearts are wholly under the dominion of sin." [26] The regenerate, once given a new heart wherewith they can endeavor to live a holy life, are confronted with the further problem of actually attaining godliness. Spiritual rebirth, the transition from self-love to disinterested benevolence, is merely the beginning of a saintly life. The regenerate soul must strive to walk in the path of virtue, and grow into eternal life. "The strait gate" is the end, the climax, of Christian life, and not its beginning. It is the goal of those endowed with a holy disposition, and the unregenerate cannot be conceived as striving to enter in at such a gate. They prefer the ways of sin, and find their joy in the ungodly exercises of their depraved dispositions.

Hopkins is not oblivious to the force of Mayhew's contention. He does not ignore the fact that there are those who, to all appearances, are really wicked and yet seem to be very anxious to go to heaven.[27] But he is quick to point out that their desire is for "deliverance from natural evil," and not for a regenerate life. Men may desire safety under a conviction of conscience, and may feel that happiness is to be had no other way but by sharing in the salvation which is by Jesus Christ.[28] But such an interest in the Gospel has no connection with a genuine relish for a virtuous life. "It is but to delude sinners," to make them believe that their dissatisfaction with the distresses which result from their wickedness is a sign of godliness.[29]

Therefore, the Gospel has no promises to the unregenerate. It would be mockery to tell a man who is not bent on salvation that if he strove hard enough he would attain it. A sinner anxious to be saved must necessarily have the wrong idea of the nature of salvation, an idea congruous with his unholy dispositions. To promise salvation to such a person would be to encourage him into thinking that he loves God and has an adequate idea of heaven; that, although motivated by self-love, he can earn his way into heaven, and enjoy the blessings promised to the pure and the godly.

Hopkins will have no middle way between the love of God and the love of one's self, between salvation and damnation. They are mutually contradictory. Salvation is impossible except through the operation of the Holy Spirit, by the grace of God, and the redeeming work of the Saviour.

"Men being washed by regeneration and renewed by the Holy Ghost, the hard, rebellious heart being subdued in a degree, and a new and opposite bias, which is by our Saviour called an *honest* and *good heart*, being given, the light and truth of God's word enters into the mind, and it discerns the things of the Spirit of God in their reality, beauty, wisdom, glory; and in this view and sense of divine truth the heart approves of the divine character, comes to Christ for life, or believes on him, and sincerely, and heartily asks for the Spirit, or that living water which Christ gives, and which comprehends all good things." [30]

Hopkins did not appreciate the fact that for men of Mayhew's mentality it had become next to impossible to distinguish between the regenerate and the unregenerate. To separate men into the saved and the damned had become artificial and absurd. Looking around him, Mayhew saw that men were more or less good and more or less bad. They seemed to be capable of both good and evil, and there was no telling which side they would swing to next. If they strove to be good, they became better; if they did not, they became worse. Hence, obviously, the wise thing to do was to exhort men to forsake their evil ways and climb the steep hill of righteousness.

For Mayhew, the end of religion was the good life.

Piety, no less than politics, was to be judged by its moral fruits. It was instrumental to the making of decent and happy citizens. Good citizenship required justice, honesty, charity, and the like virtues, which constituted the first principles of social welfare. The purpose of religion was to encourage, cultivate, and accomplish these virtues in the lives of men.[31] And all this requires effort. Men are not at all times inclined to be virtuous. Therefore, clearly, men must strive to enter in at the strait gate. The Calvinist was of another mind. Nothing was more inimical to the interests of his piety than that man should consider himself accomplishing salvation through his own goodness and power. It was the essence of the religion of the Calvinist to attribute all wisdom, power, and goodness to God, and to glorify Him alone. The enlightened liberalism of Mayhew amounted to an indifference to the glory of God. Hence the dialectics. Throughout the disheartening details of the controversy and the diversity of the issues involved, this fundamental spiritual conflict recurs with a significant constancy and precision.

To demonstrate the inability of man to save himself, Hopkins tried to show that in regeneration something happens which otherwise would have been impossible:

"Regeneration does not consist in any exercise of the mind, or any enjoyment; but by being regenerated a foundation is laid in the mind for holy exercises, for hungering and thirsting after righteousness, and eating and drinking in a spiritual sense." [32]

This initial point is imperceptible.[33] It becomes known when the regenerate begins to give signs of relish for holiness. It is but the "foundation of all the discerning of the things of God's moral kingdom, and of all right exercises of heart; this change, I say, is wrought by the Spirit of God, immediately and spontaneously, and altogether imperceptibly by the person who is the subject of it . . . These views and exercises of the regenerate, in which they turn from sin to God, or embrace the Gospel, are often in the Scripture spoken of as included in that change which is called *a being born again*; . . . all the change which is perceptible, and in which man is active, consists in this. And this is sometimes called, by divines, *active conversion*, to distinguish it from regeneration, or that change in which men are passive." [34]

This is clearly an apology, and it put Hopkins in a difficult position. Empirically, he cannot see much that is wrong with Mayhew's conception of growth into godliness. He accepts that saintliness, "true discerning of the things of God's moral kingdom," is attained through discipline and effort. But then, how is it that man is saved by the grace of God and the internal operation of the Holy Spirit, and thus alone? The answer of Hopkins is that all effort toward holiness is preceded by an imperceptible and immediate operation of the Spirit. He thus saves the Calvinistic scheme of salvation, and at the same time, grants the necessity of human striving. It was clever and dialectically impregnable, but nevertheless it was futile. It is necessarily hard to demonstrate an imperceptible fact, and when men are determined to disbelieve it, it is wellnigh impossible. Such a notion of regeneration was a dialectical necessity in the scheme of Hopkins, but it had no practical place in that of Mayhew.

This initial evasion in the thought of Hopkins had further consequences:

"Though the Spirit operates in a sense and degree in

regeneration, yet, as he does not regenerate men as being given as an abiding principle of life, but this change is produced as an unpromised favour, which neither unites them to Christ nor gives them an interest to any promise in the Bible, there appears great propriety in promising the Spirit as an abiding principle of eternal life, which comprehends all good things to those exercises or acts by which the regenerate actively unite themselves to Christ . . . and our being directed to believe on Christ in order to this, and ask for Christ in this sense, with a promise that he shall be given, is no argument that, in order to thus believing and asking, we must not first be born of God; therefore, the doctor's argument is wholly without foundation." [35]

Hopkins makes regeneration not only imperceptible, but also insufficient for salvation. It neither involves an "abiding principle of life," nor does it "unite them to Christ." The "abiding principle of eternal life" is promised on the basis of those "exercises and acts by which the regenerate actually unite themselves to Christ." Such a theory of salvation was both complicated and meaningless. Regeneration became merely an "X," which filled a gap in a theological structure; a mere postulate in an ideology. Thus, at least one Calvinistic doctrine lost its empirical significance. It became merely a "doctrine."

Hopkins could not avoid the question, Are there no "means" of salvation? Is there no benefit to be derived from an acquaintance with the Gospel on the part of the unregenerate? To answer these questions negatively would have been to maintain that there should be no effort made to present the Gospel and the benefits of holiness to sinners, which was contrary both to the churches'

practice and to his clerical common sense. Therefore, he
tried to establish the necessity of "means" without grant-
ing their efficacy.

"All those things, those institutions and exercises, which
tend to instruct mankind in the knowledge of truth; to
excite the attention, to convey truth to the mind, and
hold it up in its view; all these, I say, are in a more re-
mote sense the means of grace and salvation. Such are
all those things, those circumstances and events in the
natural and moral world, which are adapted to instruct
mankind. Such, in a special manner, is divine revelation,
and all those institutions and appointments therein, to be
attended on by men. Such are reading the Bible, public
and private instructions, religious conversation, serious
meditation on things divine, etc., and particularly prayer,
which is the most solemn way of meditating on divine
truth." [36]

That these "means" are necessary for salvation was no
less obvious to Hopkins than to Mayhew. To deny it
would have meant a repudiation of the "institutions and
exercises" of organized religion. In New England, religion and church-membership had been inseparable ideas.
Divine grace without good works was unthinkable. Antinomianism was a heresy which no respectable Puritan
could tolerate. From the beginning, he admitted that the
grace of God is the only cause of salvation, and proceeded
to abhor any one who concluded that therefore going to
church is unnecessary. He had somehow combined piety
with common sense, and reason "got over" the contradiction as best it could. Hopkins' solution to the problem
was that means are necessary for the cultivation of godliness, but that they do not produce it. [37] Of course, the

distinction is somewhat subtle, and failed to carry conviction to the champions of striving.

The compromises of Hopkins were far from satisfactory
to those who could not appreciate his great concern to uphold the ideas of divine sovereignty and human depravity.
The venerable Rev. Jedidiah Mills attacked him at a
most vulnerable point.[38]   In order to show the insuffi-
ciency of "speculative knowledge" for salvation, Hopkins
had gone so far as to insist that those who have such
knowledge and resist the Gospel call are more odious in
the sight of God than those who are completely ignorant
of divine truth.[39]   In 1767 Mills replied:

"I appeal to the common sense of mankind, is not this
strange divinity?   What! is there no possibility that the
drunkard, the thief, the liar, the profane swearer, the
adulterer, the murderer, the blasphemer should become,
on the whole, less vicious in God's sight while unregenerate, by reforming all this atrocious wickedness, tho' on
no higher principle than that of natural conscience, awakened by the common influences of the spirit . . . to a
sense of the majesty and perfections of God, the ill desert
of sin, and fears of divine wrath, than he would be, continuing the practice of all this wickedness? . . . Strange
absurdity this!" [40]

Hopkins appeared to Mills to contend that a better man
is a worse man, and of course it was absurd.   Surely, a
murderer, a blasphemer, etc., is not a better man than one
who does not indulge in such wickedness, or is doing his
best not to!   It seemed an abominable idea that a "hardened sinner" should be less odious in the sight of God
than one who is "awakened" and penitent.   Mills practically identified the idea of sin with the legalistic concept

of guilt. The more odious the crime, the greater is the guilt, or sin. The less of a criminal a person is, the better man he is, and at a higher level of Christian character. "There is such a thing among the unregenerate under the gospel, as being in a state nigh to and far from the kingdom of God." [41] Mills granted readily that one who "sins against a greater degree of light, is, in that respect a greater sinner." [42] But, he would not grant that "he is so, on the whole, all other respects considered." [43] What irritated him is that a greater doer of evil should be considered a lesser sinner. He was almost statistical.

"For instance, suppose A and B are favour'd with equal degrees of light, and suppose B has three degrees of strength of bias and inclination to sin, more than A, which there can be no reasonable doubt may be the case; can it once be doubted here, whether B is more vile and odious in God's sight than A sinning against the same degree of light?" [44]

The truth is that Mills was unable to understand and appreciate the meaning of Hopkins' contention. For the latter regeneration is a definite event which marks the beginning of a new life. The sinner is one who is not regenerate, and the further one is from regeneration, the more of a sinner he is. The "awakened sinner" is one who fails to embrace the Gospel in spite of the fact that he knows it to be the standard of a good life. He knows the good, and refuses to live by it. Therefore, his condition is far more serious than that of a person who is ignorant of the truth and the light of divine revelation. The latter may sometime come to know the truth, and repent; but the former has known it, and failed to repent. And without repentance there can be no salvation. Nothing short of a change of heart can turn the sinner into a saint. This is what neither Mayhew nor Mills could comprehend. As they saw it, to be a saint is to lead a good life; and the better a man's life, the more of a saint he is. Unfortunately for his cause, Hopkins himself was not immune to the moral principles which had captured the hearts of his opponents. His contention that the "awakened sinner" is a greater sinner than one who is ignorant and hardened, assumed that there are degrees of sinfulness, and made the attack of Mills pertinent. In fighting the heresies of others, Hopkins had appropriated their axioms and interests, and thus had produced a brand of Calvinism, "the new divinity," which was perplexing and unattractive. It was Calvinism soiled and bruised in its struggle against the humanitarianism of the age, exaggerated here, distorted there, sheepish, worried, and weakening. It annoyed many of the orthodox, irritated the enlightened, and filled the land with discord and trouble.[45]

Mills claimed a great dislike for dispute, but he produced one of the most heated documents of the controversy. He saw in the exponents of the "new divinity" the very "instruments of the adversary."[46] He claimed to be a more genuine Calvinist than Hopkins, and a defender of real orthodoxy. Thus assailed by both the orthodox and the unorthodox, Hopkins came forward with a long, dull, but significant vindication of his theory of *the true state and character of the unregenerate, stripped of all misrepresentation and disguise.*[47] His defense of orthodoxy was becoming more dialectical and unpalatable than ever.

"Mr. M.'s unregenerate sinners 'frame their doings to turn unto their God.' They seek salvation as the greedy merchant seeks goodly pearls. They labor not for the meat which perisheth, but for the meat which endureth unto everlasting life. They follow on to know the Lord, and seek first the kingdom of God and his righteousness. In a word, they deny ungodliness and worldly lusts, and live soberly, righteously, and godly in this present world." [48]

Hopkins admits that if this is true, then there is no argument. Therefore, he does his best to show that the unregenerate are not quite so "blameless and fair" as Mills would make them, and proceeds to paint as dark a picture of human nature as possible.[49] He had, as it were, unconsciously fallen into a trap. The objection of Mayhew and other friends of mankind to Calvinism was that it ignored the grains of goodness in human nature. It seemed absurd that man should be described as a filthy worm of the earth, a creature devoid of all excellence and power. And a theology which emphasized such an estimate of his "true state and character" had all the earmarks of a pernicious lie. Hopkins was on the wrong side of the fence.

He had not only set himself against the sentiments of Revolutionary New England, but he had also appropriated one of its most basic principles. The great importance which he attaches to the idea of the more heinous sinfulness of the "awakened sinner" discloses a strong bias to consider the selfish will as definitive of sin. Hopkins protested against Mills' description of the unregenerate "as being under an impotence which does in some measure, if not wholly, excuse." [50] The "awakened sinner" has the power to turn to God, but he lacks the inclination.[51] The greater is this contrariness of the will, the greater is the sinfulness.[52]   In short, the wilfulness of opposition to God is the measure of sinfulness.[53]

Such a view of sin was a curious hybrid of Calvinism and Arminianism, and it introduced confusions which no amount of disputation could eliminate.   It admitted various degrees of sinfulness.   Regeneration became an enigma, and salvation a matter of a gradual attainment of good character.   The doctrine of human inability assumed a dubious character, and total depravity became meaningless.   Hopkins had allowed himself to be dominated by the moral emphasis, and thus completely vitiated Edwards' conception of sinfulness as a lack of the sense of divine glory.   Transferring depravity from man as man to his "will," Hopkins exposed himself to a confusion which, from a Calvinistic point of view, underlay all the heresies of subsequent New England theology. Hopkins was too near Edwards to grasp the implications of his moralism, and waxed sufficiently dialectical to miss a full view of its conflict with the fundamentals of the piety of his master.   In Hopkins, Calvinism was suffering from focusing attention on its enemies instead of on its God.

The Rev. John Smalley, of New Britain, Conn., an outstanding defender of New England Theology, wrote *Two Discourses on the Consistency of the Sinner's Inability to comply with the Gospel; with his inexcusable Guilt in not complying with it, illustrated and confirmed.*[54]   These discourses throw a clear and helpful light on the troubles of orthodoxy.   The perennial problem put before Calvinism, and now presented by its enemies with a triumphant insistence, was, if the sinner is unable to save himself, how is it that he is to be blamed for his sinfulness?   The conception of guilt as inseparable from free-will and responsibility, which had now become a moral axiom among enlightened thinkers, called for a categorical answer from the Calvinists. Smalley, like Hopkins, set himself to show that the sinner is both able and unable to "comply with the Gospel."

He does not mince words. He declares openly that the heathen, the idiots, "quite delirious persons," and all those whose "natural capacity was impaired or lost by the fall," may not and will not be punished for not embracing the Gospel.[55] "A man's *present* duty cannot exceed his present strength."[56] It is obvious to Smalley, as well as to all other men of "reason and common sense," that natural inability to do that which is right cannot be sin, for it "consists in, or arises from, want of understanding, bodily strength, opportunity; or *whatever may prevent,* our doing a thing, when we are willing, and strongly disposed and inclined to do it."[57] Such inability is radically different from "moral inability," which is "the want of heart, or disposition, or will, to do a thing."[58] The inability of sinners is *moral.* They can, they have natural ability; but they will not, they have not moral ability.

However, Smalley is a Calvinist. The above distinction, which he presents clearly and categorically, much in the vein of thoroughgoing Arminianism, does not lead him to accept the conception of "free-will" as necessary for moral responsibility and guilt. Moral inability, a wicked disposition, is as much governed by necessity as natural inability, inability due to a physical defect or circumstance. The sinner *will not* love God. But if this is due to a defect in his moral constitution, then how is the sinner to be blamed for the perversity of his will? Smalley's answer is genuinely Edwardean. One is to be praised for his good motives and dispositions, another is to be blamed for bad ones, quite apart from the question as to whether they are free or not. Therefore, the distinction between natural and moral inability is useless as a safeguard for the conception of "responsibility." Smalley's sinner is "guilty," but he is hardly "responsible." Thus, there is no moral judgment in the free-willist sense. Morals is a matter of approbation and disapprobation. In the last analysis, Smalley's distinction amounts to a smoke screen intended for the eyes of his opponents; at heart he remains an Edwardean.

And yet, his rigorous apology for the heathen, the idiots, and the like, makes it evident that he could not remain indifferent to the growing humanitarianism of the age. It exhibits a "failure of nerve," which marked the beginning of defeat. On the basis of his own ethical principles, moral delinquency is no less detestable in the heathen and the idiots than in others. "Natural" misfits may be quite as much rogues and scoundrels as the "moral." They may trample upon every rule of decency and godliness. In so far as they disobey God, they live apart from God; or, what is the same thing, they are punished as consistently as "moral" sinners. This is what the new romanticism could not accept, and Calvinists like Smalley had to save their good name by compromise. The sturdy empiricism of Calvinism was too much for the humane heart of the new age. Smalley had to admit that those who sin "from, want of understanding, bodily strength, opportunity," etc., "will not be punished for not embracing the Gospel." He also, like Hopkins, vitiated Edwards' principle that a sinful state is a state of blind-

ness to the glory of God, and that the punishment of sin
is the consequence of it.[59]

The opponents of the "new divinity" were not satisfied.
In fact, they were irritated. The complicated and bewildering defenses of Hopkins and Smalley were too obviously subterfuges. Moreover, they disregarded the liberal atmosphere in which individual and social justice,
human rights, and the happiness of the majority, were
substantial ingredients. On the Calvinist side, there was
enough of real orthodoxy in the new divinity to worry the
more conventional Calvinists, who feared that they too
would be discredited by such extravagances.

William Hart, pastor of the First Church at Saybrook,
speaking for the Old Calvinists, viewed the situation with
alarm, and made some *Brief Remarks on a number of
False Propositions, and Dangerous Errors, which are
spreading in the Country.*[60] "Too many" of the "covenant
people" have accepted the "abominable doctrine" of Hopkins and Whitaker,[61] so that "the stones of the street" are
expected to "cry out." [62]

"If the convinced sinner can't yet act upon the first and
highest motive, yet in acting as he ought on the subordinate principle, he acts right as far as he goes, and as God
wills him to do, though he does not go so far as he
ought." [63]

"If men will not be influenced by the lower, there is
no probability that they will ever have given them the
higher." [64]

Hart boldly accepts salvation as a matter of progressive appropriation of the divine will, a process of piece-
meal and gradual conformity to the commands of God.
In fact, his chief contribution to the controversy is his

vehement insistence that the regenerating power of the Spirit is strictly *moral;* that He acts as the "Spirit of truth, righteousness and love." [65] The manifestation of this moral power is "faith," and this leads to repentance and regeneration.[66] His triumphant quarrel with Hopkins and Whitaker is that they have made regeneration a purely mechanical event, something like a change in blood pressure. There is no initial, secret, immediate, physical regeneration. Under the moral influence of the Gospel, man is influenced by the moral power of the Spirit, and faith and the rest follow. It is through the Gospel that men are transformed.[67] To deny this is to deny the moral power of the Gospel, for powers are either mechanical or moral. Nor does Hart stop here.

"There is in man a natural faculty whereby he is rendered capable of discerning and distinguishing between moral good and evil, as well as natural, and readily perceives the one to be right, amiable, and worthy of esteem and honour, the other wrong, hateful and blame-worthy, immediately, as soon as these objects are seen by the mind in their true light, or as being what they really are, without any further reasoning about them." [68]

This is a weighty statement. Man has an inborn capacity to understand and embrace the Gospel. As man, far from being depraved, he possesses a faculty whereby he can really and truly follow the commands of God. His will, as such, is not contrary to that of God, but in harmony with it. When man is brought face to face with the true and the good, his mind perceives them, and his heart approves of them. This is his natural reaction to God and to the Gospel. Significantly, it is also the basis of conscience and moral government.[69]

The enmity of the sinner to God is, thus, neither innate nor fundamental, but a mere "secondary passion," a consequence of particular wrong affections and deeds, indulged in in opposition to the law and the will of God.[70] Having come under the influence of these, the sinner becomes an enemy of godliness, not because he does not know or approve of it, but because it is against his interests.[71] He knows the good, but he wills to do the bad. He approves of virtue, but he wills to follow evil. And the more he perseveres in wickedness, the more he hates God. But this hatred is a purely "relative" matter, and arises from "interested views."[72] In fact, it is hardly real; it is due to misunderstanding and rationalization. The sinner cheats himself into believing that he loves evil.[73]

"The true and effectual cure of this kind of enmity, is accomplished by correcting these unhappy misapprehensions, and giving the mind a just view of the true character of God, and setting his actions and dispensations in that true light wherein he himself has placed them."[74]

The doctrine of total depravity is thus discarded. Original sin is out of question. Salvation is brought about by presenting the mind of the sinner with the true light of the Gospel. When this is done, he will readily accept it, because he is inherently a righteous and intelligent being. He has sinned because of certain acquired habits and interests. When he discovers their evil tendencies and character, he will relinquish them, and turn to the path of righteousness.

Hart hated the "new divinity."

"This new system, or rather chaos of divinity, is a hard-hearted, arbitrary, cruel tyrant, a tormenter of souls; it scandalously misrepresents the character and conduct of

God, and implicitly blasphemes the dispensation of his grace to the sinful world; it offers as great affront to reason, common sense and experience, as the doctrines of Rome; and the highest possible abuse to human nature." [75]

"It is greatly wished that all who have the office of teachers of religion to others, would themselves learn of Jesus Christ, to give a honoring representation of his Father's more than paternal *kindness and love toward man*, and breath Jesus' compassionate tenderness towards poor perishing sinners, in their doctrine." [76]

In such a statement, one can hardly fail to recognize the beginnings in New England of the "sublime beliefs" in the dignity of man and the "paternal love and kindness" of God, which have become the first principles of an enlightened Christian faith. Hart's opponents had insulted human nature and obscured the tender love of the heavenly Father; two charges either one of which alone was sufficient to disgrace the "new divinity" in the eyes of those who believed in a merely good God, and loved mankind.

Beautiful as Hart's sentiments on God and man were, he was far from invulnerable. His defiantly moralistic description of the process of salvation made the "operation" of the Spirit of God in the hearts of sinners unnecessary. To all appearances, provided the sinner acquired a true knowledge of the Word, or, what amounts to the same thing, provided he came under the moral influence of the Gospel, he was quite sufficient unto himself. This is precisely the conclusion which Hopkins, and after him, Whitaker,[77] had been trying to combat. The latter advocated the "mechanical" hypothesis of the operation of the Spirit, not because he thought that he had discovered its precise mechanical character, but because he would not have it described as "moral suasion" or "light." The perversity of the sinner is not merely "moral," an abstract "unwillingness" due to a misapprehension of Gospel truth. The roots of evil are seated in sentiment, in feelings and dispositions, in the relish of the heart for wickedness. This taste of the heart for sin, this stubborn propensity to evil, is more and other than "moral," and cannot be eliminated with "moral suasion." [78] The malady of the sinner is quasi-physical, therefore only a "mechanical" operation of the Spirit can effectuate regeneration. Whitaker was well aware that the description of the power of the Spirit as "mechanical" was not amenable to accurate demonstration, and was open to "moral" objections. Therefore, he gave his theological reason for adopting it, namely, the principle that it is the Spirit of God that saves the sinner.

"We agree that the motives have no power till the spirit exerts *some kind* of energy, so that their efficacy is only with, and never without it. Now since we agree in this, our differing about the *kind* of this energy, will not help Mr. H. nor free his doctrine of these consequences, because neither the *physical*, nor the *moral* energy of the spirit is in the power of any man . . . He must either assert . . . that there is something inherent in the truth that regenerates; or, which is nearly the same thing, deny the necessity of both the physical and moral energy of the spirit in regeneration." [79]

This put Hart on the defensive. Nor did the *Animadversions* of Hopkins afford any relief.[80] Besides returning upon Hart some of his compliments and appeals to authority, Hopkins repeated in no uncertain terms that before the Spirit can let in "light," He must give the unregenerate a "light, sweet, attractive sense," which will enable him to appropriate the truths and the commands of the Gospel. "The letting in the light" must be preceded by a change of heart, which can only be caused by an *"immediate* operation, quite different from moral suasion, or the power of holy truth and love." [81]

Hart the would-be Calvinist is irritated. Hopkins has misrepresented him, "concealed his sentiment from his reader, and substituted a very different one in its place." [82] *Of course* Hart believes in the enmity of the sinner to God, and when he described it as "partial," he meant "corrupt," and not "in part." [83] The controversy was degenerating into a quarrel. Hart certainly believes in the total depravity of man as a "general doctrine." "No sound Calvinist" could believe otherwise. But surely, he does not have to accept Hopkins' interpretation of it! [84]

"You appear to have a great disposition to make your readers think me an Arminian . . . I suffer you to enjoy the pleasure. Perhaps I may soon have the opportunity to let the public know more fully what my sentiments are relating these matters." [85]

The controversy continued, becoming increasingly more furious and complicated.[86] There was no end to repetition, compromise, and misrepresentation. Both sides were determined to prove themselves genuine Calvinists in spite of the fact that at heart they represented fundamentally divergent types of mentality and temperament. The idea of salvation, which Hart the Old Calvinist shared with Mayhew the Arminian, grew out of views on virtue and human nature which made Hopkins' and Whitaker's theory of regeneration superfluous and even pernicious. The former had come to be profoundly convinced that men "have naturally some degree of true virtue, and that their natural corruption is partial, as limited and restricted by some remaining degree of true virtue in the heart naturally." [87]   Hart never failed to reiterate this basic conviction.   Therefore, to him, Hopkins' Calvinistic notion of benevolence as a free gift of God, effectuated by the operation of the Holy Spirit, was essentially unpalatable. Hart could make little of Edwards' "true virtue" or Hopkins' "spiritual sense."   Therefore, in spite of his vehement claims to the contrary, the doctrines of divine sovereignty, total depravity, justification by faith, which constituted the essentials of Calvinistic piety, occupied little place in his thought.   And therefore, he did not appreciate the earnest protests of Hopkins and Whitaker. The latter, although they were deeply conscious of the disastrous tendencies of their opponents' moralism, could not resist its common sense and human appeal, and allowed themselves to be dragged into controversy and confusion. The vision of Calvinism was being darkened by the common sense of the new age.   It was losing its reality as human experience and, therefore, its appeal to the hearts and the minds of men.   The logic of Calvinistic piety was being transformed into a vast, complicated, and colorless theological structure, bewildering to its friends and ridiculous to enemies.   It was like a proud and beggared king, hiding his shame with scarlet rags and yellow trinkets!

CHAPTER IV

THE WANING GLORY OF GOD

Consistently with his supreme delight in God's sovereignty, Edwards conceived "true virtue" as "benevolence to Being in general." [1] Every individual existent occupies a certain place in the order of things or "Being in general." In order to gain an adequate appreciation of anything, therefore, it is necessary that "Being in general" be the standard of judgment. A disinterested approach to the facts of life, with a view to determining their true light in the glory of creation, to understand and to appreciate them as elements in universal Being, is the foundation and substance of "true virtue." Therefore, an adequate "sense of proportion" is a prime requisite for the exercise of all truly virtuous affection. Although an initial disinterestedness is the essence of true virtue, its exercise is conditioned upon a correct view of the relative significance of events in the order of reality. Empirically, it is exhibited in an intelligent love for things in particular, according to their meaning in a larger whole of which they are elements. Being in general is the complete wholeness or essence of Being.

Affections which particular objects arouse in men because of their immediate influences upon them are necessarily distinct from true virtue. Interested love or "the love of complacence," in contrast to the "love of benevolence," is based upon self-love. In such love, the appreciation extended to an object of interest is determined by its significance for the person who does the appreciating. The center of reference is the self, as if it were the point around which all creation moves. That which is delightful to it and amiable to its interests, is good; that which is otherwise, is evil.

The principles of social morality, mutuality, sympathy, self-love,—are necessary for "preservation." [2] As physical beings, men seek to appropriate the means of livelihood and prosperity. Such interests bring men into groups, in which certain principles of good conduct must be held up for the mutual benefit of those concerned. Honesty, sobriety, industry, faithfulness, are thus necessary for human welfare. However, such morality is motivated and exercised differently from "true virtue." The virtues which it demands and encourages are "natural" and "secondary." [3] A love based upon a supreme interest in anything in particular, be it the self, or the derivative interests in things directly or indirectly related to it, completely distorts the true meanings of events in their relation to "Being in general." Animal and social morality, which is based upon the principle of self-love or self-preservation, is in a way the direct contrary of "true virtue." Through it, things are seen, as it were, upside down. Instead of being appreciated for what they are and because of their position in the world, they are invested with values which are instrumental to ends entertained by any given person. Since disinterested observation reveals a realm of events in which no particular event is an ultimate value, an egocentric universe is an illusion produced by self-love. Every particular thing is both an end and a means, it comes and it goes, leaving behind it a new universe. No event, nor even the universe at any given moment, is of ultimate significance. Therefore, true virtue must be a benevolent regard to an object as included in a harmony of all existence, which is none other than "Being in general."

For a truly virtuous person the supreme object of love is God. The events of the world, in their successive appearances, are partial, "*ad extra*" communications of the infinite internal glory of God. Therefore, a benevolent regard toward the universe, a consent of the heart to its course and "constitution," implies the harmony of the will with the facts of existence, a delight in them not merely for their own sake, but as evidences of the handiwork of God. Creation is a dim and partial "reflection of the diffused beams of the glory of God." Therefore, the glory of God as communicated to and exhibited in His creation is an object more worthy of benevolent regard than any particular thing in heaven or on earth. Furthermore God, in whom all successive existences, past and yet to be, have their source and their being, is infinitely greater than His creation. God's internal glory is far greater than its manifestations in the world, so that, compared to Him, all things are as mere dust. And thus, "a benevolent propensity of heart to Being in general, and a temper or disposition to love God supremely, are in effect the same thing." [4] Such is "true GRACE and real HOLINESS."

"This consists in the expression of God's perfections in their proper effects,—the communications of the infinite fullness of God to the creature—the creature's highest esteem of God, love to, and joy in him—and in the proper exercises and expressions of these." [5]

"God's last end in creating the world" was to communicate *ad extra* the infinite fullness of his internal glory.

Considering the nature of true virtue, this is a self-evident proposition. To glorify God is the last end of true virtue or holiness, and conversely, God, who is infinitely truly virtuous, could have no other end in creating the world than His own glory. God is internally moved to create a glorious world, and this is His reason for doing it. The world exists in order to show what it is. "We may justly infer what God intends from what he actually does." God's ends are the same as His acts.

"The most proper *evidence* of love to a created being arising from the temper of mind wherein consists a supreme propensity of heart to God, seems to be the agreeableness to the kind and degree of our love to *God's end* in our creation, and in the creation of all things, and the coincidence of the exercise of our love, in their manner, order, measure, with the *manner* in which *God* himself exercises love to the creature in the creation and the government of the world, and the way in which God, as the first cause and supreme disposer of all things, has respect to the creature's happiness in subordination to himself as his own supreme end." [6]

God's love for His creatures is subsumed under His love for His own glory. In creating the world God had "respect to the creature's happiness" only in so far as true happiness consists in the worship and the service of God, in seeking the glory of God, which is the proper exercise of true virtue.

Such holiness or virtue is incommensurate with natural or secondary virtue. These two are distinct in temper, perspective, and consequence. They are two different affections, different in origin and in quality. Men of true virtue live in a world which is different from that in which

men of natural virtue live. To the eyes of true virtue the
natural world is a supernatural world. The events of life
are clothed with the qualities they have in God's sight.
The natural affections are transformed in the new perspective; they lose their individual qualities in the all-absorb-
ing appreciation of their interrelatedness, and this appreciation becomes the dominant temper of the soul. Such a
soul is a new soul. The holy man is a new creature.

The controversy over regeneration which we described
in the last chapter was not altogether futile. It failed to
bring about a mutual understanding between the two parties, but it precipitated other considerations which clarify
the nature of the difficulties involved, and put its essen-
tials in bold relief. Toward the end of the controversy,
Whitaker put the problem of regeneration in a way which
was highly provoking. Hart, said Whitaker, either accepts that regeneration is the work of the Spirit, or he denies it. If he accepts it, then he must admit the error of
his contention that "men have naturally some degree of
true virtue." If he denies it, he must also deny that divine
grace is a free gift of God, and relinquish his claim to being
a Calvinist.[7] This is the issue which "moral suasion" had
concealed and confused, and Whitaker forced it upon Hart
with clarity and precision.

Hart is again aroused. "Bread of Deceit is sweet to
Man. But afterwards his Mouth shall be filled with
Gravel." And he proceeds to explain:

"In my account of the moral sense natural and essential
to men as a moral agent, you think you find a 'good definition of a spiritual taste,' or holy love to spiritual good:
But in this you err. That approbation of reason and the

moral sense to things morally good, which I spake of, as quoted above, is not the same thing with a supreme love and preferring choice of them by the heart; which is essential to true virtue. . . . The approbation of the conscience or the moral sense, and the ruling affection and choice of the heart, are frequently as far asunder, in sinful beings, as the city of God and the kingdom of Satan." [8]

After Whitaker's challenge this was unavoidable. Hart was quick to sense the implications of such a statement, and hastened to argue that they do not necessarily follow. He tried to reinterpret and soften it, but the task proved unrewarding. In response to the sharp and clear challenge of Whitaker, he was forced to express sentiments which no amount of subtlety and dialectics could reconcile. As both he and his opponents saw it, salvation is either through the power of God or through the power of man. Beneath the perplexing details of the controversy, it was clear that they were confronted with a deadlock. And so long as Calvinism's formidable barrier between "holy love" and secular morality remained intact, it could not be otherwise.

Therefore, a year after the conclusion of his spectacular duel with Hopkins and Whitaker, Hart wrote his *Remarks on President Edwards's Dissertations concerning the Nature of true Virtue: Shewing that he has given a wrong Idea and Definition of Virtue, and is inconsistent with himself*. Hart recognized that Edwards' *True Virtue* was the "root of the tree" which had brought forth the turpitudes of his opponents.[9] He, a professed Calvinist, now struck at the roots of Calvinism.

He had an uncanny sense for the weaknesses of his opponents, real or apparent. He based his case against Edwards upon the following statement of the latter: "True virtue most essentially consists in benevolence to Being in general." [10] Hart's bold rejoinder was:

"Does not this represent being simply considered as the supreme object of virtuous regard, and make it an idol, virtue itself idolatrous? Does it not in effect represent love to God as the result of our own virtuous love to simple being, virtue's idol, rather than of his virtuous attraction, and quickening love to us while we were sinners?" [11]

This was a clever *ruse de guerre,* but none the less a complete misrepresentation of Edwards. Hart understood "Being in general" to mean "all and every being"; he thought of God as one being among the many; therefore, he took "Being in general" to be distinct from and more than God. "Being in general," according to Edwards, is not the totality of all things, nor is it any particular being. In a physical sense, it is *no* being. It is Being in general, a metaphysical, and not a physical, being. It is, as it were, the metaphysical counterpart of benevolence, the divine constitution.

Hart's own notions concerning the nature of true virtue reveal a mentality which made him incapable of understanding the thought of Edwards. He was possessed of a passion other than that of Edwards. He was living in another world; in a society of men struggling to be honest, sober, and happy; in which Edwards' idea of godliness was sentimental "enthusiasm" and metaphysical jargon. Hart's thought was the reflection of the practical and moralistic temper of the age.

"Moral virtue (or holiness) in the most comprehensive sense of the words, includes all that is morally good and right in moral beings, and, as such, worthy of approbation, praise, and reward." [12]

"Virtue is a complex thing . . . includes various affections equally original and essential to virtue . . . These are all perfectly harmonious. Their result is honor and happiness." [13]

"True virtue . . . in general, consists in right and equitable dispositions and actions towards God and our fellow servants." [14]

The general import of such passages is clear, and to be readily distinguished from Edwards' description of true virtue. Holiness is here identical with "moral virtue," which rests upon "approbation and praise." Love to God is but an application of this general principle. It is one of the affections which go into the making of a virtuous person. God is supremely good and praiseworthy. He is the author of the blessings of life, and as such, reveals himself to us as a benevolent Father. He excites us to approbation and love. We approve of God and men for the many good qualities they possess, and our own virtue consists in "right and equitable dispositions and actions" directed towards them. And the reward of us all, God and man, is "honor and happiness." All distinction between religion and morality, as "affections," is thus obliterated. Their objects may be different, but they possess the same quality of affection, and are grounded in the approbation of that which is good and conducive to honor and happiness. As Hart saw it, Edwards had fallen into great error by describing true virtue as a certain unique sort of taste or disposition, and had thus obscured its essentially and exclusively "moral" character.

"The truth is, this marvellous scheme has changed the

natural, moral beauty and glory of true virtue, into an image made like to the beauty of an equilateral triangle or a chess-board." [15]

In the mind of Hart there is a sharp and all important distinction between ethics and esthetics. Moral approval of the behavior of responsible beings and the appreciation of the beauty of physical beings fall into two radically distinct categories. The first defines virtue, the second is totally irrelevant to it. The first is a "moral" affair, the second a matter of enjoyment, an esthetic affair. Edwards' description of virtue as a kind of "taste" or "relish" made it dangerously like delight in a beautiful scenery or a handsome physique. This was to liken the excellences of moral agents to the "beauty of an equilateral triangle or a chess-board," and hence intolerable.

If virtue is a matter of being in possession of a given number of moral qualities, then there must be many varieties of saints and sinners, and many degrees of goodness and wickedness.

"A distinction ought to be made between the denominating character of the agent, and that of particular actions which he does. These do not always agree. Both virtuous and vicious men are generally imperfect in their respective characters in this life." [16]

"Some particular actions, in both, are governed by, and denominated from the weaker principles and springs of action, in them, and are inconsistent with, and belie their true, prevailing, denominating characters." [17]

There are gradations in the "principles and springs" of action; these may be "evil," "weaker," "middle," or "truly virtuous." [18] All but that which is "evil" is "friendly to virtue," [19] and is not "sinful or vicious." Below "true virtue," in which the free choice of that which is good is the denominating character, there are an indefinite number of degrees of goodness and sinfulness. Even where the "denominating character" is virtuous, goodness must vary with the frequency and the persistence of actions which are governed by it. Hart is an inveterate moralist, and his theory of ethics involves a radical moral atomism.

According to him, Edwards has reversed the whole process of growth into sainthood. This begins with a benevolent regard for certain, limited facts of experience. Then, "when the mind is so opened and enlarged, as to take in its view, his whole family as being such, and objects of his benevolent regard," "virtuous love or benevolence becomes general, and extends to all." [20] Of course, in such a scheme, any strict theory of regeneration is meaningless.

In truth, Hart has roundly discarded the "spiritual" half of Edwards' description of virtue. His views constitute an account of what Edwards calls the "love of complacence," natural, secondary, and negative virtue. This shift is of supreme significance for an understanding of the decline of Calvinism in New England. The common sense ethics of a secular age was undermining the piety of Calvinism. Its ministerial champions were neither so clear nor so clever as an Edwards or a Whitaker. But their ill-concealed belief in the power and dignity of man, their supreme concern with social virtues and human happiness, and their general conformity to ethical and theological views which grew out of these, made them popular and powerful.[21]

Once again, Hopkins undertook to vindicate Edwards.[22] It is an interesting defense.

"Love to Being in general is obedience to the law of God, commanding us to love God and our fellow creatures; for these are being in general and comprehend the whole of being. He who does not exercise universal benevolence, does not obey the first nor the second command; but he who loves being as such, or simply considered, which is the same as being in general,—I say, he who loves being in general, loves God and his fellow creatures, and, therefore, obeys the two great commands."

"If being in general was something distinct from God and the creature, and more than these, and not included in them, the objection [that 'according to this notion . . . love to God as well as our neighbour is the offspring of a general indeterminate benevolence'], would appear to have some foundation." [23]

"The law of God requires universal goodness, or love, and nothing else, in which Mr. Edwards says all true virtue consists." [24]

Hopkins did not quite lose sight of the difference between holy love and social morality. So far he was a true disciple of Edwards. But he lacked the intellectual grasp of his master, and therefore could not but modify his teaching at every turn. His dialectical acumen was an inadequate substitute for the vision and understanding of Edwards. He grasped the logic of Edwards' Calvinism, but the contents of Edwards' soul were beyond his capacities.

He equated "Being in general" with "God and our fellow creatures," and thus made it stand for the *sum* of all being. In this way he eliminated "virtue's idol," but on the other hand, he introduced a new and insuperable difficulty. For if "Being in general" stands for the totality of being, then, before one can love any one particular being, he must needs love all particular beings, which is impossible.

The consequences of such a misinterpretation were far-reaching. Almost unconsciously, Hopkins gave "Being in general" the still more limited meaning of God and our fellowmen, or "intelligent creation." In this way, the whole Calvinistic perspective has come to a vanishing point. Holy love, as a spontaneous conformity of the will to the decrees of God as revealed in the facts of life, is replaced by another love, inspired by a good God seeking the happiness of men. Intelligent creation is distinguished sharply from unintelligent creation, its physical milieu, and the events which constitute the latter have become irrelevant to holy love. The world in which we live is now mere "nature," a dumb environment supporting mankind. Hopkins realized little that this was a death-blow to that "natural piety" which belonged to the essence of the theology of which he was the outstanding advocate. With such a limited perspective on life, Hopkins impoverished the Calvinistic "glory of God" beyond recognition. He had drunk too deeply of the humanitarian spirit, which was reducing Calvinism to a formal legalism by forcing it to think in its own terms, though not toward its own conclusions.

Hopkins said explicitly: "I say, he who loves Being in general loves God and his fellow creatures, and therefore, obeys the first two commands." That is precisely what Hart and every enlightened enemy of Hopkinsianism believed. It was axiomatic to the new age that the essence of religion is just this "universal goodness, or love, and nothing else," which Hopkins offered as the definition of holy love. His charges against Hart, at this point, derive their force from being subtle misrepresentations, the most ironical one being that the latter has made moral discernment identical with discernment of structural and natural harmony! [25] For, the whole quarrel of Hart with Edwards and his followers was that that was just what *they* were doing!

The extent to which Hopkins had become humanized is still more evident in his *Inquiry into the Nature of True Holiness*. One can hardly imagine a conception of virtue that could be more plausible to Revolutionary New England than the following:

"This [holiness] is love to God and our neighbor, including ourselves, and is universal benevolence, or friendly affection to all intelligent beings. This universal benevolence, with all the affection or love which is included in it, and inseparable from it, is the holy love which God's law requires, and is the whole of holiness." [26]

"Divine love comprehends wisdom, justice, truth, faithfulness, and every moral perfection and excellence whatsoever." [27]

Hopkins' meaning and intent is clear. Holiness is the same as "friendly affection," and benevolence is very much like the love of a friend, a kindly regard for the good of others. It is a good will extended from one man to another, a sentiment of sympathy and attachment between persons, a humane partiality for the happiness of others, as well as one's own. "Universal benevolence" is none other than this lovingkindness directed toward and embracing "all intelligent beings." "Divine love," which is identical in nature with such benevolence, "comprehends" Edwards' "secondary negative virtues." The striking contrast between these views of Hopkins and the Calvinism of Edwards or Bellamy can be easily seen in the following citations from the latter:

"When God is seen in his infinite dignity, greatness, glory, and excellency, as the most high God, supreme Lord, sovereign Governor of the whole world, and a sense of his infinite worthiness is hereby raised in our hearts, this enkindles a holy benevolence, the natural language of which is, 'let God be glorified' . . . that all worlds might join together to bless and praise the name of the Lord; and it appears infinitely fit and right, and so infinitely beautiful and ravishing, that the whole intelligent creation should forever join in the most solemn adoration; yea, that the sun, moon, stars, earth, air, sea; birds, beasts, fishes, mountains, and hills, and all things, should in their way display the divine perfections, and praise the name of the Lord, because his name alone is excellent, and his glory is exalted above the heavens." [28]

"And thus a sight and sense of the infinite dignity, greatness, glory, and excellency of the most high God lays the first foundation for a divine love." [29]

The attitude of man toward such a deity must necessarily be different from his attitude to his fellow creatures, as different as God is from man. To regard the eternal and almighty Sovereign of the worlds with that "friendly affection" which one may extend to a schoolmate or a fellow-citizen, amounts to nothing less than damnable presumption. The God of Calvinism stands in a category infinitely superior to that of any and every created thing; therefore to define holiness as "love to God and our neighbour, including ourselves," is blasphemy.

The "idea of God" implied by Hopkins' conception of

true virtue is illuminating. It involves a classification of God with man as "intelligent existence," as one person among the many, although superior to all others. Herein can be seen the moral sources of the notion that "God is a person." It is important to note that such a conception of God, upon which modern theology has been very insistent, grew out of a "moral" conception of virtue, as benevolent regard extended from one person to another. This idea of God is a reflection of the modern conception of social morality, whereby God's relation to the world as *Creator* is made secondary to his relation to men as their "heavenly Companion" or "Father." The modern problem of the "personality of God" is essentially connected with, and cast in the forms of, modern psychological and moral concepts, in which man's relationship with the world in which he lives appears to be irrelevant to any moral consideration. Thus there are God and men, who are personal, and the world, which is impersonal. This fact is still more strikingly exemplified in the humanitarian religion of Channing.[30]

Coming back to Hopkins:

"Let it be observed that this love of our neighbour, as it regards the highest good of the whole as its chief object, and respects the good of individuals as included in this,— and as the greatest good of mankind consists in being voluntary subjects and servants of Christ, in belonging to his kingdom and promoting the highest interests of that,— this love I say, is not really a distinct thing from seeking the glory and kingdom of God, as they perfectly coincide." [31]

This is triumphant humanitarianism. The "kingdom of God" is that state of society in which "the highest good of the whole" shall have become a fact. When men become "voluntary subjects and servants of Christ," when they embrace "wisdom, justice, truth, faithfulness, and every moral perfection and excellence whatsoever," then the kingdom of God will be at hand and the glory of God shall become manifest. The last end of God in creating the world was the establishment of this moral kingdom. Hence the substance of religion is to serve God in and through the service of man, a disinterested affection toward God expressed in and through a disinterested affection toward one's fellowmen.[32]

It is not hard to see the consequences of this ill-concealed loss of interest in the glory of God. The great and humanly insuperable chasm between the natural and the supernatural, between the states of the regenerate and the unregenerate, between the sacred and the secular, the spiritual and the carnal,—was all but obliterated. "Total depravity" became a strong name for a mild disease of the soul. "Regeneration" became an exaggerated description of a secret and imperceptible something which bridged the gap between awakened sinfulness and defective holiness. And God lost all His perfections except His "mercy and goodness," ready to be transformed to some sort of purely tender and affectionate kindness. Calvinism had unconsciously adopted the ideals of its humanitarian rivals, appropriated their philosophy and their social moralism.

A further consequence of this compromise was that Hopkins transformed the "love of Being in general" into "obedience to the law of God." Calvinism had always claimed to be the religion of the Bible, and to have accepted the Word of God as the rule and guide of a godly life; hence the incipient legalism which has always been associated with it. But a little reflection will show that in living Calvinism there was a temper of the soul which saved its bibliolatry from a strictly authoritarian and legalistic quality. The Bible was the seat of authority in matters of religion and conduct because it was the Word of God, the sovereign Creator and Governor of the world. The application of such reverence for the Word of God to the idea of theocracy gave the Puritan a religion which was other than a mere legalism. The conception of theocracy involved the belief that New England was destined to be a "new Canaan," a land of godly people governed by a godly government, God being sovereign over all.[33] This belief nourished an idealism which gave to New England Calvinism a liberating quality, a sense of predestined greatness, a vision of the coming of the glory of God amongst the people of the land.

When all hope of the realization of such a theocratic state in New England was gone, Edwards transferred its enthusiasm to the individual's relationship to God, and discovered the glory of God through the communion of his own soul with God's universal kingdom, the world. Thus he preserved the sublimities of the belief in theocracy, except that in the new picture of divine glory the civil government of New England was a negligible light.[34] The vision of the Puritan Fathers was gone, but the glory of God continued to shine, and none the dimmer for all that. When this vision, as well as the vision of theocracy, deteriorated, Calvinism became legalistic in the usual sense of the word. Instead of the rich and colorful "holy love," the barren and colorless "obedience to the law of God" dominated Calvinistic thought. The glory of God was then sought in the majesty of His law, which, though necessarily violated, was none the less infinitely binding.

There is a subtle connection between humanitarianism, moralism, and legalism, which is well evidenced in the course of Puritan religion. Puritanism was legalized through the same process whereby it was moralized. The element of legalism in Puritan religion is, of course, nothing accidental. Puritan divines never tired of tracing the reasons for "the controversies of God with His people" to the failures of the latter to conform to the moral and institutional regulations of the Scriptures.[35] The churches of New England were social institutions, the officers of which assumed the functions of priests, prophets, lawgivers, and policemen in disguise. Throughout the seventeenth century, the divine office of the ministers as guides of the consciences and the conduct of men was never frankly questioned.

The first half of the eighteenth century saw a rapid emancipation of civil government from clerical control. Public peace and welfare was now a state problem; and the laws to be enacted and enforced to that end became matters which concerned lawyers and policemen, and not Gospel-ministers. But the clergy of the "instituted churches" were not to be dismissed in any summary fashion. The state was too lenient with the "lawful liberties" it allowed the people, and wickedness filled the land. During the opening decades of the eighteenth century we find the clergy engrossed with the task of making people good.[36] The laws and the methods of civil government were obviously inadequate to establish the rule of righteousness according to the Word of God. It was clearly the duty of the Gospel-minister to inculcate and encourage obedience to the law of God. Therefore, the clergy turned their energies to the problems of practical moral reform, and the "instituted churches," together with their institutions and "exercises," became means to that end. The people had to be exhorted to conform to the regulations concerning the conduct of good life as taught by the Scriptures. To make people good became the supreme task of the churches, and legalism followed as a matter of course. Thus the Word of God became restated as a body of laws, comparable to the secular *moral* law formulated by the humanitarianism of the age, and Calvinist and humanitarian applied themselves to the task of moral reform.

The progressive legalization of New England Calvinism is seen in the writings of Edwards, Bellamy, Hopkins, and John Barnard. Edwards' analysis of the nature of true virtue is based upon the conviction that there is a profound disparity between holy love and secular morality. The *Religious Affections* and *True Virtue* are complete antitheses of any authoritarianism and legalism. The Ten Commandments are strikingly neglected. The knowledge of the rules of righteousness is based upon the knowledge of that constitution through which God makes His glory and perfections, moral and natural, manifest.[37]

With Bellamy, Edwards' philosophy of morals underwent a marked change. His *True Religion Delineated* [38] is one of the most exalted tributes to divine glory in Puritan literature. It contains passages describing the "eminent display" of the perfections of God "as they are revealed in his works and in his word," which surpass even Edwards' descriptions, as expressions of awe and reverence in the presence of the "glorious Monarch of the Universe." [39] However, Bellamy's conception of God was

one of a "moral Governor," a "glorious Monarch of the
Universe"; and thus, it stands in marked contrast to Ed-
wards' well-rounded and essentially metaphysical concep-
tion of the deity. Bellamy's God is more like a grand
Sultan, a Judge enthroned on high, a King of kings.
Hence it is not surprising that the "divine law" occupies
a dominant place in his thought. In his *The Law our
Schoolmaster* he writes:

"The nature of justifying faith . . . implies the seeds
of every moral virtue and every Christian grace. For they
are comprised in a hearty approbation of the law, and ac-
quiescence in the gospel." [40]

"Justifying faith is founded only on truths revealed in
the written word." [41]

"Justifying faith is wrought by the Spirit of God, en-
lightening our minds, spiritually to understand the truths
of the gospel already revealed in the written word." [42]

The glorious Monarch of the Universe has revealed
His will in the written Word. The laws of the Holy
Book are *the* revelations of the will of God concerning the
conduct of life. Justifying faith is evidenced in a certain
enlightenment of the mind, whereby men come to a spiritual understanding of the truths of revealed religion as
given in the Scriptures. As revealed, the laws of the Book
are unconditional regulations formulated by God, and
derive their imperative authority and dignity as absolutes
from the fact that they are commands of the great moral
Governor of the universe. The laws of the King are perfectly just, and it is the duty of all men to obey them.
To disobey the law is to insult the sovereign Law-Giver,
and is punishable with eternal damnation. [43]

Hopkins had little of the "natural piety" of Bellamy.

The glowing descriptions of the "Alpha and Omega, the Almighty" are absent from his theological discourses. Calvinism emerged from his pen as an imposing theological structure, dialectically plausible, but seldom vivid or attractive. He was the astute apologist of Calvinistic theology; therefore his dialectical victories were achieved through the surrender of that which he set himself to defend. He marks the transition from Calvinism to moralism. The title of his sermon *On the Necessity of the knowledge of God's Law in order to the knowledge of sin* [44] is itself significant. The aim of Hopkins' sermon is to show that sinners must know the perfect law of God which condemns them; that they must recognize their obligation to love it, though naturally they cannot but hate it.

The law "is the eternal rule of righteousness, which is essential to the being and glory of God's moral government and kingdom, and is in a sense the foundation of it, pointing out and declaring the duty of rational creatures, or moral agents, as what is fit and proper to be required of them, and containing the rule of God's conduct towards them, as their moral Governor." [45]

A more thoroughgoing religious legalism is hard to conceive. Without the law there would be no divine moral government, and the glory of God's moral government rests in the written law of God. Thus, in a sense, the very excellence of the perfections of God is made manifest in the excellence of the divine law, for the divine perfections are seen in the divine moral government.

"This law of which I am speaking, consists in two main branches; one points out our duty to God, and the other our duty to our fellow creatures and to ourselves. This is all contained and expressed in the law of the ten commandments, published to the children of Israel by God from Mount Sinai, and afterwards wrote by God himself on two tables of stone, and laid up in the ark, which was placed in the holy of holies, under the mercy seat or propitiatory." [46]

Furthermore, all "right kind" of religion has "its foundations in the knowledge of God's law." [47] "Yea, the grace of the gospel could not be revealed in all its greatness in any other way. The law must be first extant in all its strictness, extent, and glory, and must be well understood, in order to men's knowing their own character as sinners, and understanding and embracing the way of salvation by grace through a Mediator." [48]

The consequence of such concern with the Law, and its becoming the foundation of religion, was that obedience became definitive of true virtue. Self-love, which was the opposite of benevolence, or, the source of all malevolence,[49] became the source of disobedience to biblical law. As self-love concerned the utility of things to one's self, it was implied that the Law had no such utility, or that it was irrelevant to it. And thus, obedience to the Law became a mere matter of obligation.[50] The Law demanded conformity and threatened punishment without impressing the sinner of its own excellence, for to do so would be to impress him with the enjoyable consequences of obedience. This was legalism triumphant.

It had been hard enough for men to derive a sense of God's glory from the glory and the government of the world, or from the idealism of a theocratic religion; to acquire a sense of the glory of the Law, or of divine glory as revealed in the Law, was well-nigh impossible. With the waning of the glory of God, the Law had become merely an unlovely and unlovable body of regulations. Hopkins himself was under no illusions on the subject. He knew that many men who know the requirements of the Law "may feel themselves so uninterested in the matter as to give themselves no trouble about it in this view, but live at ease, and, with the greatest carelessness and stupidity, run on in sin with greediness." [51]   Therefore, he took it that nothing less than regeneration could make men love the divine Law.

Other Calvinists were not prepared to leave the matter wholly in the hands of the Spirit. The brand of Calvinism which emerged from the controversies during the pre-Revolutionary generation was a religion based upon the certainty that highest human happiness is to be attained through obedience to the law of God as revealed in the Scriptures. Thus the incipient legalism of Calvinism and humanitarian interests were combined to shape a new religion. Calvinism could no longer ignore or combat the right and the desire of men to be happy. Therefore, it set out to prove that happiness is best achieved through obedience to the "divine commandment." This new interest is presented with clarity and confidence in a series of nine sermons by John Barnard, on *The Imperfection of the Creature, and the Excellency of the Divine Commandment.* [52]

"The great End and Design of these Commandments of God . . . is to make us

1. Truly Wise:
2. Truly Good: and
3. Compleatly Happy." [53]

The "divine commandment" requires nothing which is

unreasonable or impossible to perform.[54] It is a fine and "broad" commandment, setting forth our reasonable duties as human beings, and designed for our happiness.

"A due regard to the Commandment will influence us to walk wisely, and surely, and help us to shun many inconveniences, which we should be apt, otherwise, to run ourselves into, through the prevalency of our too eager passions, and unbridled sensual appetites." [55]

"In the mean while, that we may be enabled, patiently, and cheerfully, to bear what He appointeth for us, He assureth us, in His Word, of His Fatherly love, and compassion, to us, under all, and that He meaneth all for our real benefit and advantage; that we may be more weaned from a vain and thorny world, by our too fine regards to that with which we often hurt and wound ourselves, and may be more at liberty to mind, and secure, our spiritual and eternal interest . . . and finally, to be the means to promote and encrease, our future crown of glory. And who can think seriously of these mighty advantages of the divine Commandment, or have any perception of them, without seeing, that here is enough, not only to keep him from sinking into despondency, in the day of affliction, but to enable him to count it all joy when he falls into diverse temptations?" [56]

Thus was New England blinded to the glory of God. The glory of God was sought in the goodness of man, and goodness was transformed into obedience to law. The ideal of the union of the human will with the will of God was translated into the ideal of a perfect practice of "secondary" virtue, and this was proclaimed as the condition of happiness. The Calvinist gospel had degenerated into the maxim, "Obey God, and you will be happy." The unregenerate continued to be happy by being bad. What is happiness to a saint may be misery for a worldling. If men obey the laws of God or of social morality in order to be happy, they must necessarily be miserable. Such is the constitution of God which no man can alter.

Piety is the love of God because of God's own glory, and not because the laws of God are useful for the attainment of happiness. Calvinists who exhorted men to become "compleatly happy" by fulfilling their "obligation to obey" the written Law of God, offended piety, and succeeded in making themselves amusing to the worldly-wise. A Calvinism which ignored the foolishness of the search for happiness, itself became foolishness. The profound tragedy of Edwards' theology was transformed into a farce by his would-be disciples, who used his language and ignored his piety.

CHAPTER V

SINNERS AND SAINTS IN FULL COMMUNION

In the year 1750, the people of the First Church at North-ampton "publicly rejected" Jonathan Edwards, and "re-nounced their relation to him as Pastor of the Church." [1] One reason was his bold opposition to the "principles which the great Mr. Stoddard brought in and practised"; [2] his insistence that none but those who love God may partake of the Lord's Supper. Some of the Northampton people thought this man Edwards was an impossible person, without a sense of humor and tolerance. Since the middle of the previous century the churches had learned to admit people of a decent sort, who neither have nor profess to have a really "gracious heart." The Synod of 1662 had authorized the Half-way Covenant, whereby the children of such people could be baptized in a lawful way. As early as 1679, before the "Reforming Synod," Solomon Stoddard advocated the policy of allowing all those who "make a serious profession of the true religion" and are not "scandalous" in their conduct to become church-members of "compleat standing," including the "lawful attend-ance" of all the functions of the church. This was not however a mere reversion to the Anglican practice; for in his *Instituted Churches* he declared the Lord's Supper to be a "converting ordinance," and in his *Appeal to the Learned* he defended the same view against the "excep-tions" of Increase Mather. [3] Stoddard was a practical man as well as pious. It is plausible to common sense that all the means within the power of the churches should be utilized for the difficult task of bringing men to the Christian way of living. Those who seek the prosperity of the church of God are always inclined to think of it as an institution for the education of men into the good life. Such a conception of the church underlay the objection of the people of the First Church at Northampton to the theory and practice of Edwards. His way "tended to keep the church of Christ *small*, and hinder the growth of it." [4] Surely, if none might be allowed to full communion but those who have a "gracious heart," then great majorities of good people who "profess the true religion" would be kept out of the churches. The result of such a policy could be none other than the depopulation of the churches and their ultimate ruin. It was hard enough to find people who "owned the Covenant" in a "moral way"; to insist upon "gracious sincerity" was absurd. It was clear to Stoddard and those whom he left to the charge of Edwards that "moral sincerity" is quite sufficient a "qualification for communion." In "owning the Covenant," the believer bound himself to God and to the other people in the church, promising to "profess" the truths of religion and to live a good life. What more could be expected from him than that he should do this with "moral sincerity"! Edwards hesitated for a long time, but at last he came forth with his convictions.

"He that visibly makes the covenant of grace his own, promises to perform those internal duties, and to perform all duties with gracious sincerity. We have no warrant, in our profession of God's covenant . . . to leave out those great commands, *of believing with the heart*, of *loving the Lord our God with all our heart and with all our soul . . ."* [5]

Once more, the grand conviction of Edwards that true godliness is fundamentally a matter not of morals but of the "affections" was the determining element of his thought. The church of God is a community of saints, and a saint is one who is possessed of the "religious affections," one who is regenerate and has a "gracious heart." The covenant with which a member of the church binds himself to God is a "covenant of grace," so that none but those whom the operation of the Holy Spirit in their hearts has regenerated into the spiritual life may or really can "own the Covenant."

The Lord's Supper, for Edwards, was a genuine spiritual feast, a supernatural phenomenon, partaken of by saints, for "mutual renovation and confirmation." [6] The visible eating and drinking of the ceremony was the seal of the covenant of grace, the outward sign of that spiritual eating and drinking, whereby the saint entered into communion with the living Christ. Obviously, only the gracious of heart could "take" and "eat" and "drink." According to the Old Calvinists, the Lord's Supper was a genuinely sacramental function, the one institution which was frankly recognized as mystical and symbolical of union with Christ through a spiritual eating and drinking of his spiritual flesh and blood. Even Calvin, who rejected Roman Catholic sacramentalism, retained this celebration of the soul's union with Christ. The Lord's Supper was, as it were, a "synoptic vision" and concentrated realization of the quintessence of the Christian gospel by the human heart.

"Our taking the bread and wine is as much a *professing*

to accept Christ, at least as a woman's taking a *ring* of the
bridegroom in her marriage is a profession and seal of her
taking him for her husband.   The sacramental elements
in the Lord's Supper represent Christ as in covenant, as
truly as a *proxy* represents a prince to a foreign lady in
her marriage." [7]

"To suppose persons ought thus solemnly to *profess*
that which at the same time they do not at all imagine they
experience in themselves, and do not really pretend to, is
a very great absurdity." [8]

What Edwards could not understand was how a person
who is not of a "gracious heart" can "profess" to love
God; and how one who is not filled with the divine Spirit
of holiness can claim to be of a "gracious heart."   Therefore, it seemed absurd to think that one ignorant of holy
love should be able, honestly and really, to partake of the
blessing of the Lord's Supper.

The same principle, of course, applied to church-membership.   He was profoundly annoyed to see the church of
God containing within itself "*two* distinct kinds of *visible
churches*."

"One company consisting of those who are *visibly gracious* Christians, and open *professors of godliness;* another
consisting of those who are visibly *moral livers*, and only
profess common virtues, without pretending to any special
and spiritual experiences in their hearts.   I appeal to those
acquainted with the state of the churches, whether this be
not actually the case in some, where this method of proceeding has been long established." [9]

Such a church could not possibly appeal to the man who
had written the *Religious Affections* and *The Nature of
True Virtue.*   It "carried the face of a glaring absurd-

ity." [10] Unfortunately, Edwards was speaking a next to forgotten language. His impeachers could make little of his grand distinctions between visible graciousness and visible morality, between holy love and secular love, between godliness and goodness. They stuck to their views. Edwards was ruining the church by closing its doors to many decent and useful folk. He claimed that it is better to have a small church shining clearly with Christian holiness, "so as to induce others to resort to it," than to have a big church filled up with lukewarm and worldly members who profess that which they neither experience nor pretend to experience. The lukewarm and worldly majority did not agree with him, and ultimately he was dismissed. The attitude of the public was expressed nowhere better than in the essay of Solomon Williams which he wrote against Edwards: [11]

"All those persons whom God has taken into the external Covenant, are bound to the external Duties of it, except such as God hath expressly excluded; but he hath expressly excluded none but ignorant and scandalous Persons. From hence it follows that if there be any unconverted Persons in the external Covenant besides them, 'tis their Duty to attend." [12]

Williams makes much of his conviction that a sacrament is a "converting Ordinance only to Church Members." [13] But since the conditions of church membership are a knowledge of the truths of the gospel and general good behavior, it follows that all those who are neither "ignorant nor scandalous" and have accepted the "external covenant," are eligible to partake of the Lord's Supper. This notion of an "external covenant," whereby a prospective member promises to attend to the "external duties" of the church,

became the focal point of an interesting controversy between Joseph Bellamy and Moses Mather. Edwards answered Williams with a thorough and elaborate book, but
it served no immediate purpose. He went to convert the
heathen Indians of Stockbridge.

Superficially, there was nothing new in the contentions
of Williams. The practice of "covenanting" dates back
to the beginnings of Congregationalism in England. The
dissenters of Gainsborough, the founders of Plymouth, the
churches of Salem, Boston, etc., had extremely brief and
simple covenant forms, which contained no specific injunc-
tions concerning belief or practice.[14] The early settlers
took it for granted that only the elect of God, those whom
God had visited with His grace, could promise with sincerity "to walke in his waies, according as he is pleased to
reveale himself unto us in his blessed word of truth." [15]
This is especially clear from the Charlestown-Boston Covenant.[16] Therefore, the prospective church-member of
"compleat standing" made a public relation of his experience of saving grace and promised to live a godly life as
prescribed by the Word of God. Such promising did not
mean that a man's salvation was conditional upon his good
works. Salvation was the condition of good works, and
not vice versa. Sainthood was a free gift of God, which
obligated the saint to live as required by his privileged
state. This point is significant, in that, the temper and the
intent of the early covenants is alien to the later notion
that God makes conditional promises to those unregenerate
persons who "own the Covenant" of a given church. Such
a conception of covenanting with God was advocated when
the churches became alarmed by the increase of ungodliness among the people. The more "ignorant and scan-

dalous" the people became, the more it was necessary to be of "charitable judgment." It became necessary to emphasize the knowledge of correct doctrine and good behavior as among the conditions of church-membership. "Directions" and creeds were added to extended covenant forms, which were used in place of the early simple formulæ.[17]

However, it seems never to have occurred to the seventeenth century Puritan to distinguish between visible and real sainthood. Even Stoddard, who advocated the access of the unregenerate to the Lord's Table, did not entertain the notion that the sinner is in covenant with God. But he had prepared the way. And we find Solomon Williams definitely convinced that an unregenerate person who "owns the Covenant" is thereby entitled to the duties and privileges of an "external covenant," as distinguished from the "covenant of grace" which may be owned only by the regenerate. In the two cases, the word "covenant" is used in two very different senses. The first is a conditional covenant, whereby the salvation of the sinner is practically conditional upon his fulfilling the conditions set forth in the covenant which he owns. It is a contract between God and man. The second is an unconditional covenant, whereby God bestows freely, according to His own sovereign pleasure, the regenerating gift of the Holy Spirit upon those whom He wills to save. It is just this unconditional covenant that the controversy over regeneration[18] tended to render meaningless. Therefore, while Hopkins and Hart were busy considering the "true state of the unregenerate," Joseph Bellamy and Moses Mather were engaged in a heated controversy as to whether or not any unregenerate persons may be said to be in covenant with God, or in other words, as to whether or not they should be allowed to become church-members of "compleat standing."

So long as the division of mankind into two absolute categories, the saved and the damned, was accepted, it was easy to argue that only the elect belong to the visible community of saints, which is the Church. But at this time such a dichotomy was no longer considered tenable. There were many people who did not claim a "gracious heart," who, nevertheless, were decent and "Christian" folk. In fact, the "enthusiasts," who made the loudest claims to a regenerate state, had now come to be regarded as suspicious characters. Moreover, the unregenerate constituted the "three-quarters of the Christian world." [19] Something had to be done so that these would not "be shut out of the church," [20] both for the good of their own souls and for the sake of the dignity and usefulness of the churches.

Furthermore, after the Great Awakening, there followed the various steps leading up to the separation of church and state, begun with the establishment of the Provincial Government in 1692. The various dissenting churches, among which the Church of England was the foremost and the most aggressive, had come to enjoy the tolerance and even the favor of the government. The church of God was no longer a unified power in New England, and an effective cöoperation between the religious and civil forces of society was now out of question. Civil government and religion were now two different things; each with its own methods and interests. The latter was fast becoming an individual concern, and its problems were of little interest to the state, except in so far as these were

directly related to social peace and order. The people
were taxed for the support of the churches and their ministers, but beyond that little protection was afforded to the
churches, established or otherwise. Religious restrictions
on suffrage had been removed long since, and membership
in no particular denomination was compulsory. Hence,
the very existence of the churches depended upon their
popularity. It was now necessary to please and tolerate
the ungodly; to be of wise and charitable judgment. As a
matter of fact many churches had already learned to practice such leniency.[21] But the thing was as yet a theoretical
taboo. It had to be fought out theologically, and Moses
Mather, "pastor of the church of Christ in Middlesex,"
started the debate.

He wrote a treatise on *The Visible Church in Covenant
with God: or an Inquiry into the Constitution of the Visible Church of Christ. Wherein the Divine Right of
Infant Baptism is defended; and the Admission of Adults
to compleat standing in the Visible Church, though destitute of saving Faith, shown to be agreeable to the revealed
Will of God* (1769). The contention is clear. There
are two covenants; the covenant of grace and the external
covenant. There are two churches; the invisible church,
constituted by all those who are under the covenant of
grace, or the regenerate; and the visible church, constituted by the regenerate and the unregenerate who are
church-members, and comply with its various duties and
obligations.

"The external covenant, and the visible church thereby
set up, are intended as means to bring mankind to a compliance with the terms of salvation prescribed in the cov-

enant of grace. Or, in other words, for the conversion of sinners." [22]

Mather has no difficulty in showing that this external covenant is a continuation of the covenant between God and Abraham. The ordinance which established the covenant relationship between God and Abraham was the circumcision of the fore-skin. Every circumcised child in Israel was a member of the visible church thus instituted.[23] With the coming of Christ, Baptism was substituted "in the room of circumcision," [24] and thus the visible Jewish church continued to exist as the visible Christian church. The Abrahamic covenant was external; it was based upon the circumcision of the flesh, and not upon a "circumcision of the heart." In the same manner,

"The rule of the Church's proceeding in the admission of members, is, a credible profession, and visibility of grace, and not a gracious state. According to this rule, the Church may admit such as are not regenerated, when they make a credible profession of true grace; and when they are admitted, they are real members of the visible Church, and entitled to all the privileges of it." [25]

"But to suppose, regeneration is a qualification necessary to a person's being admitted into the church, is to suppose, the work must be done, before the means God hath appointed for doing it, are to be used." [26]

Mather's conception of a covenant is that of a set of conditions assented to by two contracting parties, putting both of them under certain obligations. *If* the unregenerate profess belief in the gospel-truths and are good, they are entitled to "all the privileges" of the visible church. *If* they take advantage of these privileges, they may be blessed with a "regenerate state." Entrance into both covenant relationships is conditional upon the fulfillment of certain requirements, which qualify the candidate to certain "privileges." Once more, novelties in political theory are reflected in theology. At the time when Mather wrote his treatise, Mayhew had already done his work, and the political ideas of Locke and Sydney had permeated into the social atmosphere of New England. The relationship between the king and the people was now conceived as one of mutual obligation. *If* the people obeyed the government and conformed to its laws, they could demand safety and protection. *If* the government established peace and prosperity, *if* it respected the natural rights of the people as free Englishmen, it could expect obedience and respect. The state and the people were two "high contracting parties," and quite ready to protect their own rights. The king was sovereign, not to do what he pleased to do, but to serve the interests of the people whom he ruled. God also was sovereign, not to save whom He willed and damn whom He willed, but to bless with His grace those who performed duties of the visible church. He had bound Himself to unregenerate church-members in an external covenant, and fulfilled its conditions, provided they did their part.

According to Mather, the Lord's Supper is a part of the external covenant, therefore the unregenerate church-member must partake of it.[27] The sacraments do not "seal pardon and salvation to any man absolutely; that he shall, in fact, obtain them; but only conditionally, that is, if he has sincere faith. . . . Whether the receivers of the sacraments have faith, or not, they still remain seals to the truth of these Gospel declarations of mercy."[28] In a sense, this is a significant and revolutionary statement. A sacrament is neither a sign of spiritual union, nor a medium of the gift of the Spirit, as Stoddard had supposed. It is a "seal to the truth of the Gospel declaration of mercy." It symbolizes the promise of God that He will have mercy upon those who have sincere faith. There is not a trace of the Calvinistic notion of spiritual union left in this notion of the meaning of the Lord's Supper.

Mather is certain that it is absurd to expect perfect sanctity from every member of a church, proving thereby that a regenerate state is not a qualification for communion.[29] If the sacraments are seals of perfection, no one can honestly partake of them.[30] "Moral uncleanliness" alone can bar one from the Lord's Table.[31] The thing to be considered in admission to communion is not whether the candidate is regenerate, but whether he is a "moral liver." Murder, fornication, or robbery, are scandalous sins, and no man given to the practice of them may become a church-member. But a man free from such glaring evils, who has a certain knowledge of the gospel-truths, should be admitted into the church as a member of "compleat standing"; thus he will be a party in the external covenant, and run a good chance of salvation.

The common sense plausibility of all this is obvious. In a community in which large bodies of people are conventionally well-behaved and willing to profess belief in the truths of religion, it is inimical to the interests of a church to exclude such on the basis that they have not experienced "saving grace." Besides, it is well that people of doubtful character should be placed in an environment in which they can grow in strength and goodness. Mather, as well as Mayhew, Mills, Hart, and others, sensed this strongly as a matter of certainty, and scriptural proofs, as usual, were not wanting.

Bellamy was scandalized by "Mr. M.'s external graceless covenant." [32] A covenant unites two parties in a certain agreement. The terms of this agreement constitute the contents of the covenant relationship into which they enter; and if they are sincere, they mean to act according to the promises they make to each other. [33] This is what is meant by a covenant, and nothing else. It is absurd to think that two men may sign a covenant without agreeing upon the terms contained in it, and without intending to carry them out. Such covenanting is hypocrisy, and people who do it, are knaves. [34] The covenant between God and Abraham was the "covenant of grace," and not an "external, graceless covenant." [35] The Israelites, when they entered into covenant with God, "professed, not merely to give the assent of their understandings to this truth, namely, that the law of God ought to be the rule of their lives, but to use the modern phrase, they professed the consent of their wills." [36] When they disobeyed the law of God, He "regarded them not, but their carcases fell in the wilderness." [37] Circumcision and the other external practices of the Jewish people were the *signs* of the covenant between them and God, which demanded a gracious heart and the conformity of the will.

"We ought in all cases to consent to a covenant in our hearts, before we are active in sealing it with our hands; for to seal a covenant with our hands, when we reject it in our hearts, is, in the sight of God, to lie; but lying is not a means of grace." [38]

It is true that an unbeliever may profess to have faith, but that only shows that he is a hypocrite, and not that he has a right to make such a profession. "Indeed, it was always expected that tares would, more or less, be among the wheat; but the apostles did not think it their duty to sow tares knowingly and on design. In that age of the church, this was thought to be the work of the devil (Matt. 13. 39). And methinks he may now, in our age, do enough at it, without any help from the clergy." [39] The church should require that every candidate to church-membership of "compleat standing" have a gracious heart. The candidate, knowing the rule of the church concerning the matter, should look into his own heart, and decide as to whether or not he is sincere.[40] The fact that a church can never be certain that a given prospective member is sincere, does not alter the case, nor does it mean that it is not necessary to be sincere.[41] There is no such thing as an external, graceless covenant. There are no such things as "religious duties" which may be performed in an "unholy manner." [42] A sacrament is a sign of the covenant of grace, and not a means for the conversion of sinners.

"This end might as well be obtained, if you tarried as a spectator. Those who stand by as witnesses, when a bond is signed and sealed, may know what is done, as well as those who are parties, and who bind themselves." [43] "An impenitent sinner under legal terrors may forsake bad company, lay aside the practices of uncleanliness . . . he may spend much time in hearing and reading the word of God . . . in secret prayer, and in trying to get his heart deeply affected with eternal things, etc., without lying." [44] But he may not visibly act as though he had grace, which is what he would be doing in partaking of the Lord's Supper.[45] This cannot but give him the impression that external compliance with the ordinances of the church has a virtue of its own; whereas, the truth is that, without faith, it is useless. The right way to approach a sinner is not to tell him that he may, as a sinner, enter into some sort of graceless covenant with God, but to "hold up the perfect law of God close to conscience, to show him his duty and his sin. . . . Hold up the gospel way of salvation, with all its evidence, that he may understand and believe it. . . . This will tend to increase genuine conviction of all sin and guilt, and to prevent delusive and false hopes, and to shut him up to the faith." [46]

Bellamy was a tireless preacher, and no less zealous for the salvation of sinners than any one else. But, so far as he could see, the notion of an "external covenant" did little else than gratify the sinner's vanity in making him think that he could come into a right relationship with God without a complete surrender of himself to the mercy of God. However, he failed to attach much significance to the fact that sinners "who stand by as witnesses" are not of much use for the doing of the churches' work. A church is run by its members, and not by people who stand by and watch. Moreover, it is comforting to many an established and useful church-member to know that he may go to the Lord's Table without having to worry overmuch about the true state of his heart. Bellamy should have known better than to think that all this argument about the number of covenants with which God has bound Himself to His people was for the special benefit of the sinner. After all, it is just as important to look after the prosperity of the churches as to look after the regeneration of sinners. Perhaps Bellamy could have answered this undignified argument, but it is not proper for theologians to talk of such matters. The subject was left in the background, and it spurred Moses Mather to another effort.

"I allow as well as he, that the covenant of grace is set forth in it (the covenant with Abraham): but what he endeavours to prove is, that *this was the covenant of grace, and nothing else.* Whereas, what I represented in my former piece, was, that this covenant is an external covenant with the visible church. And his showing that the covenant of grace is included in it, doth not in the least, affect my arguments; for what I asserted was that the covenant of grace was here exhibited." [47]

Mather resented the designation of the "external" covenant as a "graceless" covenant, and called the latter a "graceless phantom" in Bellamy's own head.[48] To defend himself, he had to admit that the external covenant is an "exhibition" of the covenant of grace. But he was not consistent. If the practices of the visible church are exhibitions of the realities of the invisible church, then there is no sense in the claim that the external covenant includes the covenant of grace, as though it were a more comprehensive covenant. If this is the case then, the external covenant includes elements which are graceless, which cannot be said to exhibit the covenant of grace. The truth is that although he resented Bellamy's charge that he advocated a "graceless covenant," he was unable to take the covenant of grace seriously. In fact, his notion of the nature of a gracious heart was hopelessly confused. He interpreted Bellamy's demand for "gracious sincerity" as a demand for moral perfection.[49] Perfection is contrasted with the "imperfect services of mankind." [50] "Whatever God commands to be done, he requires the performance to be, not in a gracious, but in a perfect manner." [51] And, since no man can claim such perfect obedience to the commands of God, it is absurd to make it a condition of entrance into a covenant relationship with God.

Mather's discussions of matters related to the question in dispute show that the very pattern of his thought made him incapable of understanding Bellamy's mind and feeling the force of his contentions. He was conscious of the fact that so long as the idea of a profound disparity between a regenerate state and an unregenerate state is maintained, the choice is between a gracious and a graceless covenant. Hence he argues, much in the vein of Mills and Hart, that "our wickedness and estrangement from God" does not "consist in our original and native corruption; but in this contracted viciousness which by use and custom, we bring upon ourselves." [52]

"As the moral law so plainly requires the proper place and exercise of self-love in the heart, and is so evidently predicated upon this consistent principle of our nature; therefore, no act, exercise or conduct, in which the proper exercise of this faculty in the heart is denied, can, with any propriety, be called obedience, or conformity to the moral law." [53]

It is not necessary to repeat at length that such moralism jeopardized the whole Calvinistic philosophy of piety and salvation.[54] In the present dispute it finds a further application in the transformation of the conception of the church as a visible community of saints to that of a visible community of men who have intentions of obeying the law of God as well as they can. This thing called "grace" had become something indefinite, esoteric, and rare. And surely, it could not be required for church-membership!

"It is not all the declamations that can be uttered that

will make it appear possible for a man to covenant, upon this footing, with a good conscience, without the grace of assurance. This scheme therefore, does evidently shut out ninety-nine in a hundred of true believers, out of the church; if not more." [55]

The veil of dignified theological discourse is thrown aside. In his second answer to Mather, Bellamy tries to show that it is Mather's scheme that makes it impossible for the unregenerate to profess the covenant with any degree of intelligent honesty.[56] It is true that the law of God demands perfect obedience. If such obedience is the condition of full membership in a church, then no honest man can claim to be eligible to such membership. A man who promises to obey the divine commands contained in the Scriptures must know them all and promise to obey them perfectly and at all turns.[57] This is surely impossible for any human being, regenerate or unregenerate. Therefore, no man can honestly own the external, graceless covenant of Mather. On the other hand, "the covenant of grace requires repentance toward God, and faith toward our Lord Jesus Christ, as the conditions of *its* blessings." [58] It is no harder to know the state of one's heart than to know the state of one's mind. It is easier to have a good heart than to have a clear head, to know the nature of one's dispositions than to know the adequacy of one's opinions.[59] "It is very evident, that there is a great degree of scepticism among the professors of Christianity in this age, and as much among the learned as among the unlearned; as is obvious to every man who is acquainted with books and men." [60] Surely, Mather is not making things easier by setting belief in correct doctrine as the condition of church-membership. Conformity to orthodox dogma can no longer be made essential to a Christian status. But a gracious heart, being easily distinguishable from a graceless heart and within the reach of even the ignorant, is the *sine qua non* of a covenant relationship with God. Bellamy is clear in his own mind, but he is uncertain as to the success of his plea. His pathetic utterances and his appeal to "the plan on which the churches of New England were originally formed," reveal a background of strong public opposition.

"How unkind must it be in the people, to necessitate their ministers to counteract their consciences, by continuing an unscriptural practice, in condescension to their ignorant, unscriptural notions! But how much more unkind still must it be in clergymen who know the practice to be unscriptural, to lift their voices on high, and raise a popular clamor against those ministers who, at no small risk, venture to lay aside the practice, that they may approve themselves to God and to their own consciences." [61]

The debate about the nature and the number of covenants binding God to His people was far from being a mere battle of wits among quarrelsome clergymen. It was the struggle between Calvinism and the new humanitarianism applied to the problems of church government. It brought the conflict into the field of practical interests, and revealed the fact that Calvinism was losing its grip upon the masses of the people. Joseph Bellamy was acutely conscious of this fact. The unregenerate had become sufficiently numerous and powerful to rule the conduct of the churches (for the parish system gave them control of the choice of a minister), and to convince many of the clergy that leniency is the best policy. The process of compromise begun with the Half-way Covenant had gone far enough.   The religion of the first settlers was being distorted beyond recognition.   The doctrines of orthodoxy, formulations of a natural piety so dear to Bellamy's heart, were being dissolved in the waters of worldliness.   Bellamy was provoked.   In a brilliant series of dialogues on *The Half-way Covenant*, between a minister and his parishioner, he told his opponents what he thought of their scheme.   Mark the impudence of the parishioner, who starts the conversation in the following manner:

"Sir, I am dissatisfied with a part of your public conduct, and am come to open my mind freely to you, if you will be so kind as to allow me an opportunity."

After some kind remarks by the minister, he goes on:

"I have lately moved into the parish.   I had owned the covenant in the town I came from; my other children have been baptized; we have another child for baptism, and I hear you refuse to baptize the children of any but those who are in full communion.   This gives me pain." [62]

However, the minister has little difficulty in showing the parishioner that his demand is absurd.   Baptism means to "give up your child with all your heart to the Lord forever to be educated for God, and to be for him, and for him alone, in time and to eternity." [63]   No significance is attached to the baptism of a child unless its parent has a full understanding of the meaning of the rite, and unless he himself is a godly person.[64]

"And do you love God to that degree, as thus to give him your child forever?   If so, why not you give yourself to God, first of all?   You love your child, but you love yourself better. . . . Give yourself to God, through Jesus Christ his Son, that you may become the temple of the Holy Ghost, and thus ratify what your parents did

for you, when they dedicated you to God in baptism. . . .
Then bring your dear child, and consecrate it to God in
sincerity and truth." [65]

The argument is simple and direct. The parishioner
accepts it, and goes away. "Adieu, my dear sir." The
victory of the minister has been easy. The parishioner returns soon after, having made up his mind that he has
given in much too quickly. He is now sure that he can
"turn the tables." He is well armed with the arguments
of Moses Mather. He is very much concerned about those
weak and scrupulous souls who ought to "attend the means
of grace" in order to their strengthening and their salvation.[66] Therefore, he claims, it is not right to "excom-
municate all baptized persons who neglect to come to the
Lord's Table." [67] But the minister observes with sorrow:

"Do look through the country, and observe the conduct
of those in the present practice of owning the covenant,
and getting their children baptized. Are they brought up
for God? The youth learn to dress, and dance; but do
their parents appear to understand that they have devoted
them to God?" [68]

The parishioner is again convinced, and is willing to
"drop the affair." But he comes back more aggressive
than ever.

"I am willing now to make a profession, and publicly
to enter into covenant with God, and I have no objection
against the form used in your church. I can make that
covenant, and speak truly in the sight of God, notwithstanding I know I have no grace." [69]

The rest follows quite naturally.

"Therefore, I mean to adopt the words of the covenant
in a different sense; even in the sense in which an uncon-

verted man, who is at enmity with God, may use them, and yet speak true." [70] The minister is infuriated by this "gross and scandalous dissimulation." He would rather have it that "nine tenths should be shut out of the church, if need so require," than that people should come in "by wilful lying." It would be better for their own souls, and "in the sight of pagans, Jews, and Mahometans, and in the sight of the ungodly in the Christian countries." [71] As to the parishioner, "Eternity, an endless eternity lies before you. You have slept in sin long enough; it is high time you should awake . . . My dear sir, farewell." The parishioner does not return for some time.

Unfortunately, living parishioners are not quite so easy to handle. If Bellamy thought that his real opponents were as docile and easy to convince as this imaginary parishioner, he must have been very much surprised when he received a letter from "the Parishioner." [72] After telling Bellamy in no uncertain terms what he thinks of his dialogues, the author of this letter states a conviction which has now come to be quite common, and which Bellamy had evaded in his dialogues. *"A graceless person, morally sincere,* may with truth and propriety own your covenant and avouch the Lord Jehovah to be his sovereign Lord." [73] The whole letter is an elaboration of this contention. Holiness to this man, as to all those who opposed Bellamy, meant little more than "obedience to God." [74] "Yea, obedience to God and holiness are convertible terms." He was a formidable man, this parishioner. Bellamy's views are "of the most dangerous tendency of any broached in the Christian world: Deism itself not excepted." [75]

"These principles deny the present state of the unregenerate, to be a state of probation: They deny him to be a moral agent: They deny the justice of punishment for any sin, except perhaps of original sin; for every other sin, so called, they make to be the irresistible effect of the first. Yea, these principles vacate all the obligations of natural and reveal'd religion, and thence burst the bands of social life, strike at the foundation of civil government, and even at all God's moral government of the world." [76] They are "embarrassments" which "tend to the dissolution of the church of Christ," and must be "removed out of the way." They are nothing but absurd and harmful "extremes." [77]

Bellamy could not ignore this staggering blow. He held a fourth conversation with his imaginary parishioner, in the course of which he admitted that the "unconverted" of his opponents are really "gracious," and that "he who loves God supremely, with *moral sincerity*, does love God supremely, in reality." [78] He added that such love is "gracious and holy"; but he had surrendered at least to the letter of the contention of his opponents, and that was all they wanted. He even went so far as to claim that his scheme made it easier for people to join the church than that of his opponents.[79] In a way, he was a far more shrewd churchman than the latter. He made his parishioner say:

"I never looked upon myself to be a church member, in this sense of the phrase [as one in full communion]. I never meant to join with the church, nor did the minister or the church mean to receive me as a church member . . . I never voted." [80]

It was with such men that the practice of the Half-way Covenant and Stoddardeanism was filling the churches! Bellamy felt, perhaps with justice, that it is better to have a small membership of earnest people than to have crowds of useless covenanters. Nevertheless, it was not merely a delicate matter of policy which disturbed Bellamy and his orthodox partisans. They were certain that their enemies were playing into the hands of the humanitarian Arminians, who, by this time, had become a genuine menace, and were felt to threaten the very existence of orthodox Calvinism. This is the author's advice to the parishioner who has again succumbed to the arguments of his minister:

"If it should come to pass, as I fear it will, that in the course of this controversy, numbers should openly fall off to the Arminian scheme, in order to defend their lax manner of admission to sealing ordinances, I advise you, to keep by you, and to spread every where among your acquaintance, the Westminster Confession of Faith, and larger and shorter Catechisms; a book which will be of excellent service to teach people sound doctrine, and guard them against Arminian errors." [81]

But neither Arminianism nor the fear of hell could change the minds of those who had set their hearts to the task of making the churches prosperous. Bellamy's correspondent answered him with one of the most venomous products of the controversy.

"My minister, make a penitential confession and renunciation of those shocking principles and no more call them the important doctrines of the gospel. They are calculated to sap the foundations both of morality and Christianity; they will naturally excite in some horror and distraction, in others stupidity, and in both, immorality." [82]

This is what Calvinism meant to some men of Revolutionary New England; a system of horrors and theological nonsense. The churches had to have members, and men had to be taught goodness and decency. The church could no longer afford to be a community of Calvinistic saints. "Divine grace" was neither known, nor necessary, nor wanted. All moral men, willing to obey the Ten Commandments and professing the truths of the gospel were encouraged to become church-members of "compleat standing," and thus "increase the church of God." However, New England was not sufficiently enlightened to throw orthodoxy overboard. The doctrinal scheme of Calvinism, if not its spirit, continued to define the form of the religion of the people. Therefore, in theory, some churches discontinued the use of the Half-way Covenant; while, in practice, none but extreme "enthusiasts" demanded more than "moral sincerity" from a prospective church-member. Once the distinction between "gracious sincerity" and "moral sincerity" was blurred beyond recognition, there was not much excuse for the Half-way Covenant and Stoddardeanism, which, after all, were inconsistent with the scheme of orthodox theology.[88] The practical question was settled. A quasi-gracious moral sincerity was now sufficient for "qualification for communion." It was no longer necessary to have an "external covenant," and interest in the controversy dwindled away.

New and powerful enemies were invading the camps of orthodoxy, among whom the Baptists were the most dangerous. The strength of the Baptists had been on the increase since the separatistic movements arising from the Great Awakening. During the Revolution they argued quite cogently that it was no more right for the Massachusetts and Connecticut governments to tax them for the support of Congregational ministers than that the English government should tax Americans for the benefit of the English. During a revival in 1780, two thousand were baptized upon the profession of "saving faith," and by 1790 they could boast of 266 churches in New England.[84] Their orthodoxy made the Baptists specially formidable. They based their plea for adult baptism upon the sound argument that none but the gracious of heart can enter into a covenant of grace. Babies are not regenerate, therefore they are outside the covenant of grace. Orthodoxy had justified the baptism of infants by clever handlings of the Abrahamic covenant and by tortuous treatments of the practice of baptism in the New Testament. Pedobaptism was a plausible ecclesiastical practice, and in the absence of any vigorous opposition it was defended with some semblance of logical and scriptural verification. But with the ascendancy of the Baptists, the Calvinists were forced to come to the defense of their practice. The most powerful clergymen of the time turned their attention to the task, and many pamphlets were issued between 1773 and 1795 vindicating the ancient practice of the Calvinistic churches. Unfortunately, the Baptists were orthodox Protestants, and the idea of an "external covenant" could not be used against them without putting the established church in an unorthodox light. Therefore, the Calvinists came forward with the stock argument that the Abrahamic covenant was "extended" to his seed.[85] Theologically, the controversy was quite barren. Both sides were equally anxious to demonstrate their orthodoxy. The doctrines of divine sovereignty, human depravity, salvation by regeneration, were reasserted as ancient and inviolable truths. Apart from this, the effect of the controversy upon the Calvinistic churches was a further externalization of the covenant of grace. This covenant had to be broadened to include the infants. Otherwise, the Baptists and the Calvinists went their own ways.

When the dispute with the Baptists cooled down, the question of church-membership again came to the fore. After all, it was never really settled. Thanks to the "new divinity" and the Baptists, the Half-way Covenant was no longer a vital issue for the orthodox.[86] But qualification for communion was another matter. Practice had made it clear that even "moral sincerity" was difficult to ascertain and to achieve. There were some scrupulous souls who doubted their moral state as well as their gracious state. Even the moral state implies an inward quality which is not always easy to designate; therefore, some more reliable test had to be found. The policy of the churches was as undetermined as ever. There were those who still insisted on "saving grace"; others considered a conformity of the will to the laws of God sufficient; others were inclined to be even more lenient, in practice if not in theory, and admit those whose moral state was somewhat questionable. In the early nineties, the churches were again in commotion over the matter, and Moses Hemmenway came to the rescue.

He wrote *A Discourse concerning the Church. . . . Designed to Remove the Scruples and Reconcile the Differences of Christians.*[87] The book is readily one of the most amusingly dialectical discussions of New England religious literature. Hemmenway has a strong feeling that Christians do not really differ one from another as much as they think they do,[88] and that they have been quarreling about "speculative niceties."[89] His method of reconciling apparent differences is to draw distinctions, and thereby to demonstrate that there has been much ado about nothing. Holiness, which is a condition of communion, can be analyzed into several different kinds.

"Now all the subjects of this *invisible, federal holiness,* have also an *inherent holiness,* which is inward and invisible. Their hearts are purified from the defilement of sin; they are sanctified thro' the truth . . . There is also a *visible holiness* or saintship, and that both relative and inherent, which belongs to those who are so in covenant as to be entitled to those external privileges which are granted to regular and rightful members of instituted churches . . . On this account they are termed holy, as being the subjects of an external federal holiness. . . . There is also an *external inherent holiness* consisting in a profession and conversation conformed visibly to the gospel. . . . There is an outward cleanness of hands, as well as an inward purity of the heart." [90]

The "external covenant" has come in from the back door, bringing in two more even more external. Of course, there being so many kinds of holiness, one can hardly be sure as to the class of saints to which he belongs. Even if he understood these different kinds of holiness, he would find his heart shifting from one to the others, passing through all sorts of intermediate stages. Thus, probability, and not certainty, must be his guide.

"If, after careful examination of myself by the word of God, I find more hopeful marks of sincerity, not invalidated by evidence of hypocrisy, I find more reason *in myself* for comfortable hope, than self-condemnation. This I call *credible evidence of sanctification in view and account of conscience.* And this I think all who come into church communion ought to have. But to make it a rule, *that none may come but those who judge on sufficient grounds that it is on the whole most probable they are true saints* must leave the consciences of all doubting Christians in inextricable perplexity." [91]

Similarly, Hemmenway has a set of distinctions to solve the practical problem of church-membership and the right of access to the Lord's Table. These are two different matters. "The right of admission is a *right to have a privilege granted* to the subject. The right of access is a *right to do certain actions.* The former might be called, for distinction, a *passive right or title,* the latter an *active right or warrant.*" [92] External inherent holiness is sufficient for the first passive privilege, but a "manifest preponderancy" of "invisible, relative or federal holiness" is necessary for the second. [93] "It is not the want of grace, but the want of credible evidence, which renders one unfit for admission." [94] This may be said to summarize Hemmenway's contention in so far as he may be said to have a consistent contention. One does not need to have grace, provided he has evidences of it. And since such evidences are never absolutely certain, "in reference to practice" there is not much difference between the two contending parties which Hemmenway seeks to reconcile.

Naturally, this performance was unsatisfactory to the "Edwardeans." One of the greatest of these, Nathanael Emmons, took issue with Hemmenway. [95] The book of Emmons is a revelation of the Calvinism of the time. He is greatly disturbed because,

"Many churches lay aside the confession of faith, and admit many members without any public evidence of their belief of the essential doctrines of the gospel, and without any public evidence of their experimental acquaintance with religion." [96]

He objects to Hemmenway because,

"He has so framed his Discourse from beginning to end, as to lead the undiscerning readers to mistake *morality* for *religion*. He allows *moralists* to call their morality by the agreeable name of holiness . . . Yea, he assures them, that they are real saints in their kind, as those who are born of the Spirit, and bear the moral image of God . . . This is an alarming consideration. No persons are more in danger of being self-deceived, than those of this description." [97]

But, alas for his cause, Emmons is as much of a moralist as the objects of his denunciation. To be "born of the Spirit" is to bear the "moral image of God." By making the inward image of God moral, and this the test of sanctification, he has eliminated the theoretical basis of the controversy between the "new divinity" and the liberals. The whole case of Hopkins and Whitaker against Mills and Hart, in the grand dispute perpetrated some thirty years previously, rested upon the distinction between "mechanical" and "moral" regeneration. Jonathan Edwards based his case against his parishioners upon a sharp dualism of the natural and the supernatural, which he had developed in his *Religious Affections* and *The Nature of True Virtue*,[98] and did not hesitate to designate morality as a "natural affection." Bellamy's quarrel with Moses Mather rested upon the conviction that nothing less than "gracious sincerity" is the condition of entering into the "covenant of grace." And now, Emmons objects to Hemmenway because his "visible holiness has no *moral quality*, and therefore can exhibit no real evidence of inward sanc-

tification in any person or being in whom it appears." [99]
It is a fact that Hemmenway, in his zeal for reconciling the
Calvinists to each other, exposed himself to this charge.
And yet, however inconsistently, he insisted upon "credible evidence of sanctification in the view and account of
conscience." Hemmenway's concern was to eliminate a
now esoteric "grace" as the condition of access, while that
of Emmons was to establish the *moral quality* of the profession of faith as against further externalization. Nevertheless, the fact remains that both made "moral sincerity"
the condition of access to the Lord's Table.

Emmons defines the covenant of grace as "the promise
of God to save sinners, on the condition of their believing
in Christ," or "through *faith* in the Mediator." [100]   Belief
and faith are thus used synonymously, and the covenant
of grace is conditioned upon "belief."   "Believers are *in
Christ*, and therefore all the promises apply to them.   Unbelievers are *out of Christ*, and strangers from the covenant of promise, and therefore have no title to covenant
blessings." [101]   The *form* of such a statement is Hop-
kinsian, but it has neither the force nor the meaning of
the original.   When one substitutes the words "gracious"
and "graceless" for "believers" and "unbelievers," the
difference becomes evident.   Emmons' Calvinism was primarily a matter of belief and obedience.   The difference
between "Christians" and "moralists" is that the former
believe a body of doctrinal truths, while the latter do not.
Calvinism thus degenerated into a scheme of theology
plus an independent set of "duties."   Its holy fire was
quenched, and its theological ashes lay exposed to the
four winds.

Hemmenway's answer to Emmons breathes ease and

satisfaction.[102]   "Our churches" are "admitting members
to full communion upon their making a full profession of
Christianity." [103]   The idea has become fixed that whether
saint or sinner, a "doubter" may be either gracious or
graceless.   Neither the church nor the doubter can be
sure that he does *not* have saving faith.[104]   Therefore, both
the church and doubter should be charitable.   There are
too many shadings and variations in the inner life.
There is no fundamental and discernible difference between being moral and being religious, and presumably
these also shade into each other.[105]   Hemmenway is unable to see wherein the religion of Emmons is different
from his own.   Therefore, he claims that Emmons had
no excuse for accusing him of "mistaking morality for
religion."   Emmons' criticism stands if the saints of Hemmenway are non-moral, but the latter refuses to allow
such an interpretation of his views.[106]   Hence, the controversy is over.   As to whether or not a sacrament is a converting ordinance, which is the other focus of the controversy, it does not make a particle of difference which it is,
because the "doubter" has the right of access either as a
saint or as a sinner; and this, because the distinction between a saint and a "morally sincere" sinner has become
a purely dialectical matter.   Hemmenway thinks "good
evidence of sanctification" is not reserved to "true
saints." [107]   Emmons thinks it is.   Obviously, if "good
evidence of sanctification" is *the* condition of access, then
a man who has it will have access, whether he is called a
"true saint" or not.   The real problem had been, should
such a man have access to the Lord's Table or not?   Once
this is decided, this controversy is also over, and the rest

is so much "talk," which may amuse the controversialist but cannot edify anybody.

Emmons gave the debate its finishing touches with a distinction between a "doubting sinner" and a "doubting saint." [108] The former is not born of God; the latter is. "A doubting sinner has *no* evidence of grace." [109] He may think he has, but he is mistaken. Now, surely, the distinction between a doubting saint and a doubting sinner is so fine that it is psychologically meaningless. A doubting saint doubts because he is not sure that he has grace. A doubting sinner doubts for the same reason. If "grace is the only evidence of grace," then the evidence which makes a sinner doubt his sinfulness is an evidence of grace. Emmons is aware that "*uncertain* signs of grace may be *probable, highly probable,* and *most probable*"; [110] to which one may add that they may be probable, slightly probable, and least probable. The churches' judgment must be based upon such probability. [111] As for the prospective communicant,

" 'If his hopes that he is *sincere,* be as great or greater *than his fears* of the contrary, then there is no such ill consequent to be feared as may hinder his communicating; but it is his best way to do it, and wait on God in the use of his ordinance. But if the persuasion of his gracelessness be greater than the hopes of his sincerity, than he must observe how he is like to be affected, if he do communicate. If he find it is like to clear up his mind, and increase his hopes by the actuating of his grace, he is yet best to go: But if he find that his heart is like to be overwhelmed with horror and sunk into despair, by running into the supposed guilt of unworthy receiving, then it will be worse to do it, than to omit it.' " [112]

This is all sufficiently flexible to be amenable to the calculations of common sense. Even Hemmenway could not have done better. When sincerity becomes so complicated, and the "evidence of grace" so fickle, it is silly to have qualms of conscience about "unworthy receiving." Such introverted and confused Calvinism was sickly and meaningless. Emmons has fears that he is a "young and adventurous advocate," presenting unpopular opinions through a "very unpopular argument." [113] The difficulty lies even deeper. His highly rarefied notion of holiness, complicated with the distinctions of an impossible introspective psychology, was too evidently an apologetic of orthodoxy to appeal to the "young and adventurous." Edwards' "true virtue" was buried under a mass of distinctions invented in order to make the church acceptable to men of secondary virtue.

CHAPTER VI

THE FATE OF THE DAMNED

THE belief in the "next life" was integral to the Christian "scheme of salvation." In popular religion salvation was primarily the certainty of reaching heaven. Theologians and wise men elaborated and interpreted it in divers ways so as to render it rationally plausible and practically edifying. The questions relative to it were always difficult to handle. Where reason failed, revelation in the Scriptures supplied the necessary descriptions and "proofs." Matters dealing with divine government in the present, theodicy, sin and salvation, could be dealt with empirically and rationally. But the next world, its nature and structure, was a homiletical, rather than a theological, concern. In serious theological treatments, the next life was spiritualized, detemporalized, and rarefied, thus being made pleasing to reason, but meaningless to all but the wise. That an idea is not the same idea for everybody is no new doctrine.

Jonathan Edwards' personal religion was fundamentally irrelevant to the question of life after death. His conversion had come about through a new "relish" for God, and his piety was nourished by intense living and adequate understanding. His great treatises have little bearing upon the next world. The spiritual life appears in them as a quality of being which has no connection with questions of duration and locality. In several sermons, preached for the benefit of unregenerate New Englanders, he gave pictorial and realistic presentations of heaven and hell, which he derived from the Scriptures; and his eloquence was boundless when he enlarged upon the necessity of immediate repentance. Nevertheless, his belief in "eternal damnation" was a reasoned affair.

"God is a being *infinitely* lovely, because he hath infinite excellency and beauty." [1]

"If the obligation to love, honour, and obey God be infinite, then sin, which is the violation of this obligation, is a violation of infinite obligation, and so is an infinite evil . . . Sin being infinite evil, deserves infinite punishment, an infinite punishment is no more than it deserves. Therefore such a punishment is just." [2]

Edwards' almost infinite sense of his obligation to honour and serve the divine Being left no room for doubt that the lack of such a sense, together with the wickedness it engenders, is an infinitely evil and cursed state, the essence and foretaste of damnation. Hence he had no difficulty in maintaining the *justice* of eternal damnation against those who had come to doubt it. But in his own mind, the question is hardly a matter of justice. The lack of "holy love" *is* by nature infinite damnation. The sinner's punishment inheres in his sinfulness, and grows from it. This punishment is infinite, more in quality than in duration.

"Eternal life" is independent of time and space. Edwards was too good a thinker to believe that anything which exists in time and space can continue to exist endlessly.[3] That which is infinite must also be eternal,[4] otherwise eternity would have to be more infinite than infinity; which is impossible. Therefore, infinite damnation must also be eternal. However, "absolute eternity" does not consist in an indefinite number of years or ages.[5] It transcends duration and locality. All things which endure as spatial entities, the physical events constitutive of the world of existence, must perish. In the last days, when the righteous and the wicked appear before the judgment seat of God, heaven and earth shall disappear like smoke. The world of nature will cease to be, and the supernatural world will remain as an absolutely eternal reality. In this world all things will take their eternal place, the righteous in heaven, the wicked in hell, where they belong, according to the quality of their being.[6]

"There shall be an everlasting separation made between them (the saints) and wicked men. Before, they were mixed together, and it was impossible in many instances to determine their characters; but now all shall become visible; both saints and sinners shall appear in their true characters and forms." [7]

Edwards, in his appeals to the wicked of the day, however, falls back upon descriptions of the "future life" which are commensurate with the minds of his audiences; and one is irresistibly led to believe that he was thoroughly sincere in these popular presentations, in spite of his more reasoned reflections on time and eternity. "Eternal life" meant to him more than a *mere quality* of life; it represented the absolute reality of infinite being. He knew that conceptions of heaven and hell derived from the world of sense are hopelessly inadequate as descriptions of the infinite fullness of supernatural realities. Therefore, he used scriptural and popular imagery with perfect honesty, even to the point of improving upon their concreteness. And yet, the fact remains that his primary concern was the life of godliness here, and not the fate of the damned hereafter. In the last analysis, eternal life meant a regenerate life, a life of godly regard for the positions of events in the eternal order of being.

It was the preaching of Edwards that initiated the Revival at Northampton, and opened the way to the Great Awakening. The "conversions" of these emotional upheavals were brought about primarily through an exaggerated concern with the fearful destiny of sinners in the pits of hell. The Great Awakening brought the belief in hell-fire to the forefront of the people's minds, and the Calvinism of the time presented itself as a religion of condemnation and damnation. When the horrible phenomena of the everlasting sufferings of hell were viewed in the light of the "liableness and exposedness" of many decent folk to such a state, people of humane tendencies were scandalized, and questioned the extent and the nature and the application of hell-fire.

Soon after the Awakening, Charles Chauncy began to doubt the Calvinistic doctrine of damnation. He sympathized with Peter Clark's attitude toward the damnation of infants.[8] But as a Calvinist, knowing its connections with other less obnoxious doctrines, he was unwilling to commit himself to a denial of "eternal damnation," until 1782, when he published anonymously a pamphlet entitled *Salvation for All Men.*

The stage was already set for a controversy about the fate of sinners in the next world. Infants had been cleared from any genuine complicity in the sin of Adam.[9] The total depravity of mature and conscious sinners had been denied in all but theory.[10] It was now high time to doubt and repudiate the everlasting tortures of the fires of hell.

In the year 1770, John Murray arrived in New England, and went around declaring the "constraining influence of the love of God." He was a disciple of James Relly, the author of *Union*, and adopted the views of the latter to the effect that as all men sinned in Adam, so they all are saved in Christ.[11] Murray was not much of a thinker, but he was an effective and tireless preacher. He is strikingly neglected in the writings of the time.[12] Nevertheless, subsequent discussions of the Atonement show that he had been a powerful although indirect influence in the re-making of New England theology.[13]

It was the Rev. Charles Chauncy of Boston who aroused the Calvinists, both Old and New, and forced them to defend their belief in the endless punishment of the unregenerate in hell-fire. His first timid and anonymous tract on the subject was little more than a series of excerpts from the writings of English universalists.[14] Immediately a storm broke loose, and he was answered by six Calvinists, among whom were Samuel Mather and Samuel Hopkins.[15] Chauncy's position is stated succinctly and effectively in a letter he wrote to "the friend of truth," entitled *Divine Glory brought to view in the Final Salvation of all Men*.[16] The following statements from this brief letter reveal the kind of arguments which forced the Calvinists to run to the defense of the doctrine of eternal damnation.

"Nor can I calmly resign up a number of my species to everlasting misery, notwithstanding all you have said to prove it consistent with the justice of God, and essential to his glory."[17]

"*You* expect to look down from heaven upon numbers of wretched objects, confined in the pit of hell, and blaspheming their creator forever. *I* hope to see the prison-doors opened; and to hear those tongues which are now profaning the name of God, chanting his praise. In a word *you* imagine the divine glory will be advanced by immortalizing sin and misery; *I*, by exterminating both natural and moral evil, and introducing universal happiness. Which of our systems is best supported, let reason and scripture determine." [18]

Chauncy presented an elaborate theological and scriptural defense of his views in *The Mystery hid from Ages and Generations made manifest by the Gospel Revelation: or, the Salvation of all Men the grand thing aimed at in the Scheme of God.*[19] There are a number of propositions which, to him, are self-evident.

"As the First Cause of all things is infinitely benevolent, 'tis not easy to conceive, that he should bring mankind into existence, unless he intends to make them finally happy. And if this was his intention, it cannot well be supposed, as he is infinitely intelligent and wise, that he should be unable to project, or carry into execution, a scheme that would be effectual to secure, sooner or later, the certain accomplishment of it." [20]

To deny that all men will be "finally happy" amounts to a denial of the "infinite benevolence" of God. But to deny this is impossible, therefore all men will be finally happy. God is wise and powerful, as well as good. Therefore, there is nothing in heaven or earth which will prevent God from attaining this end. "Shall we set up man in opposition to God, and say that his foolishness and obstinacy are an overmatch for the infinite wisdom, knowledge, and power of God?" [21] Indeed, no! God will use "such means" "as shall prevail upon all men, and prepare them, in a *moral way*, as *moral agents*, for an *eternal reign*

in happy life." [22]   Many men will go to hell and remain
there for long periods of time, according to their degrees
of sinfulness.[23] This is necessary for their complete puri-
fication from sin. But when they at last attain such purity,
through the moral influence of God, they shall go to
heaven. The sufferings of this world and the next are
not punishments for sin. They are disciplinary measures
employed by God for the salvation of men in a "moral
way." [24]   Men suffer, not because suffering is a just consequence of their sins, but because suffering is the means
for their attainment of eternal salvation. It is utility, and
not vindictive justice, that motivates God in allowing men
to sin, and suffer, and go to hell. The end of the scheme
of God is to make men forever happy; He is moved by
benevolence to man, not by a desire to display His justice.

However, God is *righteous*, as well as just.[25]   His
righteousness demands that He punish sinners according
to the degree of "moral depravity they have contracted in
this" "state of existence." [26]   If men were infinitely sinful,
it would be just that God should subject them to endless
punishment. But,

"It does not appear to me, that it would be honourable
to the infinitely righteous and benevolent Governor of the
world, to make wicked men *everlastingly miserable*. For,
in what point of light soever we take a view of sin, it is
certainly, in its nature, a *finite evil*. It is the fault of a
finite creature, and the effect of *finite* principles, passions,
and appetites. To say, therefore, that the sinner is doomed
to *infinite misery* for the *finite* faults of a *finite* life, looks
like a reflection on the *infinite justice*, as well as goodness,
of God." [27]

This is a fair application of the philosophy of sin and

godliness which had emerged from the controversies on regeneration and the "external covenant." [28]   Chauncy cannot but feel that the difference between a good man and a bad man is a matter of degree, and often quite negligible.[29]   All men have their finite faults, and are greater or lesser sinners.   Therefore, it does not appear entirely just that God should take a man slightly more virtuous than another, and send him to the eternal happiness of heaven, and consign the other slightly less virtuous man to eternal hell-fire; for thus, many people, who are far from being incurable sinners, would be doomed to eternal misery.[30]   When one remembers that God is "amiable and interesting," the "benevolent Father" of men, such a thing becomes unthinkable.

It gives Chauncy acute pain to think that the number of the saved will be as few as the Calvinists seemed to make it.   It is true that the Scriptures represent the righteous as very few indeed, but Chauncy cannot believe that only these will ever get to heaven.   This leads to his third argument.

"Nor can it be any other than a base and gross reflection on the *Saviour of men,* whose proper business and office, as such, is to defeat the design of the *Devil,* and rescue mankind out of his *destroying* hands.   I say, it cannot but reflect great dishonour on him to suppose, that the *Devil,* notwithstanding his *mediatory interposition,* and all that he could do in opposition to him, should *finally* get the better of him, by effecting the *everlasting damnation* of the *greater part* of those whom he came from heaven on purpose to save.   To me, I own, the thought is shocking . . . The consideration of hell as a *purging fire* is that only which can make the matter sit easy upon one's mind." [31]

Chauncy works out a complete eschatology to suit the idea of the salvation of all men. Upon death, the wicked will pass into the "next state" of existence,[32] which will be in hell. They will stay there so long as they persist in their enmity against God. In the meanwhile, the Saviour will apply himself to the task of winning them over to godliness in every way that is consistent with their nature as moral agents.[33] When they become properly disciplined, they will suffer a "second death" and pass to the "last stage" of their existence, the eternal bliss of heaven.[34] The "Judgment Day" of orthodox theology, usually thought to be the coming occasion of the final judgment of the righteous and the wicked, according to Chauncy, will be the beginning of a "new dispensation, with respect to both the righteous and the wicked." [35] During this period Christ will rescue the sinners in hell one by one, and transfer them to heaven. When He finishes His work by rescuing the last sinner in hell, this second period will be over, and He "will now give up his *mediatory kingdom to the Father*, who will, from this time *reign immediately himself*; making the most glorious manifestations of his being a God, and Father, and Friend to all, in all things, without end." [36] And thus will come the last and eternal act of the cosmic drama, when all men will be in heaven, and God, having accomplished His last end in creating the world, will be "all in all." [37] Chauncy is naturally not very much disturbed by the fact that the Devil and his angels will be left in hell-fire.

The human appeal of Chauncy's contentions was irresistible. He had segregated the doctrine of eternal damnation from its metaphysical justification, and challenged the Calvinists to defend it as an aspect of the glory of God. Having made it a moral issue, he put it in a light which made it look as an incredible and monstrous doctrine. In the course of the discussion which he thus forced upon the Calvinists, the latter did brilliant work in proving that everlasting damnation is a rational and scriptural doctrine. But their dialectical victory meant their disgrace. The more they emphasized the issue by way of defense, the more gruesome did their theology appear to good common folk. Now that the matter had become a subject of controversy, it all looked horrible and absurd. The endless punishment of great masses of half-way decent folk was incredible, revelation or no revelation. The land was full of outwardly good but unregenerate people. To consign all these to hell-fire Chauncey declared absurd.

Of the volley of answers levelled against the new heresy, that of Samuel Hopkins stands out as the most realistic and powerful.[38] It appeared before Chauncy's longer work, and makes no mention of him. But it does answer his arguments in good Calvinistic fashion, although it deviates from the thought of Edwards to a considerable degree.

"All must allow that God will answer some good end by all the sin and misery in the world, which could not be so well answered without them; or, confess that his government and administrations are imperfect and unwise; and if the evil which has actually taken place is designed, and necessary to answer the most important and best end, then it may be necessary, for the same reason, that it should continue forever, to answer the same end to the highest degree." [39]

In this world, sin and misery are *facts*. Either the universalists must allow that God uses these to "some good end," or they must think of God's government of the world as "imperfect and unwise." The latter alternative is impossible, therefore the former must be true. This good end cannot be the good of every individual person in existence, because some men are, as a matter of fact, sinful and miserable. It must be some good that transcends the good of any individual being, "the highest good of the universe." [40] Some sin is or can be conducive to the edification of him who commits it. But there are some facts of sinfulness which are thoroughly detrimental to the interests of the sinner who perpetrates them, and are or may be means to the good of others, or presumably, to the good of the "whole." Hopkins is willing to grant that God's ultimate ends are concealed from us; however, he is certain that these cannot involve the happiness of all men, because, even in *this* life, all men are not happy. He is unable to attach much weight to Chauncy's contention that sin and misery are wholly disciplinary measures. His refusal to accept such a foolishly facile generalization, and his ultimate agnosticism concerning God's ultimate plans, was thoroughly in line with the sturdy realism of Calvinistic theology.

However, the punishment of sinners does serve certain good ends which are within the limits of our knowledge. It is necessary for men to know that God hates sin.[41] The moral law is from God. Disobedience to the moral law is sin against God. God is jealous for the dignity of His moral government, and will uphold it by punishing those who transgress against it. "In the everlasting punishment of the wicked, the infinite dignity and worthiness of God, and the excellence of his law and government, are expressed and asserted in a very advantageous and striking manner; and this is one important end and design of this punishment." [42]   Vindictive justice is one of the infinite attributes of God; therefore, it is necessary that men realize the "terrible majesty of God, and the infinite dreadfulness of his displeasure and wrath," as well as His goodness and mercy.[43] The wrath of God in relation to sin is an integral part of His glory for the display of which, as Edwards put it, He created the world. And since this is best done through the "eternal punishment of any of his creatures who deserve it," it is fitting and proper that they should be thus punished.

Hopkins makes full use of the argument that sin against the infinitely glorious God is infinite evil.[44] It cannot be overemphasized that such an estimate of sin rests upon the Calvinist's attitude to the deity. Sin is rebellion against the moral government of the "infinitely excellent, great, and worthy" God. The tragedy of hell is none other than the consequence of the infinite evil of sin, displaying the full odiousness of it, and the wrath of God because of it. Hell is but the reflection of the infinite horror of sin.

This is the attitude of mind which Chauncy and the other universalists did not possess. They identified the last end of God in creating the world with the happiness of all men, and allowed Him only those attributes which were necessary to this end; namely, goodness and wisdom and power; goodness, so that He might make it His last end to make all men happy; wisdom, so that He might contrive the best means for it; and power, so that He might accomplish this end in spite of the machinations of the Devil and men's own wicked resistance. To such an end, the display of His justice was quite unnecessary. His regard for the dignity of His moral government and His own honour, was of secondary, or of no, consequence. It was only essential that He be kind, loving, merciful, "amiable and interesting." And Chauncy accepted these as constitutive of the substance of the character of God. God became just by being good.

This contrast between the goodness and the justice of God was the natural product of the humanitarianism of the age. It is of such importance for the understanding of the conflict of Calvinism with the heresies of the age that it will be well to state the view of the Calvinists on the subject. This is best expressed in the essay of Joseph Bellamy on *The Nature and Glory of the Gospel of Jesus Christ*.[45]

"Vindictive justice in the Deity has nothing in its nature inconsistent with his infinite goodness; and his infinite goodness has nothing in its nature inconsistent with vindictive justice. All the divine perfections are harmonious. Nay, all the moral perfections of the Deity are really but one—*God is love*." [46]

God is good because He is just, and He is just because He is good. He neither must nor will sacrifice the one for the other. The punishment of the sinner is both just and good, for God punishes the sinner. The salvation of the righteous is also good and just, for God saves the righteous. The exercise of His mercy upon those who repent, as well as the exercise of vindictive judgment upon those who do not, is an act of justice and goodness, and these are inseparable and harmonious elements in the character of God, comprehended under His "love." Of course, the punishment of the sinner is not always to his good, as the sinner understands it. Hence arises the notion that in order to be good to the sinner, God must suspend the exercise of His vindictive justice. The truth, however, is that the good which God accomplishes through the punishment of the sinner is not necessarily the latter's good. "God is love. Love to being in general; chiefly to the first, the great, the infinite being, the fountain and source of all being; and secondarily, to finite beings." [47] The good which God seeks and accomplishes is the display of infinite being, a good which transcends the good of all finite existence. If the misery of the sinner is conducive to such a display, which it must be because sinners are in fact miserable, then it is just and good that sinners should be punished with misery.

This was the contention of Calvin and Edwards, and of Bellamy and Hopkins at their best. It may be said to be the essence of all Calvinism. Calvinism inevitably declined when this basic element of its faith became incredible. So long as it was able to make the display of the glory of God in the facts of life convincing to its adherents, it was wholesome and strong. So long as it could cultivate a disinterested appreciation of all events as particular manifestations and instances of the accomplishment of the ultimate purposes of God, it could view the sins and the miseries of mankind as applications of that eternal constitution with which God moves and governs the world. Calvinism had re-discovered the truth that any genuine happiness rests upon an adequate understanding of the course of events, their causes and consequences, and upon the regulation of life accordingly. The test of Calvinistic piety was the worship and the service of God in spite of, nay because of, the disagreeable facts of human life. This is accomplished through the denial of the self, which Calvin placed at the foundation of Christian excel-

lence.[48]   Edwards' "true virtue" is *disinterested* appreciation and service of divine purposes.   Hopkins insisted persistently and emphatically that self-love is always sinful.[49]
In the present controversy, he bluntly accuses the opponents of endless punishment with selfishness.   "It is easy
to see that selfishness cannot be reconciled to eternal punishment on those grounds, and for the reasons, aside from
which or were it not for them, it would be undesirable and
not reasonable, *viz.*, the glory of God and the greatest
general good." [50]

In a sense this is a caricature of Chauncy's views, because these are based on fellow-feeling and human sympathy, rather than on personal selfishness.   However, the
charge is justified in so far as Chauncy identified the glory
of God with human happiness.   The change from Calvinism to the views of Chauncy had been radical and all-
important.   Before religion was God-centered, now it was
centered in man.   Before whatever was not conducive to
the glory of God was infinitely evil, now that which is not
conducive to the happiness of man is evil, unjust, and impossible to attribute to the deity.   Before the good of man
consisted ultimately in glorifying God; now, the glory
of God consists in the good of man.   Before man lived to
worship and to serve God, and now God lives to serve
human happiness.

Hopkins' Calvinism did not exclude sympathy to his
fellowmen.   Good-will to men belonged to the very essence of his religion.[51]   In the essay under consideration,
there is only one mention of the state of sinners in hell,
and that is introduced to prove eternal punishment by
showing that if "their worm shall not die, neither shall
their fire be quenched," then the worm must be given some

food and the fire fed with the necessary fuel.[52] In all other instances, eternal punishment is asserted and defended with no attempt to speculate as to its precise nature. That the wicked shall go to hell is, of course, maintained, but beyond that there is very little said in detail. Hopkins is silent concerning the various terrors which await the sinner in the next world. His concern is to describe the *nature* of true piety and the *nature* of sin against God, and to state them in terms of definite doctrines, of which eternal punishment was one. What irritated him was not that according to the scheme of his opponents too many men are to be saved from hell-fire; for he himself expressed his hopes for the best; [53] but that the *reasons* for their contentions were contrary to the spirit and the letter of that which he considered to be true piety. They ignored the majesty and the justice of God; they minimized the criminal nature of sin; they exalted man, and put God under moral obligation to make him happy. Hopkins would believe in endless punishment rather than compromise the right of God to seek His own glory and the good of the "whole."

The other defenders of eternal hell-fire failed to share Hopkins' concern for the self-respect of the deity. His interest in divine majesty, although not absent from the other writings of the controversy, does not recur with the same persuasive power. This is the case with Nathanael Emmons' *Process of General Judgment,* which was published in the same year as Hopkins' work. In Emmons' hands Calvinism lost much of its sturdy vigor and constraining realism. There is not one of the great arguments of Edwards, Bellamy, and Hopkins to which he does justice. God punishes sinners endlessly, "not for

their own good, but for his own glory." [54]   This is true
to Calvinistic form.   But, as to how the endless damnation of sinners is conducive to divine glory, he is far more
agnostic than Hopkins.   His repeated contention is that
this *may* be so; but as to why or how it may be so, he gives
the reader next to no light.   This is highly significant.
Edwards and Hopkins definitely asserted that the punishment of sinners *does* in fact display the justice of God,
which is an aspect of His glory.   In the work of Emmons,
divine justice receives little attention, and therefore, eternal punishment is a pure puzzle.   Emmons shows none
of Bellamy's relish for the vindictive justice of God, and
lacks Edwards' sense for God's hatred of sin.   Infinite
punishment as a constituted consequence of infinite sin has
no place in his thought.   He makes nothing of their grand
assertion that sin is infinite evil, which is the only ground,
and even the essence, of eternal damnation.   As Hopkins
perceived, the latter, when separated from the former, is
reduced to a diabolical fiction and an incredible justice.
In this way, Emmons had missed the whole point of the
doctrine of infinite damnation.

He has two arguments for endless punishment which
lack all force and attractiveness.   "If neither the nature
of sin can be changed, nor the guilt of it taken away, then
the damned, who have once deserved punishment, will forever deserve it, and consequently God may, in point of
justice, punish them to all eternity." [55]   This is at best a
confused statement of sin as infinite evil.   It is the *permanent duration* of evil, and not its *infinite nature*, that
justifies eternal damnation.   Of course, a sinful act is always a sinful act; but does it follow that one who has committed murder is thereafter always deserving of punish-

ment? Emmons may mean that sinners in hell will always be sinners. In that case, the eternal nature of sin has nothing to do with eternal damnation. Emmons has changed the issue from, "Does infinite sin deserve infinite punishment for the glory of God?" to "May the sinner be retained in hell forever, if this *may* be conducive to the glory of God?" The mere endlessness of damnation, instead of its infinity and "absolute eternity" has become the issue.

This unhappy modification of the question is still more striking in the writings of the lesser Calvinists who came forward against Chauncy's views. Out of the ninety-six pages of William Gordon's *The Doctrine of Final Universal Salvation*, eighty-six are devoted to proving that endless hell-fire is a scriptural doctrine.[56] Gordon presents a formidable array of Scripture passages to show that the doctrine is founded on the Word of God. He fails to realize that such a procedure could not possibly carry conviction, because Chauncy could hold forth the same authority, as he actually did, to demonstrate his more attractive theory. The doctrine of eternal damnation, as an independent doctrine, had become abhorrent, Scripture or no Scripture. And this primary emphasis on it, which scriptural exegesis necessitated and produced, merely increased its dreadfulness, and made it thoroughly unpalatable. When Calvinists tried to show that the universalists had expounded the Scriptures erroneously, and kept enlarging upon the nature and the endlessness of damnation, it became increasingly difficult for humane and ethically minded people to believe in *their* method of exegesis.

What little rational proof Gordon does offer in the last few pages of his pamphlet has little in it that can possibly be construed as sublime or profound. What we have here is a Calvinism stripped of its beauties as a religion of worship and humility, and clothed with the mourning clothes of human beings consigned to endless burning. Such a bleak figure was necessarily detestable, and people turned away in disgust.

If scriptural evidence could not save the doctrine of endless damnation, dialectical skill was no less futile. Had the latter been of any avail, Jonathan Edwards, Jr., would have vindicated Calvinism once for all, and eliminated universalism from the field of controversy. As a debater and exposer of his opponents' inconsistencies, he was without a peer. In 1789, a year after Chauncy's death, he wrote the most brilliant treatise the controversy produced.[57] It is impossible to repeat his arguments without quoting half the book; it will be sufficient to give one example to give the reader an idea of his astounding intellectual power. Chauncy had argued that God's dealings with sin are disciplinary, and not punitive. It must therefore follow, argues Edwards, that:

"*Moral evil* is not in itself odious or abominable, but that it becomes odious then only, when the disapprobation of it subserves the personal good of the perpetrator; which is the same thing as to hold, that moral evil, as such, is not at all odious, but is odious in this particular case only, when the disapprobation of it subserves the good of the perpetrator." [58]

"If sin be no moral evil, it is not blamable; and if sin or vice do not deserve blame or punishment, virtue which is the opposite, does not deserve praise and reward; and all moral distinctions are groundless, as in a moral view there is no difference between virtue and vice, sin and holiness. Therefore there is no moral government in the universe, nor any foundation of it." [59]

Still worse:

"If the punishment of hell be mere discipline happily conducive to the good of the sufferers, there is no forgiveness in the preservation of man from it . . . Forgiveness is to remit a *deserved penalty*, or to exempt from *penal evil*; not to deprive of a benefit, or of anything which is absolutely necessary to our happiness, and which is therefore on the whole no real evil, but a real good." [60]

This argument, which can be paralleled with many others in the book, reveals at once the strength and the weakness of Edwards, Jr. Its strength lies in the reduction of the contention of Chauncy to an absurdity. Its weakness is of another kind. Edwards the son had none of his father's glowing mysticism and natural piety. He was the arch-moralist among the Calvinists. In him that legalism which has previously been observed as creeping into Calvinism finds its supreme expression.[61] His mind operates wholly in terms of crime and punishment, praise and blame, good and evil. Sin is thus moral evil, and irrelevant to the glory of God. The result is that he can offer no demonstration of the infinite evil of sin except by arguing that if it were not so, there would be no endless punishment! [62] Sin is infinite evil because it is punished endlessly! This is the reverse of the procedure of his father and Samuel Hopkins.[63] Endless punishment itself he proves in several ways, of which he attaches the greatest importance to the following:

"The penalty threatened in the law . . . cannot be the temporary punishment actually suffered by the damned; because the damned would finally be saved without forgiveness. It cannot be a temporary punishment of less duration, than that which is suffered by the damned; because on that supposition the damned are punished more than they deserve. It cannot be a temporary punishment of longer duration, than that which the scriptures abundantly declare the damned shall suffer; because no such punishment is threatened in the law, or any part of scripture. It must therefore be an endless punishment." [64]

Moralism and utilitarianism are happy bedfellows, for that which is right is often seen to be useful, somehow and to somebody. Just as the moralism of Hopkins found a clearer expression in Edwards, Jr., his utilitarianism also was carried one step further. The streak of realism in his Calvinism, made Edwards, Jr., revolt against Chauncy's philosophy that all suffering must be for the good of the sinner; but it did not prevent him from making it central to his argument that moral evil is punished because "it tends to impair the good and the happiness of the universe." [65]

"All the vindictive punishment pleaded for, is that which is deserved by the sinner and is necessary to support divine law and moral government in proper dignity, and thus to promote the general good." [66]

There are two kinds of justice: "distributive justice," whereby a crime is a transgression of the moral law, and the criminal is punished because of his transgression; and there is "public justice," whereby crime is punished to promote public welfare. Distributive justice finds its justifications in its tendency to support and promote general public good. The moral law as *such*, and the punishment meted out for its transgression, are not an exhibition of divine glory.[67] God hates sin, not because, *as such*, sin is an absolute evil, but because it is inimical to public happiness. God's justice displays His glory in so far as it is conducive to this end. Edwards is one step behind his opponents. He differs from his father in making the general public good the last end of creation. His opponents differ from him in making the good of the individual the last end of creation. The process is a direct movement from the glory of God as the last end of creation to the glory of all men as the same. Edwards makes no attempt to show how the endless punishment of sinners is conducive to public good, because no such demonstration is easy to make appear plausible. In spite of his brilliant arguments, having obscured the infinite evil of sin against God and the inherent beauty of vindictive justice, he had torn off the very roots of the doctrine in Calvinistic piety. Enlightened egoism and disinterested appreciation of things describe two different temperaments. Edwards' religion was divine republicanism, and his God a President of questionable wisdom and power. In a republic, prisons filled with convicts sentenced to life imprisonment are a reflection upon its rulers, or at best, unpleasant but unavoidable social necessities. Assuming that God seeks nothing but the happiness of men, hell-fire could not possibly be put in a more favorable light.

By the year 1796 disbelief in endless damnation had assumed alarming proportions. Nathan Strong, in his *The Doctrine of Eternal Misery*, struck more than one tragic note and waxed eschatological.

"With respect to the doctrine of the salvation of all men, it is not new in the world . . . but there hath been no period, in which so many men have declared themselves converts to it, as in the present." [68]

"This error is not confined to those who are commonly called Universalists, and have formed themselves into a distinct religious sectary . . . There is a more numerous class of people, who have not, and perhaps never will openly separate from the other denominations of professed Christians; who seem to have no sense of God as a moral governor; of their own obligation to him; and of the awful penalties of the divine law . . . [who] still suppose they are travelling directly to a paradise of peace beyond the grave." [69]

"There are also many prophetic signs, shewing that we are in the period of great error and irreligion . . . Such a state of things, before the church shall put on her glory, is matter of prophecy; and we have signs enough to know that it hath already commenced." [70]

Strong has come to the realization that the only way to save the "doctrine of eternal misery" is to show that, after all, it is not quite so bad as it sounds. Since the doctrine is revealed in the Scriptures, it must be true. It must and will serve some good end. However, we may be sure that "none will be miserable but those who perfectly deserve it." [71] "It must be allowed, that an immense number of mankind in the present and in all past ages, have given too little evidence of a holy and heavenly temper, but this is no proof that there will not be many more saved, than are lost." [72] The day is coming when the earth shall be filled with the "knowledge of God and of the moral system"; the present sins and miseries of the world will teach the "inhabitants of that happy day," "the nature, tendencies, conduct, and effects of a sinful temper." [73] These shall come to a full understanding of the "scheme of redeeming wisdom and goodness"; they will mend their ways, and live in the house of God.   In the future "most successful days of the gospel," there may be "some few left in deepest sin," but they will constitute only a small minority.[74]   Therefore, ultimately, very few people will ever get to hell.   And surely this ought not to cause too much concern, because the final outcome of the process will most certainly be for "the greatest good."   The endless misery of some few incurable and great sinners is of infinitesimal significance, compared to the endless and infinite happiness of the multitudes in heaven, which will ensue from God's "scheme of redeeming wisdom and goodness." [75]

Strong's compromise was nearly surrender, but not quite.   He was willing to make concessions to mitigate the odium cast upon orthodoxy, but being a profound Calvinist, he kept the Gospel "scheme of salvation" intact. His was a belated attempt to destroy the ugly reputation which the controversy gave to orthodox religion.   The hurt was already done, and besides, apology and compromise were poor weapons against attractive heresies.[76]

The nineteenth century found the imposing theological edifice of Calvinism not only ugly but also unstable. While enemies were battering its walls, its occupants were pulling it down on the inside, pillar after pillar, and removing one plank after another as rotten and dangerous. Jacob Norton, "an orthodox clergyman of Massachusetts," gave eleven reasons in refutation of the doctrine that sin is infinite evil.[77]   To consider sin as an infinite evil destroys all distinctions between the various kinds and degrees of sin.[78]   It means that all sinners in hell will receive the same degree of punishment.[79]   It means that to indulge in one little sin is equivalent to committing the most pernicious crimes a thousand times.[80]   "Man is indeed a very ignorant and feeble being, and in all his powers and faculties greatly circumscribed." [81]   Therefore, his acts cannot be infinitely evil.

And how can the sin of such a creature "justly expose him to punishment not only endless, but illimitably great"? [82]

"Can it be consistent with the character of that infinitely glorious Being, who is the Father of all, the Father of mercies, who is infinite in goodness, boundless in love, and impartial in justice?   Upon what grounds then can any urge that sin is an infinite evil?" [83]

"Can it reasonably be supposed that sinners in the state of retribution will suffer the vengeance of endless fire, as a just reward of a single sin, or of all the sins which they had committed while in the body?   Although I would not answer peremptorily in the affirmative, yet I cannot hesitate to say that the negative of the question is probably true." [84]

However, Norton is strongly inclined to believe in the endless punishment of the damned in hell-fire.

"It is probable in the highest degree—it seems indeed hardly to admit question, that the misery of the wicked in hell will arise in a very great degree from the wicked and malignant feelings and exercises of their hearts in that doleful place of wretchedness." [85]

"And should the enmity of their hearts continue to endless duration, and to endless duration continue to increase, then it must be admitted, not only that their misery will be eternal, but that it will in a great measure arise from this source." [86]

The sinners will go to hell because of their sins in this world, and they will stay there because of "their sinful conduct in hell!" And surely, the degree of their punishment will vary with the gravity of their particular sins.

Timothy Dwight, the shining star of Calvinism in the early part of the nineteenth century, used a similar argument. He was little less doubtful of the infiniteness of the evil of sin, and believed in an everlasting "state of retribution" because he could see no reason to believe that the damned in hell will ever cease to sin.[87] Thus, both Norton and Dwight fell back upon a childish legalism such as no one could take seriously. They themselves reiterated the dogma so apologetically that the weakness of their faith was all too conspicuous. As a last resort they committed the blunder of relying almost entirely on the old stock of scriptural proofs. By this time, however, many in New England had ceased to listen to them.

CHAPTER VII

THE WRATH OF GOD AND THE CROSS OF CHRIST

THE story of Christ Jesus, the God-Man, belongs in the center of the Calvinistic gospel. The worship of God called forth the austere sentiments of awe and reverence; the worship of the Son of God called forth all the tenderness and love of which the human heart is capable. This God was also Man, a Man who had laid down His life for the salvation of His fellow-men, a Man who had mediated between an angry God and a sinful world.

The attempts of Christian theologians to give accurate and consistent explanations of the redeeming work of Christ are called "theories of the Atonement." The subject is very complicated and difficult, because a comprehensive theory of the Atonement must consider the work of Christ from several different points of view: as a sacrifice, as a payment of a debt, as an appeasement of the wrath of God, as a perfect obedience to the law of Moses, and as a revelation of God the Father. To bring these together into a uniform and consistent account taxed the ingenuity of the greatest theologians, for the ideas involved were too varied and the needs too basic to permit of a ready solution. The theory of Anselm was accepted by the Catholic Church, passed into Calvinism, and was reasserted by Jonathan Edwards, but with his own interest and emphasis sufficiently marked and clear.

According to the eternal constitution of God, punishment is the natural and necessary consequence of crime.[1] This connection between crime and punishment is *desert*. It is fitting and proper that the sinner should be punished; he deserves it.[2]   God's punishment of sin expresses His hatred for sin, and this in turn expresses His holiness. God punishes the sinner because He hates sin. "Christ suffered the wrath of God for men's sins."[3] "God laid on him the iniquities of us all, and he bare the burden of them."[4]   Laden with the sins of the world, Christ offered himself as a sacrifice, and atoned for them; "the blood of Christ washed away our guilt."[5]   Thus the sinners were "justified," or "freed from guilt."[6]

Edwards conceives the guilt of the sinner in terms of an *"unpaid debt."*   The sinner owes it to God to worship and to obey Him.   But he is unable to do so, therefore he is unable to pay his debt.   The blood of Christ is the "price" which He laid down to cover and "pay our debt; and so it *satisfies.*"[7]   "The satisfaction of Christ is to free us from misery," which was to be meted to us as the consequence of our debt.[8]   But that is not all.   "By the agreement between the Father and the Son," Christ also merited "a title to us for happiness."[9]

"Satisfaction and merit do not differ so much really as relatively.   They both consist in paying a valuable price, a price of infinite value; but only that price, as it respects a debt to be paid, is called *satisfaction;* and as it respects a good to be obtained, is called *merit* . . .   This may suffice concerning what is meant by the purchase of Christ."[10]

Edwards' conception of the merit of Christ reveals the basic soundness of his thought on the subject of the Atonement.   The merit of Christ's work, which is inseparable from the satisfaction He offered for the indebtedness of sinners to God, rests upon His perfect obedience to the commands which He received from His Father "to teach such doctrines, to preach the gospel, to work such miracles, to call such disciples, to appoint such ordinances, and finally to lay down his life." [11]   The Cross was the summing up, the climax, of the "mediatorial office" of Christ. His merit became manifest in all His teachings and doings, throughout His earthly life, as well as in the shedding of His blood.   In His obedience to the "mediatorial law," or in the conduct of His life as the Mediator between God and a sinful humanity, Christ established a new rule of righteousness which completed and transcended that law for the transgression of which mankind were exposed to eternal damnation.   Christ not only paid a debt, but also purchased "a title to us for happiness."   And this purchase He accomplished through the complete course of His earthly existence.   The practical soundness of Edwards' thought appears in this.   Justification and the Christian life are inseparable.   The appropriation of the satisfaction and the merit of Christ is evidenced in holy living.   The ideas of God's great hatred of sin, the indebtedness of the sinner to God, the greatness of Christ's self-sacrifice, which underlay the other aspects of his "theory" described above, did not obscure the common sense truth that salvation, after all, consists in the exercise of true virtue.

Nevertheless, Edwards' thoughts on the Atonement do contain a dominant theme.   An indignant sovereign deity held the world under a curse.   The sacrifice of Christ was the satisfaction or the ransom which redeemed the world from this curse.   Thus the offended deity was reconciled with mankind through the mediation of His Son.   The original atmosphere of these ideas belongs to a cultural period when sovereign lords treated their subjects as it pleased them, and prisoners were ransomed through the payment of a price. The eighteenth century was of a different spirit. The reason of the age dictated that the function of government is to establish civic order through the enforcement of its laws, which prescribed just punishments for the various crimes of the citizens of a given country. A crime became the transgression of a specific law, and was punishable according to the terms set down by the law. The enforcement of the law of the land was now the administration of justice, and justice an absolute virtue. Perfect justice became the mark of perfect government, and the maintenance of the integrity of its laws the measure of the dignity of the state.

This radical transformation in political theory, in general from sovereignty to justice, was soon reflected in theology. It gave Hugo Grotius the basis of his *Defense of the Catholic Faith concerning the Satisfaction of Christ, against Faustus Socinus.*[12] Socinus maintained that God, whose goodness is perfect, can and does forgive sinners, or cancel their debt to Him, without the inducement of a ransom; and that, therefore, the work of Christ was not a "satisfaction."[13] Grotius discovers the error of Socinus in his conception of God as an offended prince or a dissatisfied creditor.[14] His own view is that "in all this subject God must be treated as a Ruler,"[15] who administers justice according to a "penal law."[16] The omission of punishment threatened by such a law "almost always detracts from the authority of the law among the subjects."[17] A ruler must uphold the authority of his law, and in doing this "he exercises a certain virtue, which is called retributive justice."[18] As a Ruler, God could not fail to punish sinners as demanded by His law, unless He could find some other way of satisfying the law and keeping the dignity of His moral government intact. This condition was fulfilled by the punishment of Christ in the sinners' stead. God's retributive justice was thus made fully manifest, the demands of the law were fully satisfied, and God could now exercise mercy upon the sinning world without compromising His justice.[19]

The theory of Grotius, together with the philosophy of government which it implies, passed into eighteenth century New England, and found its first exponent in Joseph Bellamy.[20] Bellamy's conception of God as the "moral Governor of the Universe" has already been discussed.[21] Therefore it is not surprising to find that he appropriated the Grotian view of the Atonement. It is important for our study to get an accurate idea of Bellamy's own statement of the theory, because some of its aspects must be clearly distinguished from the parallel aspects of the "New England Theory" as it was formulated during the controversy on eternal damnation.

"The design of the incarnation, life, and death of the Son of God, was to give a practical declaration, in the most public manner, even in the sight of the whole intellectual system, that God is worthy of all that love, honor, and obedience, which his law required, and that sin was as great an evil as the punishment threatened supposed; and so to declare God's righteousness, and condemn the sins of an apostate world, to the end God might be just, and yet a justifier of the believer. And this he did by obeying and dying in our room and stead."[22]

"Thus the whole mediatorial scheme is designed, and in its own nature adapted, to do honor to the divine law."[23]

The obedience of the son of God to the divine law even unto death proved that the law of God is excellent and just. By suffering the punishment which is the just desert of an apostate world, the Son showed that such punishment is right, and in this way "he declared the Father's righteousness." [24] Such righteousness consists in the administration of justice, through the punishment of sin, which is the transgression of the moral law. The righteousness of God is primarily His "vindictive justice," which is necessary for moral government, and defines His character as the moral Governor of the Universe. In the conduct of His life, in His "incarnation, life, and death," Christ gave "a practical declaration" of the dignity of the moral law, and thus maintained the honor of the moral Governor. It was thus proven in the "highest external manner" that "God our Creator is infinitely worthy of our supreme love and universal obedience, and that our disaffection to him and to his government is entirely groundless, yea, infinitely criminal." [25] Since the work of Christ consisted in vindicating the divine law, the doctrine of imputation, the burdening of the sins of the world upon Christ, and the expiatory efficacy of His blood, receive slight emphasis from Bellamy.[26]

The dispute on the duration of punishment in hell-fire aroused a new discussion of the nature of the "mediatorial office" of Christ. Calvinistic thought on the subject labored under an inconsistency. On the one hand it was asserted that the sacrifice of Christ was a sufficient expiation for the sins of all men, or a sufficient price for their redemption; and on the other hand, it was insisted that no man is actually redeemed unless he have "saving grace." Charles Chauncy made good use of this difficulty.

The orthodoxy of his premises made his conclusions formidable.

"The human race came into the world under the disadvantage of being subjected to death, in virtue of a divine constitution, occasioned solely by the offense of the *one man Adam;* and they came into existence likewise under the advantage of an absolute assurance, occasioned solely by the obedience of the *one man Jesus Christ.* Deliverance from the power of the grave is *as absolutely* and *certainly* the advantage even *all men* are under through Christ, as subjection to death is the disadvantage that has come upon them through Adam. The advantage is no more connected with their personal agency, than was the disadvantage; but, be their character what it will, they will as surely hear the voice of the Son of God, and come forth from their graves, as they went down into them." [27]

Adam disobeyed the law of God, and the whole world was damned because of him. Christ obeyed the law of God, and the whole world was saved because of Him. Chauncy does not urge that the world at present is in a saved state. Christ put mankind in a "salvable condition." Salvation will be accomplished during the "next state," in hell, when men become "morally fit." "They will be wrought upon, sooner or later in a moral way, such an one as is adjusted to moral agents, to become righteous persons." [28] The recognition of this necessary delay in the salvation of all men, introduced the one flaw into Chauncy's argument. However, the dialectics of it was sufficiently clear to annoy the Calvinists. The righteousness of one can be imputed to many in the same way that the sinfulness of one can. Chauncy believed that he had thus demolished the orthodox contention that the imputation of

the sin of Adam to mankind rests upon "natural generation," whereas the imputation of the righteousness of
Christ rests upon the appropriation of it by a given person
and is due to a "new establishment." [29]

The broad theory that as in the sin of Adam all were
lost, so in the righteousness of Christ all were saved, finds
clearer expression in Relly's *Union*.

"Mankind now rejoice in the Justice and the Purity of
God; yea, appeal unto Him as just, as holy, as faithful,
because according unto *Union* with *Christ*, Justice hath
been satisfied, in his blood-shedding and death; where
they in him, and *He* in them, have been fully punished for
all their Iniquity." [30]

John Murray preached the same thing.

"Another Figure we have in the *Tree*—our Saviour
God is presented to us under this plain familiar Figure.—
The root is invisible, the stock is one, and visible, the
branches are many—and derive their life from the *root*
through the stock." [31]

In all this there was just enough of a semblance of
orthodoxy to force the orthodox into restatements of their
theory of the Atonement in order to discredit the absurd
contention of their opponents that sinners are or will be
somehow saved because of a mysterious imputation of the
righteousness of Christ to them, or because of a no less
mysterious "union" with Him, apart from their own personal obedience to the moral law. The universality of
the salvation effected by Christ, according to Hopkins, consists in that "he has effectively removed the difficulty, the
bar which was in the way of the salvation of any one of
mankind." [32] But this does not prove that all men do or
will take advantage of this fact. God is willing to save

men; but men perish because they "will not comply with this kind offer." [33]   Hopkins rejects the idea that God, "in a moral way," or any other, forces men into heaven.   The freedom of man does not allow such a procedure on the part of God.   This argument, which implies the complete moral autonomy of man, was made little use of by the other Calvinists who defended eternal damnation.   They took divine sovereignty too seriously to rest their cause upon such a notion of the self-determination of the human will.

The attack of Nathanael Emmons on Relly was far more effective and direct.[34]   "No divine constitution or appointment whatever could make Christ's personal suffering and obedience ours.   A divine constitution cannot alter the nature of things, nor effect impossibilities. . . . The notion that all mankind were 'with Christ through all the circumstances of his birth, life, death, resurrection, and glory,' is absurd as the doctrine of transubstantiation, of which no man can form an idea." [35]   This statement is one of the finest examples of Calvinistic realism.   In the "nature of things," it is an "impossibility" that things which are not united one to the other in one way should nevertheless be united one to the other in the same way. The "union" of mankind with Christ does not eliminate the fact that sinning men do not share the righteousness of Christ.   Men share the sinfulness of Adam, therefore his sin is imputed to them; they do not share the righteousness of Christ, therefore the righteousness of Christ is not imputed to them.   The religious argument of Emmons was even more devastating.

"If the price of redemption which Christ hath paid hath fully discharged the debt which sinners owe to God, then they now owe him nothing; and if they owe him nothing, they have nothing to be forgiven. . . . There can be no grace displayed in the salvation of the sinners by the gospel. For if they all deserve to be saved, it is an act of justice, but not of grace, for God to save them." [36]

No Calvinist failed to point this out, and to insist upon its fundamentally unchristian character. Religiously, the salvation of sinners as God's payment of a debt which He owes them or as an act of justice to them necessitated by the work of Christ, was as unthinkable as the sinners' "union" with Christ. However, the time-honored views of the Atonement as accomplished through the payment of a price for the ransom of sinners or through the offering of an expiatory sacrifice to appease the wrath of the deity, supplied the grounds for the contentions of the universalists. Therefore, the Calvinists proceeded to formulate a theory of the Atonement which would rob the universalists of the orthodox bases of their unorthodox doctrine. The foundation for such a theory was found in the eighteenth century philosophy of justice and moral government, and in the parallel theory of the Atonement formulated by Grotius and adopted by Bellamy.

In *A Sermon at Wallingford, by particular agreement, with special reference to the Murryan Controversy*, John Smalley proposed to prove the following important proposition: "Eternal salvation on no account a matter of just debt; or, full redemption, not interfering with free grace."

"What rendered the vicarious obedience and sufferings of our Saviour necessary, was, that we might have remission of sin and the rewards of the righteous, and yet the honour of the divine law and government be maintained . . . The holy law of God was not rashly given.

His own glory, and the good of the moral creation, required that there should be such a law, and that the dignity of it should be supported.   A lawless, licentious universe were infinitely worse than none.   Hence heaven and
earth might sooner pass away, or be annihilated, than the
divine law be made void, or one tittle of it fail and not be
fulfilled." [37]

Public good, public order, and legal justice, the keynotes of the political philosophy of the eighteenth century, supplied the keynotes of later New England Calvinism,—the "good of the moral creation," the moral government of God, and the glory of the "vindictive justice"
of God.   The God of Calvinism was now confronted with
the problem of letting His moral law take its full course
through a perfect constancy in the punishment of transgression, and yet forgiving those whom He would forgive.
It was the dilemma of the sovereign God trying to play
the "moral Governor."   Therefore, in his second Wallingford sermon, Smalley tried to prove: "The law in all
respects satisfied by our Saviour, in regard to those only
who belong to Him; or, none but the believers saved,
through the all-sufficient satisfaction of Christ."   The
manner of this accomplishment is this:

"Not all the curses of the law, amidst the thunders and
lightnings of mount Sinai,—nor even the execution of
those curses in the unquenchable flames of hell, gave, or
can ever give, equal evidence of the righteousness or wrath
of God, as the amazing scenes exhibited in Gethsemane,
and on mount Calvary.   Nothing could make the law appear as steadfast, or afford such full ground of faith that
every transgression shall receive a just recompense of re-

ward, as the bloody sweat,—the deserted exclamation,—
the expiring agonies, of our Divine Saviour." [88]

The new note in this revision of Bellamy's theory is the
significance attached to the sufferings of Christ upon the
Cross.   The dignity of the law of God was revealed not
so much in the obedience of Christ unto death as in the
sufferings of Christ.   The righteousness of God is made
manifest in the wrath of God, and the wrath of God in the
sufferings of Christ.   In Bellamy's thought, the Cross was
the climax and the summing up of a life of obedience,
which demonstrated the divine law to be supremely hon-
orable and worthy of obedience.   Smalley's limitation of
the atoning work of Christ to the sufferings on the Cross
had another consequence.   A fair exhibition of penal justice rests in the punishment of the criminal.   The sufferings of Christ could not have revealed the justice of
God unless Christ was accounted a criminal.   But Christ
was personally sinless.   Therefore, the sins of mankind
must have been imputed to Him.   Otherwise, His sufferings would exhibit God's injustice, and not His justice.
Thus, although the whole purpose of the theory was to
prove that righteousness and guilt are personal matters
and cannot be imputed back and forth, it rests upon a
vague notion of the imputation of the guilt of mankind to
Jesus.   The curious consequence is that whereas the sins
of men were laid upon Jesus, His righteousness could not
be transferred to sinners.   On this point Smalley is very
emphatic.

"The truth is, our *ill desert* is not taken away by the
atonement of Christ.   That can never be taken away.   Nor
doth the obedience of Christ render us *deserving* of
heaven, or *undeserving* of hell. . . . *Grace reigns* with

unabated lustre in our justification, and in the whole of our salvation, notwithstanding its reigning through *righteousness*, because it is through a righteousness *not our own*." [39]

This is the real conviction of Smalley, and the basis of his contention with the universalists. Justice is satisfied when the sinner is punished for his own sins; the satisfaction offered by Christ did not eliminate the justice of each sinner being punished for his sins. In this sense, Smalley believes not that Christ satisfied the law, but that the hatred of God for sin was adequately displayed upon the Cross. Such a display was satisfactory to the deity, so that He could now exercise His mercy upon some sinners! But it did not satisfy the moral law, for, otherwise, all further punishment of sinners would be unjust, which is absurd. The distinction is real. For the display of divine glory it was sufficient that His hatred of sin should have been made manifest in the sufferings of His Son. To satisfy the law it is necessary that each sinner be punished for his own sins. This is the one certainty. However, divine forgiveness is maintained through a dubious exhibition of God's vindictive justice in the sufferings of Christ on the Cross; dubious because such an exhibition is impossible without the burdening of Christ with the guilt of mankind; and this is impossible if sin cannot be transferred from one person to another, which has now become a moral axiom.

Jonathan Edwards, Jr., presented "His Excellency the Governor, and a large number of both Houses of the Legislature of the State of Connecticut, during their session at New Haven, in October, 1785," with an elaborate and precise statement *On the Necessity of the Atonement and its Consistency with Free Grace in Forgiveness.* Edwards, Jr., was well aware of the difficulties in the presentation of Smalley. He rejected completely the idea that Christ paid the sinner's debt, or that He suffered the punishment due to the sinner.[40] He even repudiated the idea that the law is proved to "be just, and the character of God . . . proved to be good, by the perfect obedience and death of Christ."[41]

"The obedience of Christ, even in the more trying circumstances, without any tokens of divine displeasure against the transgressors of the law, would never support the authority of the law, and the dignity of the divine government. It by no means makes it appear, that it is an evil and bitter thing to violate the law, and that the violation of it deserves, and may be expected to be followed with the most awful consequences, to him who dares to violate it."[42]

The real accomplishment of Christ was to make it appear "that sin shall not go without the proper tokens of divine displeasure and abhorrence."[43] Even Smalley had to retain the idea that the dignity of the moral law had been partially maintained through the "vicarious obedience of Christ."[44] The very merit of Christ's work rested upon His perfect righteousness and obedience to the moral law. But Edwards questions the adequacy of the obedience of Christ as an exhibition of the dignity of the moral law, or the justice of God. And in this, as usual, he is more consistent than Bellamy or Smalley. The obedience of a good man to a law may convince one that the law is good, but it does not demonstrate the vindictive justice of the lawgiver. This can only be done through the punishment of a transgressor of the law. The old question comes

back,—but how did the sufferings of an innocent Man ex- ✗
hibit the vindictive justice of God?   Edwards will not
entertain the now abhorrent notion that Christ suffered in
the sinner's stead.   But he allows that the sufferings of
Christ were "equivalent to the punishment of the sinner." [45] Unfortunately for his theory, this is not so easy
to prove as to state. The word "equivalent" was little
more than a cover for the absurdity that divine vindictive
justice was exhibited in the sufferings of an innocent Man.
Naturally, the torments of the damned in hell are far
more conducive to that end.

Confusion crept in through applying the distinction between "general or public justice" and "distributive justice."   Into the intricacies of his dialectics Edwards smug-
gled the idea that Christ satisfied the former kind of justice, but not the latter.   "Public justice" is the same thing
as public good.   Christ safeguarded public good by displaying divine justice and moral government. It is superficially plausible that Christ's sufferings should have done
this for the benefit of God's moral subjects, without satisfying "distributive justice," or eliminating the necessity
of the punishment of sinners.   In this way Christ's atonement becomes a striking public example to warn men
against sin, and thus, to establish public order.   But this is
precisely what is hard to show, unless it is accepted that
Christ was punished in the room of sinners.   Any sensible
governor who wishes to give a public exhibition of his
"vindictive justice" would prefer to hang a notorious criminal to hanging one of the law-abiding citizens of the country.   Edwards had proved that sinners may justly be punished, regardless of Christ's suffering, but he could not
show that the Cross exhibited the vindictive justice of God

for the benefit of mankind in general. If he had used his imagination, instead of maneuvering his dialectical machinery, he might have seen how impossible it is to show such a thing.

This difficulty, which made the Cross of Christ a ghastly performance of highly questionable value, was felt by Stephen West, the successor of Jonathan Edwards, Sr., to the church at Stockbridge. Contrary to the spirit and the import of the new "governmental theory," he reasserted that the death of Christ was a sacrifice necessary for the redemption of the sinful world.

In the Scriptures, "it is expressly asserted that Christ became a *curse for us*. . . . Be the evils which were implied in the curse which Christ suffered, what they may, still *they were evils*. We cannot separate the idea of *evil*, from a *curse*, especially the *curse* of God. From those evils which were implied in the curse of the law to sinners, Christ hath redeemed his people. . . . It is hence evident that Christ, in his *suffering on the cross*, was a *substitute* for the sinner. . . . For it was by *becoming* or by *being made a curse*, that Christ redeemed his people." [46]

West persistently compares the death of Christ to the Old Testament practice of sacrificing "clean beasts" as sin-offerings. "And, as the redemption which Christ hath obtained for his people is ascribed to his *blood*, or his *death*, as its procuring cause; we are naturally led to consider the sacrifice he made of himself as consisting in a peculiar and distinguishing manner in his death." [47] West works out this analogy in great detail, showing that it is because Christ was "most perfectly pure and spotless" that "his death could have been an offering of sweet savour to God." [48] Thus Christ, a perfectly sinless man, burdened himself with the sins of the world, shed his blood as a sin-offering to God, and removed the curse which lay upon mankind. Hence it is evident, why *Christ* had to *die*, and how divine displeasure with sin was displayed to the uttermost. West asserts emphatically, that if Christ did not take our sins upon Himself, He also did not atone for them.[49]

However, West keeps away from the contention of the universalists that if Christ atoned for the sins of mankind, then all men are in a saved or savable state. Therefore, his theory contains another element which coincides with that of Edwards, Jr. "Respecting *atonement*, it is to be observed that it summarily consists in an *exhibition* of the righteous displeasure of God against sin, made in some other way than in the punishment of the sinner." [50] West made the Cross a genuine exhibition of the hatred of God for sin by restating the Pauline conception that "Christ became a curse for us." But the difficulty with his version of the theory is that the substitution of Christ is valid for the good of the universe, but not for the acquittal of the sinner in whose stead He was punished! Edwards, Jr., had removed the dilemma by maintaining that Christ did not suffer instead of the sinner, but in doing this he was unable to show *how* the Cross exhibits divine vindictive justice. West's solution, less consistent but more true to the real issues, is that the work of Christ is of advantage only to those who believe in Him.[51] Only those who recognize the death of Christ as an expression of divine hatred for sin, and accordingly mend their ways and walk in the path of righteousness, benefit from the work of Christ. When they do this, the moral government of God is upheld, the dignity of the law is established, their sins are forgiven, and they escape the endless punishment of hell. They are saved because of the work of Christ, or, He has died in their room and stead. Thus, strictly, Christ burdened Himself with the sins of those only who are saved. He saved only those who are in a saved state.[52]   At this point, West is less than clear, and in the main adheres to the theory that Christ's work consisted in an exhibition of divine vindictive justice—the "governmental theory of atonement."

However, West marks a reaction to the old Calvinistic view of the Atonement as the self-sacrifice of Christ in the room of sinners. He not only reëstablished the conception of the efficacy of the blood of Christ to wash away the sins of the world, but also, through his almost exclusive attention to the death of Christ on the Cross, enhanced the miraculous interpretation of the sacrificial atonement of Christ.   In the controversies of the Calvinists with the Unitarians, which came in with the nineteenth century, we find orthodoxy committed to the belief that it was the *blood* of Christ that saved the world.[53]   It seems that the "governmental theory," which is considered as *the* contribution of New England to American theology, never really became a part of popular religion.   Nineteenth century Calvinism adhered to "salvation by blood." In this way, maybe with little wisdom and in spite of the greater gruesomeness of the conception, popular orthodoxy retained the fundamental "gospel truth" that Christ died because of our sins and in our room and stead.

The "governmental theory" itself became the official theory of the Calvinistic theologians in the nineteenth century.[54]   Its failure to capture the imagination of the people is to be explained in terms of its inadequacy to meet their religious needs. Its estimate of the work of Christ eliminated the Christological argument for universalism, but it also transformed the "gospel of love" into a gospel of justice. The infinite love of the Son of God, in a way "very God," revealed in His burdening Himself with the sins of the world and shedding His blood for the salvation of mankind, was obscured and relegated into the background. The conception of a sinless Man suffering and dying *in the place* of others, of His giving up His own life for the ransom of their souls, of His offering His blood as payment of a debt which He did not owe,—involved elements in the orthodox religion which made it a gospel of Divine love and self-sacrifice, and moved the faithful into heights of gratitude, love, and joy. Christians worshiped the Almighty God, and they loved their "Lord and Saviour Jesus Christ" as a Friend who had died for their salvation.[55] In Christ, God was revealed as a God of love, as a God who hated sin and yet loved the sinners—a God who came down from heaven, put on human flesh, healed the diseases of men, taught them concerning the good life, and died for them. Thus the Creator of heaven and earth, the Author of all things throughout eternity, was also the Father and Friend of mankind. In a complete orthodoxy, reverence, worship, and love were blended into what Edwards aptly called "holy love." The new governmental Calvinism, with its glorification of divine vindictive justice and obedience to the moral law, was of another temper.

The emphasis placed upon the sufferings of Christ upon the Cross diminished the significance of His life of obedience to the "mediatorial law." From the very beginning of Christian history, it had been well recognized that the "new righteousness" taught and exemplified by Christ had in a way abrogated the law of Moses. Although the church insisted upon the validity of the Ten Commandments, it was evident that Christ had gone beyond the requirements of the morality of the Pentateuch, and laid the foundations of a higher morality conditioned upon a radical transformation of the will or the heart. The Pauline conception of regeneration was the quasi-mystical application of a profound appreciation of this truth, and became a part of orthodox Christian theology. The disparity between the temper of Jewish legalism and "Christian freedom" always was a difficulty, but the two were held together through an incorporation of the "old dispensation" into the "new" one given by Christ. The ethical life as lived and taught by Christ was the "fulfillment" of the law of Moses, and yet it was a "new righteousness."

To the new Calvinism, the life of Christ, apart from the agony of the Cross, was theologically irrelevant. Christian living became identified with obedience to the moral law of God as revealed to Moses, and the fear of God's vindictive justice was made its foundation. All things revolved around the "moral law." God became the great Enforcer of the moral law, the blood of Christ became the evidence that God will punish transgression. Holy love faded into conformity to the moral law, and such conformity was now the measure and substance of "true virtue." Such bleak and cruel Calvinism was doomed in New England, when, with the opening of the new century, a humanized liberalism won the day, and introduced a new and softer note into the religious life of New England.

CHAPTER VIII

THE UNITARIAN REVOLT

WHILE the Calvinists were busy transforming their theology into a consistent and unlovable legalism, worldly concerns were leading others into new ways of thinking. The principles of liberty, the right of men to happiness and representative government, which nourished the zeal of the American patriots in their struggle with England and shaped the ideals of the newly freed country, had already made the theology of Calvinism irrelevant to the social thought-patterns of the period. A new, secular and humanized, frame of mind emerged from the conflict with Britain and the following preoccupation with the problems of a growing and expanding country. The temper of the new America is well revealed in the "century-sermons" preached by the clergy of the land, celebrating the coming in of the nineteenth century.

"Reflect, my hearers, on the great things God hath done for the United America, in making us a nation, and bestowing upon us privileges superior to those of any nation on earth. Judging from past events, it may be the design of his providence to elevate us above all nations—to exhibit to the world an instance of a government founded in freedom of election, a government which inseparably unites the interests of the constituted authorities and of their constituents—affords equal protection to the individual states, and secures to every citizen the just fruits of his own talents, industry and virtues." [1]

"I admire our constitution. It breathes the principles of liberty, to which I have been attached from my youth." [2]

The United America considered its freedom and increase with immense satisfaction. Timothy Dwight, patriot, enlightened utilitarian, Calvinist, and the President of Yale College, had good reasons to thank the Lord for His mercies.

"In the year 1700, there were one hundred and sixteen incorporated towns in New England, and probably 80,000 inhabitants. There are now about eight hundred and sixty towns, and probably 1,200,000 people." [3]

"The wealth of the New England states has much more rapidly increased than the number of inhabitants, and since the existence of the present American Government, much more rapidly than at any former period. In proof of these assertions, if they be supposed to need any proof, may be alleged the fences, the herds, the cultivation, the public and private buildings, the dress, the furniture, the mode of living, and the business, of the inhabitants. If we except Great Britain, we possess more than half the shipping, owned by any country in Europe. Our exports cannot be accurately estimated, because a large part of them is sent abroad from the port of New York; but those, which we directly convey to foreign countries, are very great. In the mean time it is probable, that abundance is more universally found in our houses, barns, and cellars, than in those of any other people. We do not therefore, possess merely, but eminently enjoy, also, the bounties of Providence." [4]

The same progress has been made in education, public peace, health, the diminution of crime, knowledge, and religion. [5]

"The religion of this country has exhibited a very commendable spirit of catholicism and moderation during the past century, a spirit extended perhaps as far, as can be reasonably expected from men, and producing a general and happy harmony of sentiment and conduct . . . Indeed, the existing error appears to be a tendency, in many persons, towards what is emphatically called *modern liberalism*; which is no other than mere indifference to truth and error, virtue and vice; of a more dangerous and fatal character than the most contemptible enthusiasm, or the most odious bigotry." [6]

Timothy Dwight was speaking in New Haven. His intellectual neighbors in Massachusetts, specially in and around Boston, shared his elation, but not his fear of "modern liberalism." By this time the Harvard Library was in possession of most of the literature which had produced the "modern liberalism," the works of Locke, Newton, Clarke, Sydney, Milton, Butler, and of others even more liberal or heretical, such as those of Hutcheson and Priestley. President Joseph Willard of Harvard was reputed to be an Arminian, and was in touch with the Deists of England and France.[7] As early as 1772, President Locke insisted that "foreign errors are to be met with argument alone, not by crowding down creeds and confessions upon the pain of eternal punishment." [8] Some of these "errors" were most attractive, e.g., the benevolence of God, the natural ability of man to do that which is good, his duty to do it, the subordination of theological opinion to ethical living, etc.

Liberalism in America was a humanitarian, and not a theological, movement. Boston was liberal before it became Unitarian, and its Unitarianism was primarily ethical

and social.   The controversy started by Thomas Belsham,
the English Unitarian, was preceded by a long period of
preparation, during which an alienation arose between the
religious and the secular thought of New England.   The
practical and ethical tenets of Unitarianism, which, after
all, motivated the theological uproar of the controversy,
were held by the "friends of mankind" in New England
before the Unitarian movement proper.   The dispute
about the Trinity, which became the ostensible issue between the Unitarians and the Trinitarians, merely crystal-
lized the growing estrangement between Calvinism and
the spirit of the new age, and brought it to a head.   Arianism, which was adopted by Channing, was hardly new to
New England.   As early as 1756, Emlyn's *Humble Inquiry* was reprinted in Boston, and both Jonathan Mayhew
and Lemuel Briant of Braintree were of Arian tendencies.[9]
But the heresy was checked and ignored so long as the
humanitarians failed to see, or at least elaborate, the theological implications of their political and social views.   So
long as men could manage to be Calvinists on Sunday and
eighteenth century rationalists on week-days, all was well.
The result was merely a certain indifference to theological
"truth and error."   The liberal clergy preferred to remain
in doubt, and appropriated parts of new heresies with
little consciousness of deviating from "true doctrine."
When they did deny an old truth, it turned out to be
neither important nor scriptural.   The transition from Calvinism was thus smooth and quiet.   People continued to
"believe" the "gospel truths," went to church and took
part in its practices; and since such things were irrelevant
to political and commercial activity, they were kept safe
and separate.   The churches made the necessary conces-

sions to the weaknesses of their congregations, and these respectable people satisfied both God and the clergy, as well as themselves.

Then came the pamphlet of Thomas Belsham, *American Unitarianism; or a Brief History of the Progress and Present State of the Unitarian Churches in America.* It was little more than an irritating battle-cry. Its declared aim was to describe the "radical and essential changes" which had taken place during the previous "thirty years," specially "in some parts of New England." [10] The story turns around several personalities, such as Freeman, Sherman, Thacher, Cary, whose contributions to the Unitarian cause are retold in terms of high approbation, while their opponents are censured in equally strong terms. The Unitarians are praised as "some of the most valuable characters of the present age; men of enlightened heads, of pious and benevolent hearts"; [11] Sherman, who was dismissed from his church at Mansfield, is described as an "upright, conscientious enquirer after truth" who has fallen "a victim to bigotry, ignorance, and intolerance." [12] The conflict of the Unitarian liberals with orthodoxy appeared to the author as a conflict between "virtue and learning and honour," and "craft and cunning and equivocation and falsehood and intolerant zeal." [13]

He offers little rational justification for the new "Rational Christianity"; although he gives several extensive citations of Belsham's creed, which presumably carry their own evidence of truth, or at least, of their excellence.

"*God is love.* Infinite benevolence alone prompted him to action. And infinite benevolence, combined with unerring wisdom, and supported by irresistible power, will infallibly accomplish its purpose in the best possible manner . . . Evil therefore is introduced and *permitted*, not because it is *approved*, but because it is *unavoidable*." [14]

"The almost universal desire of life and dread of dissolution, amounts to a strong presumption, that life is in general a blessing. And the disgrace universally attached to flagrant vice, proves that such vice is not common." [15]

"God cannot be unjust to any of his creatures . . . Indeed it is plainly repugnant to the justice of God, that the existence of any of his intelligent creatures, should be upon the whole a curse." [16]

"Christianity sums up the whole of human duty in the love of God and our neighbor . . . To a true Christian every day is Sabbath, every place is a temple, and every action of life is an act of devotion." [17]

Such were the great truths which the enlightened liberals thought they had discovered and set against the errors of orthodoxy. They implied that the God of historic Calvinism was not a God of love, that He was unjust to His creatures, that He permitted evil because He approved of it, and that He would not accomplish His purposes in "the best possible manner." The spirit of the new America was alien to any Calvinism. A Providence which had blessed the people of the land with all manner of good could be none other than good. What could be more evident than that God was on their side, and made their happiness His chief concern? It was no less evident that God was just because He rewarded virtue with success, and that He was love because He forgave sin. It all was reasonable. If the liberals had stopped here, the Calvinists might have forgiven them. Many Calvinists were inclined to similar opinions.

But in the imported English Unitarianism, which became the theology of these sentiments, there were some doctrinal views which flatly contradicted those of current orthodoxy.

"Mr. Lindsey's Creed.[18]

"There is one God, one single person who is God, the sole Creator and sovereign Lord of all things.

"The holy Jesus was a man of the Jewish nation, the servant of this God, highly honoured and distinguished by him.

"The Spirit, or Holy Spirit, was not a person or intelligent being, but only the extraordinary power or gift of God." [19]

"The Scriptures contain a faithful and credible account of the *Christian Doctrine*, which is the *true word of God:* but they are not *themselves* the word of God, nor do they ever assume that title." [20]

The temperamental liberalism of New England was thus combined with a doctrinal heresy brought in from England. Liberalism became Unitarianism. The emotional alienation of New England from Calvinism at last found overt expression in a theological schism, and the fight began. The Calvinists might have been seduced into believing in the "benevolence of God," but that "the holy Jesus was a man of the Jewish nation," and that "the Scriptures . . . are not *themselves* the word of God," was another matter.

Jedidiah Morse, writing for the orthodox, hailed the pamphlet of Belsham as "one of the most important events, which have taken place for many years, in reference to the interest of religion in our country." [21] "For at least a quarter of century . . . there has been in Boston a defection from those doctrines of the Bible, which have usually been denominated orthodox in Protestant communities." "From a great variety of anonymous publications it has been evident, that the defection had proceeded in the downward course to the lowest degrees of Socinianism, and to the very borders of open infidelity." [22]   Morse is gratified that such defection has at last come to the surface.   Now that the heretics appear in their true colors, orthodoxy is seen to be freed from the charges of slander, calumny, and cruelty, which have been raised against it. Morse is confident that a mere restatement of the views of the Unitarians will be sufficient to condemn them as enemies of true religion.   He quotes Belsham's statements copiously, and repeats them in his own words.   That a great fire has been kindled will be seen from the following reproductions of Belsham's tenets by the orthodox Morse.

"Unitarians hold and teach, then,

"That there is a very great preponderance of virtue over vice in the world; and with few, if any, exceptions, in every individual;

"That we may certainly conclude, from our own reason, that none of the creatures of God will ever be made eternally miserable;

"That the Holy Spirit was nothing more than the power of working miracles;

"That regeneration, and the new creation, mean only the conversion of the Gentiles to the profession of Christianity;

"That the death of Jesus is called a *propitiation* because it put an end to the Mosaic economy; [!]

"That the scriptures were not written under a plenary inspiration;

"That the Sabbath is no more holy than any other day;

and consequently, it is lawful to do the same things on that day as on any other;

"That the great object of Christianity was the revelation of a future life;

"That Christ was no more than a man;

"That on the subject of demoniacal possessions in particular, he, like the mass of his nation, was involved in gross darkness, and actually believed that to be true, which the wisdom of modern times has discovered to be false.

"Such is the Unitarianism which Mr. Belsham wishes to propagate, and of which he professes to write a history; so far, at least, as it relates to its progress in this country." [23]

Then follows Morse's own conception of true religion.

"We are sincere believers in the great doctrines of the Reformation; in the inspiration of the Holy Scriptures, in the unity and perfections of the Godhead; in the supreme divinity of the Son and Spirit; in the atonement and intercession of Christ; in the native and total depravity of the unregenerate; and in the reality and necessity of special divine grace to renew and sanctify the souls of men, that they may be capable of participating in the holy enjoyments of the heavenly world.

"Believing conscientiously, that these doctrines are essential to Christianity, we have felt it our duty to resist, so far as lay in our power, every effort to supplant them, by substituting others, which as they appear to us, can neither administer present comfort, nor lay any just foundations for future hopes." [24]

However, the pamphlet was more like a "call to arms" than a real offensive. No attempt was made to offer a genuine justification of orthodoxy, nor was it shown wherein the Unitarians were "infidels." Such a statement as the following neither alarmed the liberals, nor was it an effective defense of orthodoxy:

"If a denial of the divinity and atonement of the Saviour, *be denying the Lord that bought us,* whatever character a man who does this may sustain among his fellow creatures, ⁙ the sight of God he is an unbeliever; and whatever may be the *degree* of his guilt and punishment, he is as *surely* exposed to final destruction, as the Atheist, or the Deist." [25]

The very list of the Unitarian assertions selected by Morse as defining the character of the new heresy, suggest the kind of thing that popular orthodoxy had come to be. "Human depravity" means a "great preponderance of vice over virtue in the world." The belief of Jesus in "demoniacal possessions" must be defended against the "wisdom of the modern times." The Scriptures, "written under plenary inspiration," must now compete with human reason and the insight of men into the structure and the behavior of natural phenomena. The holiness of the Sabbath has become a grand truth of revealed religion. The divinity of Christ, eternal damnation, the person of the Holy Spirit in the Trinity,—must be accepted because they have been revealed, reason or no reason, and on pain of "final destruction."

The natural piety of Edwards and Bellamy was as foreign to the new orthodoxy as to its opponents. In a profound sense, this new "Calvinism," with its scheme of "revealed truth," was a travesty on the old. The test of this new orthodoxy was not "saving grace" and dependence upon God, but belief in a theological scheme supposed to have been revealed in the Holy Bible, and conformity to moral laws equally biblical. Orthodoxy became a mere bibliolatry; to defend its doctrines it had to turn its back on "the wisdom of the modern times." The new Calvinists, unlike Edwards, *had* to decry reason to hold to doctrines which had become, both to them and their opponents, hopeless metaphysical subtleties; they *had* to insist upon "plenary inspiration" in order to accept them.

People engaged in a dispute, seldom confine themselves to the subject of their controversy with each other. Morse did not fail to notice that the Unitarians entertained very high opinions of each other, and that they considered themselves the intellectual élite of Boston and its vicinity; nor did he overlook their characterization of the orthodox as "ignorant and malignant persecutors," and men of "bigotry and ignorant superstition." [26] In return he questioned their honesty and challenged them to come out and present themselves as they really were. Unitarian tenets "have spread *very extensively* in New England, but I believe there is *only one* church *professedly* Unitarian." [27]

"Indeed! Are these the true representatives of the apostles and martyrs, glorifying God by their *open profession* of his Gospel, and not ashamed to own their Lord before men? Is this the simplicity and godly sincerity of the Gospel? And these the men who claim all the reason, all the learning, all the charity, all the *integrity* of the community? Are these the men, who, according to the insinuation of Mr. Wells, are 'everything that is respectable,' while their opponents are 'everything that is detestable'? The conduct of Mr. Belsham, rotten as he is, in point of doctrine, . . . is purity itself compared with the conduct of these." [28]

Belsham's plea for separation met the hearty approval of Morse.

"With all our hearts we subscribe to this frank and ingenious comment. It does honor to Mr. Belsham. How different from the disguise of our Unitarians, and their whining complaints about illiberality in the orthodox in refusing to exchange with them." [29]

"It is the reproach and sin of Massachusetts, that while the orthodox from Connecticut to Georgia, are unanimous in withholding communion from Unitarians, she is lagging behind, and dallying with this awful and responsible subject. It is high time for decisive action on this point." [30]

Morse is specially grieved with Harvard College.

"It is no longer what it once was . . . The lustre of science still shines, but the Sun of Christianity is eclipsed. Young men leave the place now, not with hosannas in their mouths to the Son of David; but with burning zeal to propagate the new philosophy. Does the parent who bows the knee to Jesus, wish his son to *deny the Lord that bought him?* If not, let him well reflect what destination he gives him, to be taught the principles of religion as well as science." [31]

The thrusts of Morse were effective. He put the liberals on the defensive. He had forced it home that since they did not believe in the divinity of Christ, they should give up their claim to being Christians. For if Christ came not from God, if He is not the Son of God sent by God for the salvation of men, then He is not the Saviour of men. In denying the divinity of Christ, the liberals had denied God's "scheme of salvation," and were not fit to be called believers in the "gospel." Surely, it was only right that they should leave the Church of Christ, and go their godless way.

The liberals were alarmed. For, after all, they were

liberals, and not infidels. With a certain vagueness and facility characteristic of liberalisms, they even thought themselves to be in harmony with the really essential and desirable doctrines of orthodoxy. Belsham had carried things too far. Many were prepared to make some distinction between Christ and the rest of mankind, and they certainly were not anxious to separate themselves from the churches to which they belonged. William Ellery Channing came to their rescue.

Channing's defense was a masterly apology. He urged that the doctrine of the Trinity, which had presumably caused all this uproar, had no "immediate bearing upon the temper and the life." [32] He announced reluctance to introduce the "Trinitarian controversy to the pulpit," [33] and set forth his conviction that the Unitarians of Boston were not of Belsham's type.

"As to myself, I have ever been inclined to cherish the most exalted views of Jesus Christ, which are consistent with the supremacy of the Father; and I have felt it my duty to depart from Mr. Belsham, in perhaps every sentiment which is peculiar to him on this subject." [34]

"We are accustomed to speak of the Father as the only living and true God, and of Jesus Christ as his son, as a distinct being from him, as dependent on him, and deriving all from him." [35]

He is conciliatory but firm. "Our brethren are thus instigated to cut us off, as far as they have power, from the body and church of Christ," "because after serious investigation, we cannot find in the Scriptures, and cannot adopt as instructions of our Master, certain doctrines, which have divided the Church for ages, which have perplexed the best and wisest men, and which are very differently conceived even by those who profess to receive them. It is in particular, because we cannot adopt the language of our brethren, in relation to a doctrine, which we cannot understand, and which is expressed in words not only unauthorized by the Scripture, but as we believe, in words employed without meaning, (unless they mean that there are three Gods) by those who insist upon them. This is our crime, that we cannot think and speak with our brethren on subjects the most difficult and perplexing, on which the human mind has ever engaged. For this we are pursued with the cry of heresy, and are to have no rest until virtually excommunicated by our brethren." [36]

Although, on the one hand, Channing thinks of the doctrine as very abstruse and confused, and a matter which ought not to be made a subject of controversy, on the other, he is certain that the Trinitarian position is either meaningless or absurd. If there is only one "living and true God," there cannot be three Gods. The orthodox must choose between monotheism and tritheism. This was sufficiently clear to Channing to make him risk the much dreaded "excommunication," rather than believe that Christ is God. He wanted peace, but he also wanted victory. His attempt at reconciliation was thus a failure, and thereafter he led the liberals in their war for truth.

Channing was an eloquent man obsessed with a veritable "persecution-complex." The mere mention of separation filled him with grief, and brought forth complaints of "criminal unfairness" or "sneer and insult." He felt as one courting martyrdom.

"Let us never forget, that the most honoured condition in earth is that of being sufferers for the sake of righteousness, for adherence to what we deem the cause of

God and holiness, and let us welcome suffering, if it shall
be appointed us, as bringing us nearer to our persecuted
Lord, and his injured apostles. . . . We profess to look
up to a heavenly inheritance, and to hope that we shall one
day mingle with angels and just men made perfect. And
with these sublime hopes, shall we tremble before frail
and fallible fellow creatures, be depressed by difficulties,
or shrink from the expression of what we deem important
and useful truth? God forbid." [37]

"Most earnestly do I hope that we shall not be betrayed
by any violence of assault into a sectarian heat and obstinacy, which will discredit our profession, and obstruct this
glorious reformation of the church of God." [38]

He is even more brilliant in his fear of impending
troubles.

"I cannot but look forward with pain to the irritations,
hatreds, bitter recriminations, censoriousness, spiritual
pride, and schismatical spirit which will grow up under
this system of denunciation and exclusion, and which may
not only convulse many churches at the present moment,
but will probably end in most unhappy divisions among
the very Christians who seem to denounce us. . . . Er-
rour of opinion is an evil too trifling to be named in comparison with the practical departure from the Gospel, with
this proud, censorious, overbearing temper, which says to
a large body of Christians 'stand off, we are holier than
you.' " [39]

Channing's appeal was doubly effective. First, he mir-
rored the faith of the new age. His enlightened audiences
were already suspicious of the truth and the practical value
of orthodox theology. His belittlement of dubious doctrines was, as it were, a balm which soothed whatever un-

easiness his people entertained because of their waning faith in orthodoxy. Channing both fed the new flame and quenched the dying fire of Calvinism. Secondly, he was the very embodiment of "ethical Christianity." He appeared as a martyr to truth, a man motivated by a supreme love for brotherly understanding and peace with his fellowmen. He was against animosity, intolerance, and schism. He advocated friendly intercourse among Christians, based upon good-will and compliance with the ethical principles of Jesus. It was for this that he was being persecuted and reviled. It all was very touching and satisfactory.

The orthodox soon discovered that they had to deal with a brilliant orator who was "able to arouse the passions and inflame the prejudices of thousands." [40] Samuel Worcester, who took up their cause, protested against Channing's free indulgence "in vague declamation, poignant invective, and fervid appeal to popular prejudices and passions." [41] He was fully aware of his opponent's "advantages in this respect." Channing was carrying the people off their feet. Although "vague declamation" became the order of the day, and Worcester himself was not free from it, he tried to impress Channing with the extent of the latter's heterodoxy. The real issue between them, as he saw it, was the divinity of Christ.

"But, sir, between a being essentially divine, as by us the Saviour is held to be, and a mere creature however 'exalted,' there is, as you will readily admit, an infinite disparity . . . As your acknowledged Saviour is infinitely inferior to ours, so too are the offices and the work you assign to him. You doubtless do not suppose, that by a mere creature, atonement could be made for the sins of an apostate world, of sufficient merit for the pardon, sanctification, and eternal salvation, of all who should trust in him . . . Upon this denial of atonement, must follow of course the denial of pardon procured by the blood of Christ—of justification solely through faith in him—of redemption from eternal death unto everlasting life by him . . ."

"Now, sir, are these small and trivial points of difference between you and us? The God whom you worship is different from ours; the Saviour whom you acknowledge is infinitely inferior to ours; the salvation which you preach is immensely diverse from that which we preach." [42]

Worcester did not offer a direct answer to Channing's charge of tritheism. He did not offer to show how Christ could be God without there being two Gods. In fact, he did not even state explicitly that Christ is God. He insisted that Christ is a "being essentially divine," because such a view was necessary for the doctrine that Christ's death was "an expiatory sacrifice for sin." Worcester recognized that the doctrine of the Trinity, although abstruse in itself, was a necessary part of the orthodox scheme of salvation. Channing, through his pretended harmless denial of the Trinity, was undermining the whole Calvinistic "gospel." Unfortunately, Worcester, instead of making this the issue, allowed himself to make the Trinity and the authority of the Scriptures the two major questions in dispute.

Channing was all too willing to discuss the Trinity. He retorted in a manner true to his general method.

"Have I not, in my turn, an equal right to reproach Dr. Worcester with ambiguity and indistinctness? Has *he* anywhere told us, which of the many, very many explanations of the *Trinity* he and his brethren embrace, and are determined to impose on us as the term of Christian communion? Has he told us the precise scheme of *atonement* which he adopts, or which of the many definitions of *faith* he has selected?" [43]

Unfortunately, Worcester's presentation had been little more than a mere repetition of the bare formulæ of the doctrines in question. He had done little to show their significance as expressions of the religion of the orthodox, to present their significance for living piety and the facts of empirical experience which they formulated. He had done nothing to repudiate Channing's facile conviction that they were unintelligible metaphysical subtleties. Hence, the latter continued to proclaim them as insignificant and unnecessary for any genuine piety. Here he struck a note which belongs to the first principles of enlightened liberal thought.

"From a knowledge of the amazing power of education and other circumstances over the opinions of every mind, and from a fear that we, as well as others, may have been swayed and blinded by unsuspected infelicities attending our condition, we are unwilling to decide on the degree of truth which is required to the salvation of every individual, or to say that the errours of an apparently sincere professor of Christianity are inconsistent with a pious character." [44]

Therefore:

"According to Trinitarians, Jesus, who suffered and died on the cross, is a derived being, *personally* united with the self-existent God. According to the Unitarians, he is a derived being, *intimately* united with the self-existent God. Ought this difference, which transcends the conception of common christians, to divide and alienate those, who love the same excellent character in Jesus Christ? . . . The differences between Trinitarians and Unitarians are often verbal. Ought distinctions so subtle and perplexing, to separate those, who love the same divine character, and respect the same divine will." [45]

That Channing was sincere in his attempt to minimize the differences between the two parties may not be questioned. But, these differences *were* great, and his more unguarded and aggressive statements left no room for doubt in the minds of both the liberals and the orthodox. "Loving their neighbours as themselves," and "doing to others as they would have others do to them," which he considered as the common and undisputed principles of the Christian religion, say nothing of the fall of Adam, of the consequent condemnation of mankind, of the ransom of the world by the Son of God, and of the necessity of a new birth in order to salvation and a title to eternal joy in heaven. This is what the orthodox believed. It was their great "gospel story," the grand cosmic drama which dominated the heart and the imagination, and determined the movements of the soul. These "details" and "some inferior points connected with" the "great doctrines of the gospel," which he was so anxious to do away with, had grown out of the roots of orthodox theology in the life of the people. Being a humanitarian, and in the eighteenth century fashion, a rationalist, he was out of tune with the mentality of the orthodox, and quite incapable of appreciating the significance which they attached to their "inferior" opinions. With a glibness characteristic of men who fail to grasp the emotional significance of other people's opinions, he proceeded to evaluate and modify and repudiate as it seemed reasonable and proper to him.

+ Once more, Worcester tried to demonstrate to Channing the clarity and the truth of the doctrine of the Trinity.

"I do believe that we understand the meaning of the proposition, *Father, Son, and Holy Spirit are three Divine Persons in one God.* . . . We have indeed said, that we use the term, *person,* because we have no better word; and we are not tenacious of the name, provided we have the thing. But this accommodating concession you attempt to ridicule . . . I do believe that though they have not each a *separate* existence, but are all essentially united in one God; yet they are really and truly intelligent agents, each possessing all divine attributes, and performing in union with the other two, all divine works. And so far as I can perceive, I have as clear an understanding of the meaning of person when applied to three Divine agents united in one God, as when applied to angels or men, who have each a separate existence. I do not see, nor do I believe that you or any other man can show, why three Divine Persons may not so exist as to be one God, as well as three human persons so as to be three men; nor why the one God may not exist in three Persons as well as in one." [46]

It is needless to remark that Worcester is not quite so clear in his own mind as he would have Channing believe. He comes dangerously near making Channing's charge of tritheism correct. He reiterates the ancient idea that "person" as applied to the Trinity does not coincide with its meaning as applied to human beings. However, he soon all but forgets this precaution. When he describes the divine persons as "really and truly intelligent agents, each possessing all divine attributes, and performing with the other two all divine works," he sets forth a genuine tritheism. "Person" is no longer a symbolical approximation; it is a biological analogy. Metaphysical and functional distinctions have become physical and existential. The doctrine is no longer a mystery; it has become an absurdity. Worcester was as incapable as Channing of thinking of the word "person" in any but a biological and psychological sense. This is well illustrated in the following description of the relationship between the Father and the Son:

"It will not be doubted even by Unitarians, that the Father knows the Son perfectly, as he knows all other beings; knows him intuitively; has an immediate, intimate, complete perception of all that is in him. Even so then the Son knows the Father; has an intuitive perception, an intimate perfect knowledge of all his Father's infinite mind and will . . . Such is their coöperation, their unity of will, and of action, that all that is done by the Father is in the same manner, and at the same time, done by the Son." [47]

Worcester even goes so far as to compare the unity of God with the unity of three human beings.[48] The distinction he discovers between the two cases is one of *degree*, and not one of *kind*. If three men could see, and understand, each other as the three Divine Persons do, if they could unite their wills and actions quite as perfectly as they do, they also would become a trinity. No wonder that such theology could not defend itself against Channing's charge of tritheism. On the other hand, when some Trinitarians tried to establish the unity of the God-head by refusing to think of the Trinity as comprising three separate persons, for all Channing could see, "their three persons vanished into three *undefinable somethings*." [49] "Would the Trinitarians tell us what they mean," concluded Channing, "their system would generally be found little else, than a mystical form of the Unitarian doctrine." [50] Unfortunately, the new orthodox were not even mystics; they took the "society" of the three Persons too literally:

"When we turn our thoughts from the Trinity to the one Divine Person, inhabiting eternity in solitary existence, we find it impossible to conceive how he can be happy . . . The three adorable Persons, unlimited in all perfections and excellencies, inhabit eternity together; dwell everlastingly in each other, in mutual, perfect, unmeasurable love . . . Their own society of boundless love and boundless happiness, is the archetype and center of that holy, and blessed, and numberless fellowship of angels and of the redeemed from among men, who are to be 'gathered together in one,' around the throne of everlasting glory, with immortal joys, and unceasing praises.— Call this, Sir, mystery, mysticism, or what you please;—it is a theme on which my mind delights to dwell; and which I cannot exchange for the solitary Deity and the philosophical heaven of Unitarians." [51]

This interest in the happiness of God was surpassed only by Worcester's relish for the idea of "blood atonement." Here is the other reason for the doctrine of the Trinity. "If forgiveness of sin and justification unto life can be obtained, only through the merits of his sacrifice, and by *faith in his blood*; is it a light thing to reject this doctrine?" [52] Nothing but the blood of a *divine* being could have redeemed the world. The Man who died on

the cross was, therefore, "very God." Worcester's conception of the Atonement came perilously near being magical,
as his conception of the Trinity came equally near being
a logical absurdity. His theory of the Atonement is boldly
and unqualifiedly sacrificial. Christ, the second member
of the Trinity, came down from heaven, and became united
with human flesh so as to form "one complex person." [53]
He suffered and *shed his blood;* and thus becoming our
"great High Priest" and "Sacrificial Lamb," He became
"our propitiation." [54] In this fact, God has made us a
"gracious proposal."

It is the acceptance of the truth of this cosmic sacrificial
drama that constitutes man's main share in the covenant
between God and himself. Belief in this sacerdotal story
separates the saints in heaven from the inmates of hell.
It is the blood of the Son that has accomplished salvation.
It is this blood that the Christian must believe in. Blood
was poured, and sins were cancelled, the sins of those who
believe in "infinite atonement" by the blood of the Son.
The drama has all but lost ethical content. Justification,
reconciliation, sanctification, are relegated into the background. The moral government, the righteousness of the
Lamb, the infinity of human sinfulness, sanctification by
the Spirit, without which the historical theories of the
Atonement lose all semblance of empirical reality, hardly
come into the picture.

To "rational Christians" such a presentation of the work
of Christ appeared as a perversion of the simple Gospel
of Jesus into immoral untruth. "Unitarians," said Channing, "say nothing about *infinite atonement,* and they
shudder when they hear, what Dr. Worcester seems to
assert, that the ever blessed God suffered and died on the

cross." [55]   It was abhorrent to the new rationalism that
God should have chosen to suffer for the salvation of
others.   Such a procedure was contrary to the principles of
"sound morality," according to which any such "substitution" was unjust.   The new ethic of individualism regarded the feudal principle of collective guilt, expiable
through the suffering of a worthy representative of a
group, as barbarism.   In the new philosophy of right conduct self-sacrifice was irrational, for it contradicted the
first principle of the rights of men to seek and find happiness.   It was this ethic that the French Revolution established, and that the enlightened New England of Channing accepted as a new insight into the essence of Christianity.   Therefore, that Christ should have burdened
Himself with the sins of mankind and suffered in their
stead, was an immoral idea.

It was fatal to the orthodox that many of their best
minds were unable to grasp the true significance of the
Unitarian revolt.   They dealt with it as though it were a
movement in biblical interpretation or doctrinal criticism.
Dr. Worcester did not offer empirical and ethical grounds
for his beliefs.   He only knew that his "revealed religion"
and the "natural religion" of the liberals were profoundly
antithetical.

"The Unitarians . . . glory in excluding all mystery
from religion.   Hence the name which they assume of
Rational Christians; and hence the imposing superiority
which they affect over those, who understand the scriptures in their natural and obvious sense, and believe in
doctrines confessedly beyond the power of the human
mind to comprehend." [56]

It had come to this.   The orthodox doctrines might

seem absurd, and incomprehensible, and immoral. Nevertheless, they were taught in the Scriptures, and the Scriptures were the Word of God. While Channing was voic-
ing the sentiments of the enlightened public, Professor
Moses Stuart of Andover Theological Seminary set forth
an erudite philosophy of biblical authority. To Stuart's
mind, in the grand dispute between the Unitarians and the
orthodox, there is one question to be asked; namely, what
does the Bible teach? Once the "divine origin and authority" of the Bible is established, the business of reason
and common sense is to understand the true meaning of
the contents of the Bible, and not to pass judgment upon
the reasonableness of that which is written in it.[57] Once it
is ascertained that a given doctrine is set down in the
Scriptures, it must be accepted as truth, even though it
may contradict the "known properties" of things as given
by human acquaintance with the world. "The resurrection
of the body" is a truth taught by the Scriptures; "it is a
known property of the human body to corrupt and perish."
One who, by the use of his reason, has convinced himself
of the "divine origin and authority" of the Bible, must,
in spite of his reason, accept the doctrine of the "resurrection of the body."

Stuart claimed that his orthodoxy was "rational," and
one that should not be "exposed justly to be taxed with
mysticism."[58] There are "facts" which reason cannot
comprehend. It is rational that such facts should be accepted as real. Natural religion accepts the unity and the
"underived existence" of God as statements of fact, although a full understanding of such things is beyond
human reason. Revealed religion accepts that "there is a
real distinction in the Godhead," that Christ is divine, that

men are saved by the blood of Christ,—in the same way. This is no more mysticism than gravitation is. Orthodox Calvinism was thus hermetically sealed against contamination by reason; it was "revealed." The burden of Stuart's apology was to demonstrate that it was rational to believe the now suprarational doctrines of Calvinism.

Professor Andrews Norton of Harvard was easily the equal of Stuart of Andover. Being well versed in "Sacred Literature," he was able to show that certain ways of construing Scripture passages lead to downright absurdity. Language is intrinsically ambiguous.[59] "Almost every word is used in a variety of senses; and some words in a great variety." [60] "Beside their common significations, words may be used in an undefined number of figurative senses." [61] "In eloquence, in poetry, in popular writing of every sort, and not least in the Scriptures, a great part of the language used is the language of emotion and feeling." [62] Therefore, a literal acceptance of a given biblical passage must often lead to a complete misunderstanding of the idea which the author meant to convey.

Moreover, many passages in the Bible are "corrupt"; others have been interpolated by hands other than that of the original authors; there are "passages relating to Christ which have been mistranslated"; [63] others, "relating to God, which have been incorrectly applied to Christ." [64] In view of all these difficulties, surely, the Trinitarians cannot presume to derive their views "concerning the nature of God and the person of Christ" from the Scriptures!

Norton does not "deny that there are certain expressions in these texts, which, nakedly considered, *will bear* a Trinitarian sense." [65] But in view of the many considerations to be taken into account, in order to an adequate interpretation of such expressions, there is little reason why they should not bear a Unitarian sense. "The Common Version" of the Bible says, "Repent, for the kingdom of Heaven is at hand." But, "the proper sense of the original word" is "reform," and not "repent." Christ did not advocate repentance, as the Trinitarians teach, but reformation of character, as the Unitarians teach. As for the second part of the sentence, although an improvement in expression is not possible, it is plausible to interpret it in a sensible way. "For myself, I conceive him to have intended by the 'kingdom of Heaven,' . . . that state of things in which men should recognize the authority of God as the supreme Lawgiver, and submit themselves to his laws, as human subjects to those of a human government." [66]

As to Stuart's contention that revealed truth, even though incomprehensible, must be accepted, Norton replied, "What cannot be comprehended cannot be made known, and therefore cannot be revealed." [67] "To talk of an incomprehensible meaning, if we were to use the word 'incomprehensible' in a strict sense, is to employ terms which in themselves express an absurdity. It is the same sort of language, as if we were to speak of an invisible illumination." [68] When men say that "the attributes of God are infinite," they should either understand what they say, or they should not say it. Norton denies that he does not comprehend the proposition "the attributes of God are infinite," or that, "space and duration are infinite." [69] And it seems to him that the orthodox doctrines of the Godhead and the person of Christ do not fall within the same category.

"When I am told that the same being is both God and man, I recognize . . . a very *intelligible*, though a very absurd proposition, that is, I know well all the senses which the words admit. When it is affirmed that 'the Father is God, and the Son is God, and the Holy Ghost is God; and yet there are not three Gods, but one God'; no words can more clearly convey any meaning, than those propositions express the meaning, that there are three existences of whom the attributes of God may be predicated, and yet that there is only one existence of whom the attributes of God may be predicated. But this is not an incomprehensible mystery; it is plain nonsense." [70]

Perhaps, in passing judgments on the doctrines of Calvinism, Norton should not have ignored those numerous and weighty "considerations" which contribute to the "intrinsic ambiguity of language"; perhaps he should have been more skeptical about his ability to "interpret" the mind of the orthodox. However, he had set forth a brilliant and erudite defense of "Rational Christianity." Having established the intrinsic ambiguity of the language of the Scriptures, and the possibility of several interpretations of disputed passages, he had eliminated the necessity of belief in "plain nonsense," the doctrines of orthodoxy. Of the many meanings of scriptural expressions it was now possible to take those which seemed most reasonable to the Unitarians; yet the Bible continued to be the sole authority of Protestants.

A religious movement of any size and importance is always a complicated affair. Underneath the high-flung dialectical disputes of its champions, one must look for issues capable of capturing the hearts of their adherents and of arousing glowing public sentiment in favor of the new cause. Metaphysical heresies would die away in the minds of those who concoct them, were they not symptoms and formulations of new interests and new loyalties. The controversy on the Trinity, the Atonement, and the authority of the Scriptures, was little more than a signal for the precipitation of an open rebellion for which the cultured of New England were well-prepared. From the very beginning, the struggle was a medley of elements which had little bearing upon the theological questions supposedly in dispute. The Unitarians considered themselves as peace-loving and reasonable reformers, being oppressed by unintelligent and hard-hearted ecclesiastical authorities, who had invested themselves with "apostolick dignity," and were trying to impose their stupid opinions upon an intelligent public.

To John Lowell, "a layman," who wrote a pamphlet entitled *Are you a Christian or a Calvinist? or do you prefer the authority of Christ to that of the Genevan Reformer?*, it looked like a fight between Massachusetts and Connecticut, between Harvard and Yale.[71] The defenders of orthodoxy were graduates of colleges other than Harvard, who were plainly jealous of her, because "they knew then, and they know now, that for zeal for the truth and authenticity of the scripture, for respect to the Christian religion, and for ardour in its dissemination, the University of Cambridge yields to no other seminary in our country."[72]

In such a chaos of issues, Channing struck a new note, thereby completing the alliance between *Unitarianism* and that *secular humanitarianism* which had been growing in New England half a century since. His *Unitarian Chris-*

tianity, preached in 1819, was a clear and comprehensive statement of the faith in human power, in human dignity, in human reason, and in human rectitude.[73]   It was brilliant discourse, setting forth the principles of a theology congenial to the interests and the ideals of the new age.

"We conceive that the true love of God is a moral sentiment, founded on a clear perception, and consisting in a high esteem and veneration of his moral perfections. Thus, it perfectly coincides, and is in fact, the same thing, with the love of virtue, rectitude and goodness . . . We esteem him, and him only, a pious man, who practically conforms to God's moral perfections and government; who shows his delight in God's benevolence by loving and serving his neighbor; his delight in God's justice by being resolutely upright; his sense of God's purity by regulating his thoughts, imagination, and desires; and whose conversation, business, and domestic life are swayed by a regard for God's presence and authority." [74]

This ethical note was the real burden of Channing's message.   It soon became the center of his controversy with the orthodox and the foundation of his arguments against their doctrines.   If men are to be virtuous, they must know that which a virtuous life consists of.   They must have a "clear perception" of "God's moral perfections."   The "natural constitution of the mind" cannot be "unfailingly disposing it to evil." [75]   Such a thing is contrary to the "plainest rules of morality."   "We object strongly to the contemptuous manner in which human reason is often spoken of by our adversaries, because it leads we believe to universal scepticism." [76]   Men not only have a knowledge of the nature of an ethical life, but they also are capable of attaining it. Men are endowed with an innate capacity to do good.

Channing's theology was in an "intimate connection with moral Christianity." He could "endure no shade over the pure goodness of God." [77] Christianity is an ethical religion, and the God of the Christians must above all be good. The goodness of God must be made of such stuff as men cherish as virtuous. God is the Father who is seeking to establish that excellence which is dictated by the human conscience.

"To give our views of God in one word, we believe in his parental character. We ascribe to him not only the name, but the dispositions and principles of a father. We believe that He has a father's concern for his creatures, a father's desire for their improvement, a father's equity in proportioning his demands to their powers, a father's joy in their progress, a father's readiness to receive the penitent, and a father's justice for the incorrigible. We look upon this world as a place of education, in which He is training men by prosperity and adversity, by aids and obstructions, by conflicts of reason and passion, by motives to duty and temptations to sin, by a various discipline suited to free and moral beings, for union with himself, and for a sublime and ever-growing virtue in heaven." [78]

Such a God is "one being, one mind, one person, one intelligent agent, and one only, to whom underived and infinite perfection and dominion belong." [79] This conception of God is necessary as the basis of the ethical relationship or fellowship between Him and human beings, personal, mutual, and benevolent; a fellowship which would find its application in the intercourse of men with each other, and their pursuit of individual and social righteousness.

Calvinists who were bewildered by Channing's emphasis on the worth of man sought to discredit him by proving that his teaching was contrary to the Word of God. But their high-handed challenge to him and his followers, either to accept the doctrines of Scripture, or to relinquish their belief in the divine inspiration of the Bible, was obviously futile. There was another way open; namely, appeal to "observation and experience." Leonard Woods of Andover Seminary recognized the human interest of Channing's contentions against orthodoxy. He realized that Channing's view of human nature was far more important than his denial of the doctrine of the Trinity. Channing had denied human depravity. He had asserted that men are capable, physically and morally, of reforming their character so as to conform to the will of God. Here was a subject which was amenable to empirical and rational treatment, and Woods took it up.

"Regulating ourselves by the maxims of Newton and Bacon, we inquire, not what we should expect the properties and laws of the physical world would be, whether this or that thing can be reconciled with the infinite wisdom and goodness of God, but simply, *what is fact? What do we find from observation and experience that the properties and laws of nature really are?*" [80]

"Now this principle is applicable to the science of *theology,* as to the science of *physics.* Indeed, it will be found that it is still more necessary, and that any departure from it is attended with still greater danger than in physics. *Theology,* as well as *philosophy,* is founded on facts. The first thing to be done is in either case to determine, what are the facts on which the science is founded." [81]

In order to a disproof of the doctrine of human depravity, the Unitarians "must satisfactorily account for all the corruption and wickedness which man has exhibited, from childhood to old age, in all nations and circumstances, and in opposition to all the means which have been used to restrain him, without admitting that his *nature is prone to evil;*—a task of the same kind, with that of accounting for all the phenomena of the natural world which prove the law of gravitation, without admitting that law." [82] Perhaps neither the law of gravitation nor the doctrine of human depravity had been formulated in the way conceived by Bacon and Woods, nevertheless the appeal to "observation and experience" was appropriate, and Woods had seized the right weapon against the presumptions of the Unitarians.

However, he did not make a serious attempt to derive the doctrine of "native depravity" from observation and experience. It may have been impossible to give the Unitarians a sense of "all the corruption and wickedness which man has exhibited." Woods preferred to show that the doctrine does not contradict the concept of "free agency." "Human nature is prone to evil," but this does not mean that all men must of necessity be sinners. They are saved when, and if, they respond to the operation of the Holy Spirit in their souls.

"The sinner is so influenced by the Spirit of God, that he *freely* forsakes his sins, and devotes himself to the service of Christ. And this is the same as saying that, instead of exercising his moral agency *wrong,* he now exercises it *right.*" [83]

The influence of the Spirit is moral and resistible.[84]   It is "effectual," "overpowering," "superior," but not irresistible.[85]   Now, this is what Channing also believed.   He never denied that man is saved with the help of God; but he did deny that the power of the Spirit is other than moral and resistible.   Therefore, Woods was correct in saying that "in regard to these views *substantially*, I must say, that if Unitarians hold them, there is thus far, no controversy between them and us." [86]   Woods had become reconciled with Channing by surrendering an important Calvinist position.   For, if God is sovereign, His grace must be irresistible.   When God bestows His grace upon a sinner, He saves him.   As Woods says, "The purpose of God perfectly coincides with the acts of his government." [87] God's intentions are manifested in the facts of "observation and experience."   If Woods had adhered to this grand principle of Calvinism, instead of trying to show Channing that the doctrines of orthodoxy do not contradict "free agency," he would have made better use of the "maxims of Newton and Bacon."

"But does not God's purpose to save his people, or his agency in executing that purpose, destroy their free agency and make them machines?   By no means.   They are as free in this case as they are in any other; as free as they could be, were there no divine purpose." [88]

This is what is left of the doctrine of predestination! God has a foreknowledge of how men will act, but He in no way interferes with the exercise of their "free agency." Again, the idea that God foreknows the free acts of men may have been a high compliment to the deity, but it had nothing to do with "observation and experience."

Woods is very anxious to have the Unitarians understand that the orthodox believe in the *"paternal* character of God."[89]   All the representations of God as angry and full of wrath, as well as the corresponding "theories of atonement," are metaphorical.[90]   They describe merely the effects of sin.   God is all "goodness, mercy, or placibility."[91]   He is "a father to his kingdom; and will therefore show his displeasure against that which tends to injure that kingdom."[92]

Surely, the Unitarians could not object to such "enlightened Christianity"! But they did. In his unguarded moments, Woods had given evidences of a Calvinistic temper. He had talked in terms of election, salvation and damnation, innate depravity, in short, the scheme of Calvinistic theology. Henry Ware, Hollis Professor of Divinity in the University at Cambridge, was ill-satisfied.[93] He insisted that if Woods agrees with the Unitarians, there is no reason why he should retain the old doctrines as figures and metaphors.[94] The doctrine of election obscures God's benevolence and justice.[95] The doctrine of reprobation, the notion that God withholds His mercy when and as He pleases, makes Him arbitrary.[96] "Imputed righteousness," which Woods sometimes seemed to believe, contradicts the common principles of morality. Divine influence is inconsistent with moral behavior. Woods should drop these doctrines altogether, and thus eliminate confusion and misunderstanding.

Moreover, Woods had been unwilling or unable to offer a satisfactory demonstration of the doctrine of "innate depravity." Of all the doctrines of orthodoxy, cultured Christians hated this one most. Here at least, no compromise was possible. Ware sets himself to correct

Woods, and to give a truly enlightened view of human nature.

"Innocence, and simplicity, and purity, are the characteristics of early life.   Truth is natural; falsehood is artificial.   Veracity, kindness, good will flow from the natural feelings . . .   How early does the infant discover affection, attachment, gratitude to those from whom it receives kindness! . . .   How universally it is an object of interest to those about it!" [97]

Nor is such interesting excellence confined to infants.

"I hesitate not to say, that as much as there is of wickedness and vice, there is far more of virtue and goodness . . . I insist, that if we take a fair and full view, we shall find that wickedness, far from being the prevailing part of human character, makes but an inconsiderable part of it . . .   Even in the worst men, good feelings and principles are predominant . . .   The greatest liar does, by the constitution of his nature, doubtless speak many truths to every lie he utters." [98]

"The doctrine [of innate depravity], it is confessed, is repulsive.   The mind naturally revolts at it.   It *seems* at first, to all men, universally to be inconsistent with the divine perfection." [99]

Woods had insisted that, nevertheless, it is a *fact*, and is taught by the Scriptures.   But this is what Ware questioned.   The doctrine was so obnoxious that he would "yield his assent with caution, not till he has examined with care, and not without very satisfactory evidence." [100] And, naturally, his examination of the facts did not yield him such "very satisfactory evidence."

Woods was soon led to realize that his attempt at reconciliation had been a failure. He now turned to reassure the orthodox and win over those who were in doubt.

"It is very natural to suppose, that the habits of thinking and feeling, which have led men to embrace the Unitarian views in regard to this controversy, will give them but a poor opinion of our arguments. . . . Did not our own experience, did not a faithful comparison of our heart and life with the rule of duty convince us of the fact, that our own nature is the subject of an original and deep-rooted corruption, no external evidence could easily induce us to believe the fact in relation to others." [101]

However, in considering the sins of others and a general theory of moral evil, Woods weakened. He agreed with Ware in that:

"By their natural birth all are moral agents, and as soon as they are moral agents they are sinners; *moral agents by nature, and sinners as soon as moral agents.* I think this representation of Dr. Ware cannot easily be mended." [102]

Sin and moral agency are thus held to be inseparable. Only the actions of free moral agents can be described as sinful. Sin and guilt are profoundly identical. The emphasis is transferred from that a given law is *God's law,* to that it is a *moral law,* prescribed to free moral agents. The consciousness of sin is thus based not upon the contrast between the holiness of God and the absence of holiness in man, but upon the notion of "free agency." Sin has become identical with "free agency"!

The issue reduces itself to the impossible argument as to whether or not moral agents are depraved before they voluntarily do that which is sinful. Ware would have it that moral agents choose *freely,* and that they start with a perfectly neutral nature. According to Woods, men cannot choose evil unless they have an initial propensity to it. However, since such a propensity cannot be discovered prior to a sinful act, it must remain an inference, which can be asserted or denied at liberty. The issue has become "metaphysical"; namely, do new affections make it necessary to assume that they were in human nature as "propensities," previous to their emergence into consciousness? [103] Woods thought so; Ware did not. Significantly, Woods failed to consider the obvious objection that the same argument can be used to show that men have a "propensity" to do some things which are good.

Dr. Ware would not let Woods keep the metaphysical "propensity" which he had so freely chosen to assume. In his second answer to Woods, he went a step further, and insisted that it is natural to human beings to be good. Sin is failure to realize one's natural tendency to be good.[104] He repudiated the distinction between natural and moral excellence. The purity, the innocence, the gratitude, of children, are moral as well as natural.[105] Moral qualities, good or bad, arise in the exercise of man's natural faculties and emotions.[106]

Ware had gone too far. Woods became irritated. "But there is no end to controversy in this form." [107] The hope of compromise gone, Woods let Ware and all those interested know that he was a dyed-in-the-wool Calvinist. He identified "free agency" with the freedom of man to act according to the judgments of "right reason." [108] He reasserted the distinction between holiness and an amiable character, and described infants as depraved.[109] He insisted boldly that foreknowledge means predestination, and that "God created man's will and endued it with a power to act" as it was "his design that it should act." [110]

One can feel an element of regret in his retrospection of the controversy, and a concern to undo his errors.

"Every new examination of the subject of controversy adds new strength to my conviction, that the system which he has labored so zealously to defend, is *radically erroneous*, and of *fatal tendency*, and the system which he opposes, is the truth of God. The religious system set forth . . . in the writings of the most respectable Unitarians in this country and in Europe, overlooks *the ruined state of man*. This is the grand, fundamental error of Unitarians . . . If they should be feelingly convinced, as I hope through the mercy of God, they will be, that all men are by nature totally sinful, and totally ruined, children of wrath, and that God would be perfectly just and holy should he leave them without exception to perish forever; they would have little difficulty in respect to the other doctrines which our system contains . . . And it is very obvious to us, that where this conviction is wanting, there will always be difficulties and perplexities respecting the doctrines of orthodoxy. The controversy appears, in this view, to be as much a matter of *feeling*, as of *reasoning*; and it ought to be treated accordingly." [111]

Ware put in his own last word.

"The great articles of the Unitarian faith, I am satisfied, rest upon a foundation, that can never be shaken. The more they are contemplated, the dearer they are to my heart . . . The oftener they are presented to view, and made the subject of public discussion, the better will they be understood, the more clearly will their evidence, their reasonableness, and their foundation in the word of God be perceived, and the sooner, I am confident, shall we witness their general prevalence." [112]

The controversy between Woods and Ware was carried on at a plane of intelligence and dignity which was beyond the ordinary disputant of the day. The majority of the pamphlets produced on either side display little insight into the real issues involved in the controversy, as these were grasped by Woods and Ware. Futile discussions of the Trinity and the Atonement continued to engage the attention of both parties, and the standard arguments from reason and Scripture were repeated *ad nauseam*. In the process of the conflict it became clear that compromise between liberalism and orthodoxy was impossible. Each side was in possession of certainties which it clothed with the finality of eternal truths.

Channing was fulfilling his mission as the prophet of the new order in an admirable fashion. The Calvinists were helpless before this eloquent champion of noble sentiments and high morality. While Moses Stuart was busy expounding the Scriptures and invoking the "early fathers" on the *Eternal Generation of the Son, Atonement*, etc., Channing was boldly explaining to the public their "Likeness to God." [113] Liberal theology was in the last stages of its making.

"To me, it seems, that the soul, in all its higher actions, in original thought, in the creations of genius, in its love of beauty and grandeur . . . especially in disinterestedness, in the spirit of self-sacrifice, and in enlightened devotion, has a character of infinity . . . In truth the soul is always bursting its limits. It thirsts continually for wider knowledge. It rushes forward to untired happiness . . . Its true element and end is unbounded good. Thus God's infinity has its image in the soul; and through the soul, much more than through the universe, we arrive at this conception of Deity." [114]

"In ourselves are the elements of the Divinity. God, then, does not sustain a figurative resemblance to man. It is the resemblance of a parent to a child, the likeness of a kindred creature." [115]

"We call God a Mind. . . . God is another name for human intelligence raised above all error and imperfection, and extended to all possible truth." [116]

"The same is true of all the moral perfections of the Deity." [117]

The perplexities and the profundities of Calvinistic theology were irrelevant to this simple scheme of Unitarian religion. The methods of the ordinary orthodox against Channing were either inadequate or unfair. An anonymous Review of "Unitarian Christianity" bewailed "the extended and glowing encomium bestowed upon nature" and the absence "of reference to the Scripture," [118] a true but highly inadequate objection. It enlarged upon the similarities between Deism and Unitarianism.[119] Another Answer, by Joseph McCarrell, verged on the repulsive.

"Unless in those places where the influence of Christianity has elevated the tone of general morals, purged away the grossness and smoothed the asperity of the natural man, his inbred corruption breaks out in every species of abomination and crime. More than three-fourths of the world are at this present moment sunk in idolatry, superstition and all their attendant evils: and even in Christian countries, what an array of laws, and judgment-seats, and prisons, and penitentiaries, and gibbets, is necessary to restrain this depravity from sweeping, with hideous desolation, over the land." [120]

"How little does the history of the world contain besides a detail of its crimes. Injustice, perfidy, murder, cruelty, and oppression, blacken almost every page. Whence come the wars and fightings which have, in every age, set man against his brother, and turned our earth to a field of blood? Come they not hence even of their lusts?" [121]

Such degenerate Calvinism, having identified depravity with moral corruption, had to resort to the lie that history is nothing but a record of crime and perfidy.

Finally, it made the ludicrous charge:

"Having denied the binding force of minute regulations, and admitted views of duty so broad, as to convey (if Unitarian practice is any illustration of their theory) no definite instructions at all, this oracle of Unitarianism betakes himself to the mere intelligible dictates of nature." [122]

The crime of the Unitarians is that they have "denied the binding force of minute regulations," and are content with the "intelligible dictates of nature"! They make their own conscience and intelligence their guide, and attach little significance to conformity to particular duties prescribed by the Bible. Practical religion is, to this writer, a system of "minute regulations," set down in the Word of God; disobedience to these regulations is the essence of depravity, and exposes men to hell-fire. Intelligent Christians would of course smile at such a charge. They likewise repudiated the cynicism which made him exclaim about men:

"Give them a Mahometan paradise, and the Christian heaven they can lose without a sigh. It is the fearful looking-for of a judgment to come that makes them tremble. If because sentence against an evil work is not executed speedily, the hearts of the children of men are fully set to do evil, what a full swing will they give to their indulgence in sin, when assured, by a system calling itself Christian, that no punishment will ever be inflicted!" [123]

McCarrell's solution of the problem of suffering could have been no less revolting to the intelligent liberal of the day.

"If a deadly taint of corruption have not pervaded the mass of humankind, why do the innocent suffer? It is not required by the justice of God, but forbidden by it; for to inflict unmerited pain, is the very essence of injustice. It can do no good to those intelligences who may look into the divine administration of human affairs; for it confounds the distinction between good and evil, by treating the righteous and the wicked alike. And surely it is the reverse of goodness to inflict unnecessary misery on an innocent creature." [124]

McCarrell has accepted the proposition that the reward of virtue and innocence is happiness. It is uniformly unjust that the innocent should suffer. But since the innocent do actually suffer, they must share in a "deadly taint of corruption"; in other words, the innocent must be corrupt.

In the Unitarian controversy, Calvinism entered upon the final stages of its decline.

CHAPTER IX

THE FREEDOM OF THE POWER OF THE FACULTY
OF WILL

The sorrows of Calvinism all merged into the "problem of free-will." The one eternal complaint of its enemies was that it was "deterministic," that it reduced men to mere machines and undermined moral responsibility. Its theological scheme was highly conducive to such inferences. Its doctrines of election, predestination, efficacious grace, etc., were all apparent denials of human agency and power. Calvinism made an excellent theology of human dependence on God, but it jeopardized the "moral agency" of man. Therefore, as early as the end of the sixteenth century, Arminius voiced a protest against Calvinism, in behalf of the freedom of the human will, and the age long conflict between the Augustinians and the Pelagians flamed up again with renewed vigor.

At the beginning of the eighteenth century Arminianism appeared in New England through the missionary work of the Church of England. Deistic and Arminian literature leaked in and called forth the customary ineffective replies, until finally, Jonathan Edwards, taking his clew from the new psychology embodied in Locke's chapter on "Power," wrote his famous *Careful and Strict Enquiry into the Modern Prevailing Notions of that Freedom of Will which is supposed to be essential to Moral Agency, Vice and Virtue, Reward and Punishment, Praise and*

Blame.[1] This work put the Arminians on the defensive for at least a generation.

The fundamentals of Edwards' treatment are strikingly simple and clear. Man perceives.[2] That which he perceives may be a "motive." "By *motive*, I mean the whole of that which moves, excites, or invites the mind to volition, whether that be one thing singly, or many things conjunctly."[3] A motive is a thing perceived as an object of preference. The mind is that which perceives and chooses. When the mind is presented with several alternatives for preference, it is moved by the "strongest motive," or, it prefers that motive. This preference or choice of the mind is *volition*. Volition is an act of the mind in view of a motive. It is to be distinguished from other kinds of mental activity, such as understanding or reasoning, in that it involves a preference or choice. Thus the temptation arises to attribute to the mind a certain "power or principle," whereby it is capable of choosing. Whence the origin of the division of the mind into "faculties," each with a distinct "power or principle." Such a twist to the analysis of mental behavior was given by John Locke, and his influence on Edwards is seen in the latter's definition of the "will" as "that by which the mind chooses any thing."[4] However, with Edwards, this is a *façon de parler*. Strictly, there is no such thing as the "will." There is perception of motives, volition, and action. "The will always is, as the greatest apparent good is," which is the preferred object or perception, or the "strongest motive."[5] That which the mind prefers, it wills. Therefore, it is the mind (not the will) which wills.

Edwards will not say that "the will is *determined* by the greatest apparent good, or 'by what seems most agreeable'; because an appearing most agreeable to the mind, and the mind's preferring, seem scarcely distinct." [6] One of two physical objects is said to determine the other when they are two distinct entities in a given physical connection. The relationship between a motive and the mind is not of such a character. An act of volition is a consequence which is inseparable from the mind's perception of the strongest motive. Motivation and volition are aspects of a continuous performance. They are "scarcely distinct"; therefore, a motive cannot be said to *determine* a volition. "Determinism" derives its sting from a division of the mind into quasi-physical "faculties," whence arises the question, is a given faculty (e.g., the will) self-determined, or is it determined by something else? Where such analysis or division into faculties is lacking, there is no psychological determinism. Edwards cannot be called a "determinist" without a basic misconception of his analysis of volitional activity.

The mind is absolutely free to act on the strongest motive, because it chooses what it does choose. Given the strongest motive, the mind cannot choose any other. Such a thing would be a logical absurdity; it would mean that the mind may prefer what it does not prefer. The mind is under a "moral necessity" to will that which it does will. It is under a necessity to choose the "strongest motive." And since the strength of a motive rests in its being preferred by the mind, "moral necessity" consists in the identity of the strength of the motive and the mind's preference of it. The mind must of *logical* necessity, or by definition, choose the "strongest motive."

This is what Edwards meant by "moral necessity," and he distinguished it clearly from "natural necessity."

When the mind chooses a motive, but the choice does not result in physical action because of a lack of the requisite physical instrument or condition, there is natural or physical "inability." [7] When a man can do what he pleases, there is "natural ability." The freedom of man consists in a freedom from a physical impediment to his doing that which he is inclined or disposed to do. When he has the physical means to act according as he pleases, he is said to have "liberty." Such liberty is the only real or intelligible liberty there is. To have the freedom to walk up a number of stairs or to ride up in an elevator, is a "natural freedom" and the only kind of freedom that is possible. "Possibility" here means that a man *can* do a certain thing *if he will*. Man may or may not possess a "natural inability." His will may or may not be thwarted by a "natural necessity." When it is, he is not free. When it is not, he is free.

There is no such thing as the "self-determination of the will," because there is no "will." A volition is a preference of the mind, and must, of necessity, or by definition, be as the preference of the mind. A preference is as the character of a man, his soul. [8] Given a man's character, there is a "moral necessity," which circumscribes the nature of his volitions. But a man's character is comprised. of his motives, the things which move him to action. Therefore, a man's motives are the "causes" of his acts as a moral being, provided he enjoys "natural liberty." [9] Moral agency is thus characterized by "moral necessity" and "natural ability."

This duality of the moral and the natural is not absolute. Motives are natural as well as moral. An inclination or a disposition of the mind to prefer certain motives is itself a complex internal motivation, and as such shares the nature of a motive as that which moves.

"I suppose, that Necessity which is called *natural* in distinction from *moral* necessity, is so called, because *mere nature* as the word is vulgarly used, is concerned, without any thing of *choice*. The word *nature* is often used in opposition to *choice;* not because nature has indeed never any hand in our choice; but, probably, because we first get our notion of nature from that obvious course of events, which we observe in many things where our choice has no concern; and especially in the material world; which in many parts of it, we easily perceive to be in a settled course; the stated order, and manner of succession being apparent. But where we do not readily discern the rule and connection (though there be a connection, according to an established law, truly taking place) we signify the manner of event by some other name . . . So men make a distinction between nature and choice; as if they were completely and universally distinct." [10]

Edwards held to the distinction between a moral event and a natural event by avoiding the "naturalistic fallacy." Moral behavior involves motivation and preference. It must therefore be distinguished from natural or physical behavior, such as we discover in the "material world." Motives are natural events, but they are not *mere* natural events, because they refer to mental acts, and involve choice. Although, "choice, *in many cases*, arises from nature, as truly as other events," it is a volitional act, and as such, *moral*. [11]

Edwards' grand distinction between natural and moral necessity became a subject of violent discussion. Much confusion was caused by the disputants' forgetting that

the eighteenth century dualism of morality and nature as
an ultimate metaphysical principle is foreign to the thought
of Edwards. For him, both ethics and physics are subsumed under metaphysics. Morality is as much in Being
and of Being as the "material world." The distinction
between voluntary behavior and non-voluntary behavior
is empirical and real, but both are intelligible; they fall
within the limits of the metaphysical category of cause and
effect, or antecedent and consequent. It is necessary to
make it clear that Edwards' analysis is logical and metaphysical, and only secondarily psychological. He makes
no attempt at a classification of "motives," or at an accurate introspective analysis of mental behavior. Psychological analysis in terms of ideas, feelings, perceptions, etc.,
is irrelevant to his purpose. A "motive," something which
moves a person to a choice, may be any kind of a fact,
and its nature has no bearing upon the situation that the
"will is as the greatest apparent good is." A modern rendering of this analysis is the study of human behavior in
terms of "stimulus and response." A stimulus is Edwards'
"motive," and response is volitional behavior. Such a
study is based upon the principle that where there is no
stimulus, there is no response; where there is no action,
there is no reaction; where there is no cause, there is no
effect. The nature of a given stimulus is irrevelant to the
fact that it acts as a stimulus. An "S-R bond" may be
physical or it may be moral, and in both cases it is a "certain connection" between a "motive" and an act of volition.
Edwards' metaphysical principle of necessity is the modern
methodological principle that all action is reaction. The
excellence of Edwards' thought consists in that he with-
stood a careless attribution of mental functions to under-

lying quasi-physical structures or entities (which is also the virtue in behaviorism), *and* did not commit the fallacy of reducing one function into another, the mental and moral into the physical (which is the vice of modern behaviorism as understood by the "vulgar"). The will is neither a "faculty," nor an uproar in the cells of a muscle or a gland. Volition is not *caused* by the will, because there is no will to cause such an act. Nor is it an "epiphenomenon," *caused* by a more "real" physical condition of the body. A volition is an act in view of a preferred motive. An act is something in action, and not something *caused* by another thing, as is assumed both in "faculty psychology" and in "epiphenomenalism." Edwards did not share the materialistic prejudice which is involved in both these theories of mental activity, and which underlies the materialistic coloring of their concept of causality, that is, the determination of the motions of one entity by the motions of another; a conception which gave the "determinism vs. free-will" controversy the sting it has come to have.

A cause may be moral or it may be natural, an inclination or a snowstorm. As thus conceived, causality is the metaphysical principle that all events have antecedents and consequents. Moral and natural necessity are identical in so far as they are instances of "philosophical necessity," which "is really nothing else than the full and fixed connection between the things signified by the subject and predicate of a proposition, which affirms something to be true." [12] Thus, causality is a "certain connection," in this logical sense of predication. The mind determines a subject in the act of predication, which, as a prelude to practice, is an act of preference. The difference between natural and moral necessity "does not lie so much in the nature of the *connection*, as in the two terms *connected.*" [13] The two kinds of necessity are different as a moral act is different from a natural act, and they are identical in that between two mental events and two natural there is the same logical connection.   Furthermore, a natural event may be the cause of a moral event, an act of volition, or it may be the cause of a natural event, a physical motion. A natural event becomes the cause of a volition by first becoming a motive, an event which is the object of mind's perception and preference.   Therefore, in a sense, a natural event never is the cause of a moral event, or, its connection with a moral event, although necessary, is always indirect.   When a natural event becomes a motive, its connection with the mind's choice is a case of "moral necessity," otherwise, its connection to another natural event is a case of "natural necessity."

The bearing of such a conception of volition upon "vice and virtue, reward and punishment, praise and blame," is presented with Edwards' usual logical vigor.   "The essence of the virtue and vice of dispositions of the heart and acts of the will, lies not in their cause, but their nature." [14]   A man is judged virtuous or vicious according to the nature of his motives and preferences.   If he were to be judged according to the causes of his motivations and dispositions, and these in turn according to their own causes, and so on, then it would be impossible to judge anybody as virtuous or vicious, except the First Cause. [15]   Such a procedure is warranted neither by theory nor by common practice.   Men are judged according to their dispositions and their volitions, or, their character.

Praise and blame are grounded in the same way.   If a

man wants to give money to the poor, but has none, he is not to be blamed. He suffers a "natural inability." [16] But if he has money and does not want to give some to the poor, he is under a "moral inability"; he lacks the necessary "disposition of the heart and an act of the will"; and he is to be blamed. He has money, and he is free to give it. But he does not please to do so, therefore, he is blameworthy. If he please to give (the conditional is real in that he has money to give away) he is praiseworthy.

Again, "What is reward, in the most proper sense, but a benefit bestowed in consequence of something morally excellent in quality or behavior, a testimony of well pleasedness in that moral excellency, and of respect and favour on that account." [17]

Reward is the consequence of a given voluntary action. When bestowed by one person upon another, it is the exhibition of an appreciation, a recognition of the virtuousness or viciousness of an act. When such recognition is adequate, there is just reward. Rewards vary with the preferences of him who rewards. But the connection between virtue and its reward is necessary, because the will of the rewarder is as "the greatest apparent good." Rewards are consequences of vice and virtue, as health is the consequence of a given way of living. The distinction between reward and good health is that the first is moral, and the second merely natural.

Upon all this, the "freedom of will" has no bearing.

The Calvinists hailed Edwards' demonstration as conclusive, and made his distinction between moral and natural necessity the foundation of their defense against their opponents. The latter, although dissatisfied with Edwards' work, were unable to handle its "puzzles," and did not venture to write against him until 1770. By that time the controversy over regeneration was quite settled, and few dared deny that man must strive "to enter in at the strait gate." [18] "He can, if he will," was a sensible proposition, and man's moral freedom became a well accepted notion. It was high time for an answer to Edwards' abominable doctrine of "moral necessity." Such an answer was written by the Rev. James Dana.[19]

"To say that the mind is necessarily determined in all its acts, is making mankind necessary agents in *that* thing which distinguisheth them from the inferior creatures. Without moral liberty, it is plain their actions cannot be of a moral nature, any more than those can be called naturally free actions, which proceed from natural necessity. Abridge a man's natural liberty ever so much, his moral freedom may remain; and if it doth, the willing or unwilling mind is rewardable or punishable. On the contrary, suppose moral liberty taken away, or rather, never to have been possessed, there is an utter incapacity of moral action." [20]

"Let a man look into his own breast, and he cannot but perceive inward freedom—*inward freedom*—For if freedom be not in the *mind*, it is no where. And liberty in the mind implies self-determination." [21]

"We readily grant, there can be no act of choice without some motive or inducement. But . . . the application of commands, invitations, monitions, etc. is consistent with a freedom to *either* side." [22]

The mind determines its own volitions, and in this consists its freedom. The mind perceives several "inducements," and chooses the one it prefers, the choice being determined by the mind itself. The mind *can* bend to "either side," and thus is the "original cause" of its bending. The preferred motive is merely the "immediate cause." The objection of Dana to Edwards is that the latter has failed to determine the "original cause" of a volition.[23] Edwards has failed to show, *"whence* it is that any proposed object hath the appearance of good." "If every circumstance of things hath an answerable cause, then there is a cause why this or that motive is highest."[24]

"Mr. Edwards's business, therefore, according to this state of the question, was, to point out what *causeth an object to appear* most agreable. For if that which CAUSETH *this appearance* be the real cause of volition, then the agreable appearance ITSELF cannot be the cause."[25]

This distinction between an appearance and its cause is fundamental to Dana's quarrel with Edwards. It assumes the epistemological principle that an appearance must be caused by a reality. Accepting this principle, Dana is right in that Edwards has failed "to point out what *causeth an object to appear* most agreable." But this principle is irrelevant to Edwards' discussion, which applies to human experience taken at its face value. An appearance is something as it appears to the mind, and not an appearance caused by the mind or an external reality. In Edwards' thought there is no distinction between an "immediate cause" and an "original cause." An event as it appears is caused by another event as that appears. All we have are events as they appear to us. Therefore, the distinction between appearance and reality had no place in Edwards' analysis of causality. This aspect of Dana's critique of Edwards is an application of the controversy between realists and not-realists, which will be settled in the last days.

Dana's conception of causality is similarly alien to Edwards' thought. According to the latter:

"Choice and pleasure (so-called) is fixed by a previous necessary cause—and doing and conducting fixed by volition—Now, the immediate fruit and consequences of volition must be of the same nature with their cause—alike necessary. In other words, the will is no cause at all. For a necessary cause is not properly speaking a cause; it is nothing distinct from a meer instrument. A cause, strictly so called, must be *free;* at least so far as praise or blame, reward or punishment, belong to it." [26]

That which is the cause of another thing, cannot itself be caused. If the acts of the will are causes, and these are caused by the "motives," the will is a mere instrument, a part of a system of necessity. A necessary system is a mechanical system, and there is no freedom in it. Edwards has made "the intelligent system a curious piece of mechanism." [27] Unless the mind is an uncaused cause, a self-determining entity, *free* to choose what it does choose, it is not a *moral* cause. The freedom of the mind is essential to its being moral. Thus, there are two kinds of causality, mechanical and efficient. The physical world is a "closed system" of mechanical causes and effects; the moral world is composed of agents, who are the causes of their own actions, and may originate new chains of causes and effects. To be a moral agent is to be a self-determining cause, as it were, a real cause, as distinguished from an instrumental cause. Dana can make nothing of Edwards' distinction of natural and moral causality, and insists that on this subject the latter's thought is very much confused.[28] However, he is certain that, since Edwards' conception of causality is systematic, it must be mechanical. Dana's own doctrine that all causation, whether caused or uncaused, is the determination of one entity by another, which is essentially a mechanical conception of causation, made it impossible for him to take Edwards' description of causation and of "moral necessity" as anything but a description of mechanical necessity, and brought forth the alternative that the will is either an uncaused cause or a mere instrument.

This distinction between efficient and mechanical causation is further illustrated and established by Dana's query, How far is an act of volition caused by natural causes and how far by moral causes? [29]   Such a question assumes that a moral cause can be a component of a mechanical system. We are face to face with the problem of the interaction of mind and body. Dana does not go further than to assume that mind and body are such that they interact, more or less. Here again, Dana raised a question which has no place in Edwards' analysis. Edwards was not a "modern philosopher," and like Locke failed to feel the sting of epistemology. In his thought a volitional act is a mental act, not in the sense that the mind is an agent, but in the sense of a conscious act. To be moral is to envisage alternatives, and to prefer one to the others. A moral act is natural in so far as it involves physical behavior, and mental, in so far as it involves thinking and choosing. A moral act is at once mental and physical. The question, then, how far is an act moral and how far natural, does not involve the problem of freedom. A moral act can *cause* a physical act, because the moral is also physical; but it is also as really mental as it is physical, in as much as there is the kind of activity called thinking and choosing.

Dana's conception of causation involves a parallel conception of causes and effects. His grand assertion as against Edwards is that an act of volition is caused by the mind, and not by the motives. The mind and the motives are set against each other, and the question is asked, Which determines the acts of the will? Edwards is understood to answer that the motives are the determining causes; Dana insists that the mind (or the will) [30] determines its own actions. The use of the concept of "determination" in this connection assumes that the mind or the will partake of the physical nature of the motives; for, in order that one thing determine another, they must be commensurable. The mind or the will, therefore, must be some sort of a natural entity. That Dana entertained such a conception of the mind or the will finds further evidence in his notion that it has an "energy," "power and capacity," whereby it is the "original cause" of its acts.[31] This manner of thinking may be said to be at the source of Dana's controversy with Edwards, and to give strength to his charge that Edwards has failed to point to the real cause of an act of volition. Otherwise, the differences between Dana and Edwards are reducible to mere matters of terminology. What Dana calls the "will," which is supposed to determine action, is what Edwards calls "the dispositions of the heart," which are as much "motives" as the "external motives," which Dana calls "the motives." [32] For Edwards a motive is that which moves, and it may be internal as well as external to the body. Therefore, empirically, Dana's "self-determination of the will" is an act of choice in which an "internal motive" is the "strongest motive."

A similar confusion is involved in Dana's denial that "the will is as the greatest apparent good is."

"The truth is, that man is a compound of rational and animal affections, that without attending to himself, sometimes the one, and at other times the other, must of necessity prevail, as they happen to be strongest; and that, through the love of present pleasure, and aversion to present pain, or through mere pusillanimity, we too often decline the combat; and in contradiction to our reason, our conscience, and all the most weighty considerations of honour and interest, respecting this life and the next, suffer the animal to prevail over the rational affections." [33]

This objection is based upon an analysis of "affections" which represents merely a verbal disproof of Edwards' thesis. A "rational affection," in Edwards' terms, is an affection which an adequate intellect would judge as the greatest good; an "animal affection" is one which such a mind would not prefer. Whether rational or animal, an affection, as preferred by the mind, is a motive, "the greatest apparent good." Dana's statement that either the rational or the animal affections "must of necessity prevail, as they happen to be strongest," is an unconscious reassertion of what he set himself to disprove.

However, apart from such confusions, the fact remains that the emotional and practical contents of such words as will, cause, mind, necessity, etc., which were used as the key-words of the controversy, were profoundly different for the two men. The conflict was one of temperaments and thought-patterns, which appears even more strikingly in the less careful and logical writings of the controversy. The very title of a pamphlet such as *A Preservative against the Doctrine of Fate . . . proposed to the consid-*

eration of young Students in Divinity [34] reveals the temper which makes clear thinking on such a matter well nigh impossible.

"The sum of all the controversy," begins the author, "between Mr. *Edwards* and those he calls *Arminians,* is this, whether man has truly any free will at all, which is not moved as necessarily as any natural motions are caused? . . . Whether man is not an engine moved by God and other causes, no less necessarily than a clock or a watch, but only by more invisible causes, and to us unknown?   And, therefore, our willing and nilling is called *contingent* and *free,* when truly there is nothing in the world really *free* or *contingent.*" [35]

"If this be our case . . . then, we are no more subjects of virtue and vice than an ax, sword, or gun: nor are we any more capable of being called to account, or judged for things done in the body, than the winds and clouds are accountable for their motions.   For according to him [Edwards], we have no more power over our volitions than they have over their motions: nor can we will otherwise than we do will, anymore than they can move otherwise than they do move."

"This we think is to exempt men and devils from all guilt and blame, and to cast the whole load on God blessed forever." [36]

"We believe that God has set life and death before us . . . It pleased him to make us probationers, by giving us the power to determine our own minds to look either at temporal, or at eternal things; and according as we use or abuse this power, so we shall be happy or miserable forever.   This power is our capacity for religion.   To deny it, as Mr. E—— does, is to contradict common sense, and to overthrow morality and religion, and to encourage an atheistical course of life, under the pretence of *philosophy*." [37]

Such men, inhaling freedom in the very air of Revolutionary New England, were not inclined to sympathize with careful thinking, which they dubbed "philosophy." As usual, the thinker was suspected of being a mischief-maker. As a dogmatic orthodoxy anathematized "free thinking," so a liberalism sold to the dogma of "free-will" anathematized "pretence of philosophy." Joseph Huntington, an enlightened Calvinist, in a sermon on *The Vanity and Mischief of presuming on Things beyond our Measure*, decried that men "should please to form their own hypotheses," and say "many curious Things." [38] His clerical advice was to let "speculation" alone, and attend to the practice of the Christian virtues, with an appropriate measure of belief. "We ought never to perplex our Minds with Points of Speculation, which we are able neither to understand nor practise." [39] Such a speculation was the discussion on the freedom of will, and Huntington was quite willing to leave it alone, because so far as he could see neither side admitted the sinfulness of God and the innocence of the sinner. [40]

Huntington's advice was neglected. There were Calvinists who were not to be reconciled to the notion of absolute human autonomy, and the implied sufficiency of man unto himself. The champions of freedom insisted upon the *power* of man to choose what he willed, whether or not he could do what he pleased. They talked of his power to cause his volitions. They gave man not only "free will," but also a *power* to be an "*original* cause." This suggestion of an inherent potency in man, of a reserve of energy to be used as one will, was a direct affront to the sovereignty and the omnipotence of God. It could not but irritate the good Calvinist. The emotional significance of the word "power" was even greater than that of "cause," and called forth Stephen West's animated disapproval.[41]

"The expression *The powers of human nature, when it is used in its real analogy to the word Power as applied to inanimate, material things*, can import nothing more than a capacity there is, in human nature, of becoming the subject of certain particular sensations, apprehensions, and voluntary exertions. We have observed it to be a general law of nature, or, rather, of divine operation, that, under certain circumstances, men should be the subjects of certain *feelings, exercises*, and *sensations*." [42]

"The word Power, as applied to *natural, inanimate things*, I believe, in common use, intendeth and implieth nothing more than a *fitness or capacity for being the subjects of certain effects, from external influence*." [43]

West's treatise is a statement of what has come to be known as "Calvinistic determinism." The concept of "cause" as an "external influence," and of that of causality as the determination of the motions of one object by those of another, have become established.[44] "Nature" comprises so many things causing each other to act in a certain fashion. When a thing acts in a certain way, when acted upon by another thing, it is said to have the power to act that way. Any action is the effect of an "external cause," and takes place only when that cause acts upon it. Such interaction among things is according to a "general law of nature."

Human behavior is "analogous" to the behavior of

"natural, inanimate things." Men act in a given way under the influence of an external cause. Men's motives are related to their will as external causes of their actions, and determine their character.[45] "When *motive* is considered as *cause*, or *antecedent*, its *correlative*, is *outward action*." [46] A motive is internal to the mind, because it "importeth no more than some certain perception"; [47] but it is external to volition, which is an "exercise," and inseparable from "outward action." Thus "feelings, exercises, and sensations," cause certain "outward actions"; and when "exercises" are voluntary, there is an exercise of the will.[48] There is a direct and natural connection between feelings and outward action. Volitional action "is an effect of such human exertion as is *without volition*," and "must of consequence be an exertion in which *man* is not an agent." [49] There is thus a closed "natural" chain of cause and effect, and "voluntary actions" constitute a certain segment of it. In Stephen West we have a full-fledged "psychological determinist."

It is possible to construe West's treatise as a psychological and materialistic elaboration of the principles laid down by Edwards. His definitions of such terms as volition and causality are Edwardean. However, the truth remains that the analyses of the two men are very much different. The naturalistic metaphysics of West, and his psychological approach to the subject of moral agency, give to his work a twist which is absent from that of Edwards. The latter's conception of causality as "philosophical necessity," a principle transcending both moral and natural necessity, was overlooked by West, as well as by Dana. It was interpreted as natural necessity, and Edwards became the great "determinist," praised and reviled with equally little understanding.

After Edwards, the naturalistic bias of the eighteenth century crept into the controversy on "free-will," and gave it a new significance. Dana's complaint that Edwards had not "given the foundation of the will's determination," that he had merely dealt with "appearances," was a consequence of this naturalistic bias. West's discussions are similarly conditioned.

"The *cause* why men are influenced as they ought to be by *reasons and motives,* and the reasons and motives themselves in view of which *they are influenced,* are quite two things, altogether different from each other. The *cause* of mind's closing with reason and truth, is one thing; the *reason and truth* with which it closeth, is another." [50]

"These thing(s) I observe to shew that the word *motive,* as in common use among men, never importeth the *cause* of voluntary exertion—the *efficient reason* of its being brought into existence." [51]

This is a statement of what the modern psychologist calls "rationalization." A person *reasons* in order to choose a particular course of conduct, but the *real causes* of his actions must be sought in "natural causes," determined by a "general natural law," which is "in the nature of things." "There is a foundation in the nature of things, or in the law of divine operation, for all material things to unite with one another." [52] This constitutes a system of causality, which is the "foundation" of all "outward action." Therefore, in volition, the mind perceives the motive, and supplies the reason for a given action, but the real and efficient cause of an action is another action, according to the "nature of things, or the law of divine operation." This last phrase is West's Calvinization of the "general natural law." Having accepted the doctrine that nature is a closed system of physical necessity, as a Calvinist, he maintained that natural causes are mere antecedents, and that the *power* with which they determine their effects is the power of God.[53] So that, God is the one and only real efficient Cause. This is West's "supralapsarianism." Calvinism allied with the conception of a system of nature became "deterministic" in the modern sense of the word.

Such Calvinism brought forth a corresponding defense of "free-will." The new determinism offered no possibility of reconciliation. An impassable line was being drawn between the two opposing parties, and the problem was becoming notoriously insoluble. The Rev. Samuel West came forward with a conception of moral agency which contradicted the very foundations of Stephen West's opinions. Edwards was classified with the latter, and denounced in the same manner.

"Now, by *cause* I understand that which produces an effect; i.e., an efficient; and, by an *efficient*, I understand an agent; and, by an *agent*, I understand a mind: For, I have no idea, that anything can properly deserve the name of an agent, i.e., of an active being, but only a mind . . . If this be true, it will follow that if motives be causes, which produce effects, they are properly minds, which have a real existence; which is to me, a thing quite incomprehensible." [54]

Voilà! If Stephen West thinks that a mind cannot properly be called a *cause*, Samuel West thinks that nothing else can properly be called a *cause!* Moreover, a real cause cannot also be an effect, for to be an effect is to be passive, and a real cause is active.[55] The will is the mind in operation. That which operates is a cause. Therefore, the will is a cause, and never an effect. Men are determined by themselves, otherwise they cannot be causes, or moral agents, which is unthinkable.[56] Thus, it stands proven that men are free moral agents. As proof of the possibility of uncaused causation, Samuel West points out that such must be the nature of divine activity; and if it is possible with God, it is possible with men.[57]

In this author, there is more than a suggestion of the "transcendental ego." The "moral agent" is something quite supernatural. He is a being with a power over his body, a being even independent from his character, so that he is under no "necessity" whatsoever, although he may "certainly" act one way, and not another.[58] That he acts in a given way does not prove that he, the agent as distinguished from his "nature," does not have the "power" to act in another way. Endowed with this power, the self determines its own course, and is a *cause*. This self is not the natural man, for *he* is not an uncaused cause, nor does he have real power. And yet the self is a cause which can produce a natural effect. Thus the cause of human freedom allies itself with the dualism of mind and body, thus illustrating the connections between the problems of philosophy and the passions and practices of the vulgar.

The epistemological counterpart of such metaphysics assumed an equally dominant importance. The involved discussions of causality were now becoming inextricably mixed up with detailed analyses of "the essential faculties or properties of the mind."[59] The superabundance of terminology made current by John Locke were coming to be used and tossed about by men who shared neither his erudition nor his caution. They had now become necessary ingredients in any adequate treatment of the "problem of free-will." The "faculties of the mind" were classified in various ways, and in the accumulation of words and half-baked notions, the subject became increasingly complicated, clear thinking increasingly difficult, and intelligence and intelligibility beyond the capacities of the ordinary disputant. In the process, "freedom of will" became a logical dilemma, a psychological puzzle, and a metaphysical or non-empirical fact.

Samuel West analyzed the "essential faculties of the mind" into three: "Perception, Propension, and Volition."

"In perception, I include apprehension, judgment, and memory; for memory is only the reviving of past perceptions, with a consciousness, that we have had those perceptions before. Judgment is the perceiving of the agreement or disagreement of two or more things compared together. Apprehension is the ready and quick perception of the reality of things presented to our view." [60]

Thus, a percept is an impression of the external world upon the *tabula rasa* of the mind and a concept is a mere "copy" or (if one is rather skeptical) a mere "impression," as it appears after the thing which produced it vanishes. The mind, therefore, is a storehouse of concepts, hidden inside and sometimes revived as memories. The mind is the passive recipient of its contents; therefore, in perception the mind is not free. It is similarly affected by a "propension," which is the "influence of a passion or an affection on the mind." Therefore, this faculty of the mind also is externally determined. Volition, the only other faculty left, is the seat of the freedom of man.

"When the motives have done all they can do, the mind

may act or not act; i.e., that there is no infallible connection between motive and action." [61]

West considers this the very crux of the controversy. However, this apparent conflict is due to a confusion. By a "motive," he means a "propension," "the influence of a passion or an affection on the mind"; whereas, Edwards meant by it, *anything* that moves the mind to a choice. Therefore, West, in arguing that a motive does not necessarily determine a given volition, is merely saying that a passion is not always the "greatest apparent good." When a passion is presented to the mind, the mind may or may not prefer it. But if the mind does not prefer it, why does it not? Edwards would reply, because that passion is not the "strongest motive." West concludes that it is because there is no necessary connection between motivation and preference, and that because the mind determines its own preferences. But does the mind act according to a perception of a greatest apparent good? If it does, there is a necessary connection between motivation and preference. If it does not, it acts without a preference, without choice, without volition. West's psychological analysis merely obscured this issue, and ended in the triumphant but indeterminate assertion that "when motives have done all they can do, the mind may act or not act."

West's insight into human consciousness supplied him with another argument for freedom.

"Conscious, that many things take place in consequence of our acting, or determining, we attain the ideas of cause and effect; in consequence of which, we become capable of connecting our ideas, and of being rational creatures. If any one dislike this account of the matter, let him inform me how we came by the ideas of independence, efficiency, etc. If these ideas be not in consequence of experiencing in ourselves, that, in willing and choosing, we act independently of any extrinsic cause, from what quarter do they arise?" [62]

To this, Jonathan Edwards, Jr., retorted:

"When gentlemen speak of experience and consciousness, they ought to confine their observations to themselves . . . For my own part, I am not conscious of either self-causation of volition, or an exemption from extrinsic causality; and to be sure I am not conscious, that my volitions take place without cause or by mere chance . . . I never yet caught myself in the act of *making a volition*, if this mean anything more than *having* a volition or being the subject of it. If any man be conscious, that he makes his own volitions, he is doubtless conscious of two distinct acts in this, one the *act made* by himself, another *the act making* or by which he makes *the act made*. Now will any man profess to the world, that he is or ever has been conscious of these distinct acts? If not, let him tell the world what he means by being the efficient cause of his volitions . . . If it be meant, that he causes them by *the mind itself*, or by some *power* of the mind, and not by any *act* of the mind or of those powers; I appeal to the reader, whether this be, or can be, a matter of consciousness. . . . The existence of the mind and of its powers, is *inferred* from the acts, and we are not properly conscious of them." [63]

Such conflict of internal evidence might have led to a speedy conclusion of the controversy had it not been that the theological implications of the two positions made such peace impossible. The issue could not be discarded so long as the Calvinists saw in the contentions of their opponents consequences which negated the grand principles of the sovereignty of God and the dependence of man upon him. The "self-determination of the will" might have been interpreted as an innocent, although confused, bit of psychological analysis. However, the Calvinists were determined to oppose and refute it because it implied the sovereignty of man, his ultimate self-sufficiency, and vitiated the conception of the moral government of God. Therefore, they did their level best to stay clear from psychological discussions, and threw their weight on the side of logic and metaphysics.

"Self-determination uninfluenced by motive, is inconsistent with all religion and morality and with all virtue and vice. To love God without motive, principle, aim or end, is no religion. To love and do good to mankind in like manner, is no virtue.

"The self-determining power is, as I said, an ungovernable principle. . . . Nay, it cannot be governed by God, his providence or his grace. To be governed by either of these would be to be governed by an extrinsic cause, and under such government men would be passive. If God in his providence govern and control them and their actions, they are limited, and act only by permission, and have no power to act or not act, no liberty to either side, but are confined to one side. Where then is self-determination? On the other hand, if men determine and control all their own actions, none of their actions are controlled by God." [64]

To Edwards, Jr., it appeared that the controversy revolved around the question of necessity and contingency, and with his usual dialectical skill, he discredited the principle of "chance" as the foundation of morality. In this he was at one with his father.   In the details of his criticism of his father's opponents, the son set forth brilliant restatements of his father's views; and of all the defenders of the latter, he was his most successful interpreter.   And yet, at a most crucial point, on the subject of "necessity," he is in better agreement with Stephen West than with his father.

"If it be said, that the Great First Cause is the efficient of the sensation of heat; the same Great Agent is the efficient cause of volition, in the same way, by a general law establishing a connection between motives and volitions; as there is a connection between fire in certain situations and the sensation of heat." [65]

This attribution of "efficient causation" to God, as over against His creation, carried with it the denial of "power" to men.[66]   This combination of Newtonian mechanics with Calvinism was a most unfortunate blunder.   The distinction between a thing and its "power," and the placement of the latter in the deity, vindicated the persistent protest of the free-willists that the Calvinists had made man a mere puppet, a system of mechanical antecedents and consequents, functioning through a "power" induced from without, and according to universal "established laws." The "Creator" or "Author" thus became an immense reservoir of physical energy, perchance gas or steam, and man became one of the many bits of machinery which constitute "Creation," and are run by the "power of God."

Edwards, Jr., was not the man to mince words.

"If there be no inconsistence in bringing sickness on a man, and then healing him by medicine; where is the inconsistence in bringing sin, which is moral sickness, on a man, and whereby both he and that system are so far morally diseased, and then by punishment healing him or the system?" [67]

Enlightened Christians who believed in the goodness of God were scandalized, and preferred to believe in free-will. Nathanael Emmons gave the final touches to this "supralapsarian" Calvinism.

"Mankind are creatures, and by the law of nature absolutely dependent upon God. We cannot conceive that even Omnipotence is able to form independent agents, because this would be to endow them with divinity. And since all men are dependent agents, all their motions, exercises or actions, must originate from a divine efficiency. We can no more act, than we can exist, without the constant aid and influence of the Deity." [68]

This might be construed as a rather innocent or rhetorical outburst of piety, but Emmons' conception of human agency hardly permits such a construction. "Our moral exercises are the *productions* of the divine *power*." [69] "When he [God] works in us both to will and to do, he first exhibits motives before our minds, and then excites us to act voluntarily in the view of the motives exhibited." [70] Having thus made "power" solely a divine property, Emmons thinks of men as a succession of acts or exercises, voluntary or involuntary. [71] "Moral depravity consists in the free, voluntary exercises of a moral agent." [72] "Moral depravity can take place nowhere but in moral agents; and moral agents can never act but only as they are acted upon by a divine operation." [73]

Emmons had thus reached the limit. He tried to save the good name of God by insisting that God is not like His works, and that men act voluntarily as though there were no divine operation. Nevertheless he reduced the acts of men to a chain of exercises caused by the operation of God; and after all, this gave men much less freedom than did the vague belief that God somehow was involved in the permission of sin in general. Emmons' position was not only obnoxious to his opponents, but it was also without any empirical support. He stripped men and things of everything but "acts or exercises," and thus invested God with those psychological and mechanical "powers" and "efficiencies" which his opponents claimed to discover in man and nature. Such a conception of divine agency was no more empirical or rational than the "free-will" of his antagonists. He had made Calvinistic necessitarianism as much a metaphysical subtlety as the "freedom of will."

Nor could sensible Calvinists themselves accept such a perversion of divine sovereignty. Timothy Dwight repudiated it in the name of reason and Scripture.

"Motives in their nature are addressed to beings, supposed to be capable of being moved, or influenced, by them. . . . Motives can be addressed only to things, existing at the time when they are addressed. But the idea or exercise, which exists at that time, instantly perishes; and can have no possible influence on the nature, or character, of the new one which succeeds it. *This*, therefore, which the motive is intended to affect, is removed by the nature of the case, beyond the possibility of being affected by it. . . . Motives, therefore, can have no possible influence on men according to this scheme; and yet God proposes them to man, and blames, and punishes him for not being influenced by them. Can this be supposed of the Creator?" [74]

Emmons' "system" was obnoxious to the common sense

mind of Timothy Dwight, who swung back to a decent
Calvinism. He replaced in man a good, substantial soul,
with "dispositions and affections," [75] created in and for a
state of happiness, although now dominated by a "prevalent sinful disposition." [76]   Once again Dwight made virtue and vice a matter of motivation and disposition, and
pointed out the general innocence of "certain characteristics of human nature." [77]   Having thus rehabilitated "human nature" as that out of which moral actions grow, he
denied flatly that God is, in any sense, the author of sin.
As a Calvinist he maintained that the actions of moral
beings are foreknown by God, and retained the belief in
divine sovereignty in the sense that circumstances of birth
and education have a great deal to do with a man's moral
life, although in his particular environment every man is
to a considerable extent a moral agent. [78]

Dwight occupied a position of high authority among his
contemporaries; therefore his restatement of divine sovereignty and moral agency, although neither profound nor
consistent, was a severe blow to the supralapsarianism of
West and Emmons.

A second, and no less, devastating blow was a new and
dominant interest in the "psychological approach" to the
problem of "freedom of will."   Any discussion of volition
must involve a discussion of man, as a feeling, perceiving,
willing, thinking, being.   In this sense, the study of volition must necessarily include "psychology."   But the
"psychological approach" to the subject is a different matter.   It proceeds through introspection to distinguish between the various "affections" and "acts," to classify them
in a systematic way, and to discover their mutual relations.
In this process there emerges a terminology which derives

its meaning from its being an effective language for an implied theology, and soon assumes the dignity of a system of thought, or a science. Such a system rests and thrives upon its terminology, and may be no nearer the facts and no more intelligible than any other system.

The connection between introspection and the origin of a "faculty psychology" is not hard to perceive. The various "acts" discovered through introspection must be *caused* by some definite entities. The "will" must be that which wills volitions. But since the "will" is nothing in particular, such as an eye or a foot, it is a "faculty of the mind." Only a slight indiscretion is needed to lead one to talk of the "determination of the will," of "the power of the will," of "the freedom of the will," etc.—and one soon forgets that after all there may be no such thing as the "will," and that therefore it may be neither powerful nor weak, neither free nor determined. When such "science" becomes allied with an extraneous interest, such as divine sovereignty or human freedom, the resulting perplexities pass beyond the limits of comprehension, and it is time for the layman to seek solace in a "practical solution."

The rudiments of a "faculty psychology," derived from the work of John Locke, have already been discovered in Jonathan Edwards and his successors, especially his opponents. Samuel West definitely committed himself to the study of the "faculties of the mind." [79] However, the first full-blown, systematic treatise on the subject was written by Asa Burton, and the "faculty psychology" was predominant in New England down to the days of William James. [80]

"A faculty is a preparedness, a fitness, an adaptedness of the mind to be the subject of definite operation." [81]

"A faculty is as distinct from its operations, as a body is distinct from its motions. Hence a faculty is antecedent to its operations, and the foundation of them." [82]

"The scripture teaches us that the mind is created with three distinct faculties, whose operations are very different from each other. *Perceptions* of objects are the operations of the understanding. The *affections* are the operations of the heart. The *volitions* are the operations of the will." [83]

"The will is only an *executive* faculty. It is no more than a servant of the heart, to execute its pleasure. The will is no *primary* principle of action; its office is to obey the commands of the heart. Accordingly, for all the good or evil produced by the will, the heart only is praise or blame worthy; or every moral agent is to be blamed or praised, on account of the good or evil heart in him." [84]

"Hence the heart, or the faculty of taste, being the only property of the mind which is susceptible of pleasure and pain, is the principle of action in moral agents . . . The heart is a cause; its operations, such as pleasure and pain . . . are its *actions* . . . The first and immediate effects it produces are *volitions;* and by means of these and bodily motions, it produces all the effects necessary to reach the ends desired." [85]

Burton was a Calvinist; and although he made the "faculty of taste" the "primary cause" of action, he repudiated the pet notion of the free-willists that the mind has a power to act or not to act. He insisted that the operations of the heart are caused by "wishes or desires," caused by "objects" which "please," or "disgust." [86] That the "faculty of taste" should be the "primary cause" of action and hence the seat of vice and virtue was objectionable, for it obscured the connection between morality and volition; Samuel West before him had made the will the only "active" faculty, and designated *it* as the seat of moral agency; nor was his definition of the will as merely "the executive faculty" free from difficulties, because, as James Dana had observed, the will is not always determined by the heart or pleasure, in any obviously physical sense.

Apart from these considerations, and of greater importance, was the new vitality given to the controversy on free-will. With the faculties determined by objects and by each other, Burton had added "psychological determinism" to the metaphysical and naturalistic determinisms of his predecessors.[87] He had indeed mechanized mental behavior, and made it the effect of equally mechanical "extrinsic causes." Given such a "faculty psychology," one had to choose between mechanical necessity and mechanical contingency.

Nathaniel W. Taylor took another step.

"Generally speaking, moral character consists in a man's governing purpose, evinced to us by that course of specific action or conduct to which it leads." [88]

Taylor was belligerently convinced that feelings, dispositions, tendencies, and the like, constituting the "nature" of a person, are non-moral.[89] He denied that these are the "efficient causes" of sinfulness, although he allowed them to be "occasional moral causes." Hence, all moral agents are depraved, not because they inherit a sinful nature, but, because

"They are subjects of that supreme love of the world,— that preference of earthly good, or that selfishness, or that selfish principle, or that corrupt and wicked heart, or that sinful disposition, call it by what name you will,—which governs its subject in all its specific actions or conduct." [90]

Having made the "affections" mere moral "occasions," Taylor is free to posit a moral power or moral agency behind them.

"Moral agency implies free agency—the power of choice—the power to choose morally wrong as well as morally right, under every possible influence to prevent such choice or action. Moral agency and of course moral beings can no more exist without this power, than matter can exist without solidity and extension, or a triangle without sides and angles." [91]

Taylor's primary interest in the "moral government" of God made such a definition of moral agency inevitable. The end of God's "perfect moral government" is "the highest conceivable well-being of its subjects." [92] To this end God has instituted a perfect "moral law." This law is binding for all "moral agents," who may obey it or they may not. [93] Therefore, the conditions of a moral government are a moral governor, a moral law, and moral beings who are subject to that law. God's moral government is perfect, because His law is perfect, but the highest happiness of its subjects is not attained because they are free moral agents, and have the power to disobey the laws of God. This "power of choice" in men is necessary if there is to be any moral government at all.

As a Calvinist, Taylor claimed a belief in the "foreknowledge" of God, but in his hands the conception of "moral necessity" underwent a radical though subtle transformation. Against Henry Ware, he claimed that all that the Calvinists ever meant by "moral necessity" was "moral certainty." [94] The certainty of an action does not eliminate the "power of choice." Moral agents have a power to act or not to act, but they certainly act as they do act. Such certainty was an empirical certainty, resting not upon a metaphysical necessity, but upon a metaphysical freedom! Taylor was laboring under a serious difficulty. Moral government, he believed, requires free moral agents, and yet, the same moral government implies a system of rewards and punishments which exercise a divine "control of the action of moral beings, [so] as to secure the great end of action on their part," that is, obedience to the moral law.[95]

In Taylor the doctrine of the freedom of will triumphed. Nor could it be otherwise. Given a system of "faculties of the mind," entities related to each other as "extrinsic causes," the only kind of freedom possible was one resting upon an element of contingency in the system, a freedom due to the intrinsic power of a given faculty, the will, to act and not to act. Edwards' conception of moral necessity having been changed into one of quasi-mechanical necessity, was found unsuitable for "moral government" and "moral agency," and was discarded in favor of "free agency" and a "power of choice." Taylor introduced an ill-concealed contingency into the connection between divine purposes and human behavior, and thus saved the benevolence of God and the responsibility of men for their sins. He cut the Gordian knot, but the feat cost him the sovereignty of God, the dependence of man on God, the doctrines of election, total depravity, and regeneration. On these subjects he waxed profound and unintelligible. In truth, he had sacrificed them for the establishment of "divine moral government."

The orthodox faithful Calvinist of the day, therefore, became a frank "determinist." Otis Thompson, for example, in *A Review of the Rev. Thomas Andros's Essay on the Doctrine of Divine Efficiency*, 1821, protested against the latter's refined Calvinism.

"God governs the natural world by general laws; from which he never deviates, except in the case of miracles . . . In the system of nature, therefore, as soon as we learn the properties and combinations of second causes, in any par ticular instance, we may conclude, with certainty, what will be the result. From what *has* been, we may accurately calculate what *will* be. It would be the same in the moral world, if motives governed the will. Upon this supposi-tion, volition would follow the exhibition of motives, as invariably, as fire consumes wood, or water runs down declivity." [96]

As to divine agency, Thompson has no patience with "mere permission."

"In the divine word, *the divine agency* is represented as equally the *efficient or producing cause* of both sinful and holy exercises. In both cases, God works by means; but, in neither case, do the scriptures represent means as having power to produce moral exercises or actions, without the positive agency of the Deity. As has been observed, the positive agency of God, in causing the sins of men, is more frequently mentioned in scripture than his agency in caus-ing their good deeds." [97]

Thus Calvinist clergymen who wished to save the essen-tials of their religion were forced to return to the position which profound and "metaphysical" theologians, as well as common sense folk, had attempted to evade. Calvinism could not be liberalized. Henceforth men had to choose between being incredibly old-fashioned determinists and being sensible Christians or free-willists. Some naturally preferred to be confused, and became "moderate Calvinists" or moderate "liberals"; but the argument was over.

Note. The above treatment of the discussions of volition in New England varies considerably from that of Frank Hugh Foster, in *A History of New England Theology*, chapters III and IX. Foster criticizes Edwards for dividing the mind into the faculties of understanding and will; and says, "Thus he confounded the emotions, the action of which is necessary, with the will, the action of which is free, and attributed to the latter, as a matter of self-evidence, all the necessity of the former." [98] Evidently, Foster himself divides the mind into three faculties, the understanding, the will, and the emotions. Accordingly, he understands Edwards to maintain that "motives are 'causes' determining the will," and he asks, "Is the motive an occasion upon which the efficient will acts, or itself an efficient cause operating upon this will?" To this he adds, "Edwards' definition gives no answer." Edwards naturally could not have answered it because he knew nothing about an "efficient will." He was equally oblivious to the distinction between an "occasion" and a "cause." Foster follows Taylor and believes that an "efficient will" is the cause of moral action, while the motives are the "occasions" of such action. This is obviously an inversion of the truth. A man *wills* to do something *because* of a motive. The "will" is an "occasion" or an occurrence growing out of a given motivation.

Edwards did not include the emotions among the faculties of the mind, neither did he confound them with the will. The question as to whether or not the "emotions" are a faculty of the mind is irrelevant to the present issue, because it reflects the introspective tendency of nineteenth century psychology.   Edwards' analysis is more objective. If Edwards did any confounding, he confounded the emotions with "motives," and not with the will.   Any perceived emotion may be a motive.   A motive may be an affection, or a disposition, or an external object, or a purpose,—in short, all things which move the mind to a choice are motives.

Foster's opposition to Edwards, and his easy endorsement of his opponents, are based upon a misconception of Edwards' language in view of a later psychology.   He is misled by the fact that Edwards' empirical description of volitional behavior is couched in terms of "faculty psychology."   Edwards was influenced by John Locke sufficiently to use his terminology, but not enough to lose his own good sense.   Edwards' mistake was not that he believed in two faculties, instead of three, but that he adopted a language put into currency by Locke, and permitted himself to be dragged into a controversy about the "freedom of will."   Where there are no faculties, nor "body and mind," there is no problem of the "freedom of will."

CHAPTER X

THE BITTER END

CALVINISM thus attacked by two opposite evils simultane-
ously, by the rationalistic Unitarians and by the moralistic
Arminians, was so enfeebled that it fell into a rapid and
fatal decline. The heretics had gone their way, but they
had left behind them a body of distinctions and perplexities which continued to harass the Calvinists, and introduced the final era of confusion. An idea central to Christian theology, the doctrine of regeneration, was now subjected to psychological analysis, scrutinized in the light of
current philosophical considerations, given new "theoretical" interpretations, and so reconciled with new truth, that
it became innocuous and neglected.

By analyzing afresh the concept of the "means of regeneration," the Rev. Gardiner Spring centered attention
upon the basic problem of causation: How are the "means
of regeneration" used by the unregenerate related to the
regeneration by the Spirit of God? He arrived at the
conclusion that the problem resolves itself to a "mystery." [1] The sinner must use the "means" because they
are appointed by God. Besides, the "means" are of some
use because they eliminate stupidity, enlighten the conscience, reveal "human obduracy," and convince men of
the necessity of the operation of the Holy Spirit in order
to their salvation. [2] Therefore, it is beyond doubt that a
sinner "who pays an exemplary external regard to means"

is "more likely to be saved." [3]   But the individual can
never be certain of his own salvation, because there is no
causal connection between the use of the means of regeneration and regeneration by the Spirit.   After a man has
done all he can, the Spirit *may* come in, and again He may
not.   The coming in of the Spirit and the manner of His
operation is a "mystery."   Infants may be regenerated
without the use of means, but it is the will of God that
adult sinners should use the means, and thus prepare themselves for the probable working of the Spirit in their hearts.

Spring's dissertation was reviewed anonymously in the
Christian Spectator.[4]   The learned reviewer is dissatisfied with Spring's simple treatment and "mystic" solution
of the problem of regeneration.   Regeneration is really a
very complex psychological phenomenon, involving motivation, thought, feeling, action,—a process in which man
is genuinely active.   What Spring calls regeneration is the
culmination of this process, and never occurs apart from
adequate psychological preparation.   To be sure, "the
whole mental process of united thought and feeling, for
which we contend, *need* not occupy any measurable duration.   Along with the perception of the object, the emotion may instantaneously rise into the liveliest exercise." [5]
Nevertheless, as an up-to-date Calvinist, the reviewer is
not willing to forgo the pleasure of explaining *how* the
Spirit works in terms of psychological science.

The psychological examination of the elements which
go into the process of regeneration does not reveal an independent operation of the Holy Spirit.   The reviewer
discovers nothing in the mind but perceptions, thoughts
and feelings.   He is well aware that his analysis may be

construed as a denial of the Holy Spirit, but he meets such criticism by the amazing statement:

"Our principle is simply that of Edwards. 'God produces all, and we act all.' When we say, therefore, that the soul in regeneration chooses God as its portion, 'under the impulse of its inherent desire for happiness,' we are not excluding the influence of the divine Spirit. We are simply stating the great principle of Edwards, that 'the will is as the greatest apparent good.' " [6]

Unfortunately, this is little more than a bit of precious dust thrown into the eyes of his opponents. He soon dismisses it, and describes the function of the Holy Spirit in a way which shows that he had only a vague conception of the "principle" of Edwards which he used in self-defense. The Holy Spirit, he believes, is necessary to offset those influences which counteract the natural tendency of self-love to lead to a love of God. [7]

The examination of the motives of men leads the reviewer to the conclusion that all men desire happiness. This is the principle of self-love which is operative in all action involving preference and choice. Some men find their happiness in love to God, and others in love to mammon. Men are endowed with tendencies to that which is good and to that which is evil. When their self-love leads them to prefer the good, they are on the way to making God the supreme object of regard. [8] Normally, however, the tendency to the good is overcome by the tendency to evil, and therefore the necessity of the Holy Spirit in order that men may be saved. [9]

Here the reviewer's theology militates against his psychology. His idea that self-love may lead men to God, which is derived from his psychology, is vitiated by the idea that actually self-love does not lead men to God, which is derived from his theology. Therefore, according to his theology, self-love actually leads to selfishness, and there is no empirical ground for distinguishing between the two. However, as a psychologist, the reviewer does not believe that self-love invariably leads to evil and selfishness. Some men naturally seek and find their happiness in that which is good. He regards the volitional activities of men previous to regeneration as having a tendency in that direction.[10] Then, why the Holy Spirit? His failure to grasp the significance of Edwards' principle that "God produces all, and we act all" becomes apparent when he asserts that the Holy Spirit is merely a supplement to natural self-love. Thus, as a theologian, he accepts Spring's position, which, as a psychologist, he had repudiated. Having failed to discover the Holy Spirit in the human mind, he also asserts that His operation is a "mystery." [11]

In spite of the psychological and theological profundities which the reviewer marshaled forth in defense of his views, loyal Calvinists saw in him an enemy of genuine orthodoxy. Bennet Tyler was perplexed, and regarded him with suspicion.[12]

"He does indeed maintain that regeneration is produced by the power of God, or by the agency of the Holy Spirit; and yet, if I do not misunderstand him, he makes no distinction between the act of God, who is the author of this change, and the act of the sinner who is the subject of it . . . The consequent is not the same as its antecedent, nor the effect as its cause . . . But who could feel authorized to say, that the sinner regenerates himself?" [13]

According to Tyler, regeneration is either an act of God, or an act of man. And yet, he is as unable as the reviewer to discover any element in regeneration which is not a psychological phenomenon. He tries to defend his distinction between an act of God and an act of man by pointing out that regeneration may be "instantaneous." [14] But he is no less certain than his opponent that such regeneration "includes the perception of the intellect as well as the act of the will or heart." [15] To uphold his belief in divine efficiency, therefore, Tyler falls back on his theology. Salvation is either an act of God or it is the act of the sinner. The former alternative seems to be without internal evidence, and the latter is contrary to Calvinism. Tyler chooses to believe that regeneration is an act of God, and not an act of man. Of course, there was nothing to prevent others from making the contrary choice.

Tyler's attempt to distinguish an act of God in the human soul from any human mental behavior whatsoever was based upon a notion of divine activity which is by definition beyond all empirical verification; for, if everything that is empirical is merely human or natural, there can be no evidence that any event is an act of God. That is why Edwards said, "God produces all, and we act all." One can understand Tyler's suspicion that his opponent was doing away with the Holy Spirit. But his attempt to rehabilitate the Holy Spirit through a metaphysical postulate was little more than futile. True enough, in the theology of Calvinism, the Holy Spirit is a logical necessity, but He also is an empirical reality, a truth concerning the motions of a regenerate soul. His distinction between the natural and the supernatural, apart from the distinction between the spiritual and the non-spiritual, is either arbitrary or meaningless. Tyler's notion that an act of God is a meta-

natural act, put divine agency beyond all empirical verification, or philosophical justification.

The psychology of the new Calvinism was no less inadequate than its metaphysics. Tyler repudiated his opponent's doctrine of self-love on the ground that there is no
alternative between selfishness and holy love.[16] A moral
agent is either selfish or unselfish.[17] If he is selfish, he is
a sinner; if he is unselfish, he is a saved man. Self-love is
selfishness, to love God is unselfishness. Therefore, holy
love can never be motivated by self-love.

Such criticism was evidently based on theological dialectics, and not on psychological insight. Tyler was again
over-shooting his mark. The doctrine of self-love was
defensible in so far as all men seek happiness, and moral
agents are motivated by the "greatest apparent good"; [18]
but such good may be the love of self, or it may be the love
of family, church, country, race, etc. One man may find
his happiness in eating himself to death, another in giving
away his money to the poor. All men may be said to seek
happiness, but since they find it in different quarters, the
object of self-love, rather than self-love itself, determines
the moral character of a person. To love good and eschew
evil is moral excellence. To confuse self-love with selfishness, as Tyler did, reveals an artificial dialectics as well as
a false psychology. However, this is more than a matter
of psychological analysis; it is a fundamental perversion
of the Calvinistic religion. The burden of Calvinism was
that man must find his happiness in the glory and the service of God, and not that a man may not find happiness.
The essence of sin is that man should prefer lesser good or
"secondary virtue" to "true virtue" or the love of "Being
in general." The identification of the desire for happiness

with selfishness and sin was an ill-concealed confession that man cannot love God and be happy at the same time, that the search of happiness is not a "means of regeneration."

On the other hand, in declaring self-love or the desire for happiness an "ultimate end," Tyler's opponent confused the Calvinistic principle that all true and ultimate happiness consists in glorifying God.[19] He allowed his erudition in the new scientific psychology to obscure the fact that in seeking happiness men may fix their attention upon an object "outside" the "self," and find their happiness in making it the object of their love and devotion. His principle of "self-love" was irrelevant to the Calvinistic principle of "self-denial," and in setting it up as an "ultimate end" he had committed a profound psychological blunder, which vitiated his Calvinism and gave his philosophy the semblance of an apology for selfishness.

The moral and the doctrinal implications of the new psychology were soon discovered and established. They turned out to be the same as the moral principles and beliefs of the intelligent public of the day.

"Do you ask how it is, that self-love can dictate *either* a sinful or a holy act? The answer is, man is a moral agent. His will is free. Both self-love and free will, as well as reason and conscience, are an essential part of our constitution, as moral agents. Let the reader also carefully distinguish, when we are speaking in the nice language of metaphysical precision, and in the popular and practical language of the bible."[20]

"Speaking in the nice language of metaphysical precision," man is born with a holy principle, as well as a selfish principle.[21] In the pursuit of happiness, he may exercise either the one or the other, as he will. A man is a moral agent in so far as he uses his constitutional endowments, which include self-love and free-will. Man has two kinds of "constitution," the moral and the physical. A moral act is caused by the former, which, nevertheless, is not strictly moral, because mere "constitution" cannot be sinful or holy.[22] The author is struggling with a difficulty. He is certain that "what is constitution, is not character." [23] And yet, character must be "caused" by a constitution which is not purely physical. Therefore, man has a "moral principle," which includes self-love, free-will, reason, and conscience. But "what is constitution, is not character." Hence the dilemma. If the "moral principle" is constitutional, then it is non-moral, for "moral agency" or "character resides not in the constitution of the soul, but in the *use* of it." If the "moral principle" is not constitutional, a moral act is "caused" by a constitution which is not "moral" but "mechanical."

What we have here is the beginning of the modern distinction between human nature and its conditioning or functioning. Such a discussion throws considerable light upon the origins of the profound "problems of philosophy." Calvinism asserted that man is sinful; that man sins because he is man, or, that, man is by nature, by constitution, a sinner; for to be sinful and to sin are one and the same thing. However, to this empirical description of man there was the objection that it makes God the "author of sin." [24] Furthermore, it seemed to make man the victim of physical chance, the possessor of a "nature" given to him through no choice of his own. The first consideration contradicted the "goodness of God," [25] and the second made man a mere puppet. Both consequences were obnoxious to "enlightened" Christians. Hence it was desirable to demonstrate that the problem does not concern the "constitution" of man, and is therefore related merely to his *moral* "character."

Nathaniel W. Taylor, the liberal apologist of Calvinism, made bold to assert that depravity is not "anything created in man." [26] There are no "constitutional propensities," nor any *"disposition* or *tendency,"* to sin.[27] "There is an obvious distinction between a disposition or tendency to sin which is prior to *all* sin, and a *sinful* disposition." [28] There is no sinfulness prior to a sinful disposition and act.[29] Human nature is the "occasion" and "reason" of sin, but it is not the "cause" of sin.[30] The only plausible meaning of depravity "by nature" is that men "will sin, and only sin, in all the appropriate circumstances of their being." [31] Thus it is that God is exonerated from complicity in human sin, and man is left without excuse to indulge in sin.

"His guilt is all his own, and a just God may leave him to his choice. He is going to a wretched eternity, the self-made victim of its woes. Amid Sabbaths and bibles, the intercessions of saints, the songs of angels, the intreaties of God's embassadors, the accents of redeeming love, and the blood that speaketh peace, he presses on to death. God beseeching with tenderness and terror—Jesus telling him he dies once and could die again to save him—mercy weeping over him day and night—heaven lifting up its everlasting gates—hell burning and sending up its smoke of torment, and the weeping and the wailing and the gnashing of teeth, within his hearing,—and onward still he goes. —See the infatuated immortal!—Fellow sinner—IT IS YOU." [32]

Touching as this "popular and practical language" was, it failed to make his fellow-Calvinists overlook the opinions he had expressed "in the nice language of metaphysical precision." Joseph Harvey failed to grasp the significance of the distinction between constitution and character.[33] So far as he could see, the character of man is the cause of his behavior. As such, a man's character is no less sinful than any particular act which he may happen to perform.[34] Moral agency resides in character, and not in one's behavior. If there is no sinful heart, there is no sin and no depravity.[35] The truth is that the sinful man has a sinful character and acts in a sinful fashion. This is depravity.

Harvey was too naïve. He had accepted the distinction between character and action, and argued that both are sinful because a cause partakes of the nature of its effects. An anonymous writer made a profound psychological study of moral causation, in which he distinguished "instinctive feelings," "permanent states of voluntary affection and choice," and "particular acts of the will," from each other.[36] Such words as "tendency, propensity, disposition, principle, etc.," are used "to denote voluntary states of the mind." [37] Hence they are inapplicable to "instinctive feelings." The latter are the "occasions" of "permanent states of voluntary affection or choice," but they are not the causes of them. Therefore, sin should inhere in "voluntary affection," and not in "instinctive feelings." But, argues our Calvinistic writer, moral causation is a "special case" of "cause and effect," whereby, "a certain and exclusive effect, or where there is a series of such effects, the ultimate end, will be a true index of the character of the cause." [38] Of course, the debate, manipulated in this way, led to an impasse. The question, Are the unconscious sources of sinful behavior such that they have the same character as their effects in conscious and voluntary action? could not be answered on the basis of observation, because an unconscious state cannot be discovered to be sinful or not sinful.

The question is further complicated by the writer's opinion that there is no sin apart from the exercise of free-will. Therefore he discards the doctrine of original sin.[39] Sinfulness begins "at birth," and not before.

"A moral being, for ought we know, may be a voluntary agent from his birth, and thus, in fact, to a certain extent sinful, and that without supposing that depravity is seated in anything but the will. In this case nature itself is sinful, according to Mr. Harvey's theory, that is to say, the state of that being, from his birth, and before he has any knowledge of law and commences moral action, in the sense of Dr. Taylor, is a sinful state." [40]

Here, therefore, is a third and mediating position. Man is neither sinful before he is born, as Harvey seems to think, nor is his sinfulness delayed until he "has knowledge of law and commences moral action," as Taylor seems to think. Infants have all the faculties necessary for moral agency, therefore they are rudimentary moral agents, even "at birth." Harvey claimed that infants are born with a sinful character, because they perished during the deluge and the destruction of Sodom and Gomorrah. Taylor refused to hold such distressing views concerning infants. He considered infants to be non-moral, even as the brutes; living and dying as do the brutes.[41] He refused to see any moral significance in their sufferings or death, and attributed these to purely natural causes.[42] Such was the fate of the doctrine of "total depravity." It is no wonder that the perplexed author of the "Examination" has come

to consider "Philosophy," that is the subtleties of the controversy in question, as a "labyrinth, where thousands have
been bewildered and lost."

From such discussion of depravity emerged the "problem of evil," in a new and accentuated form. Taylor's
persistent antagonism to the doctrine of innate and total
depravity as conceived by Harvey and uncompromising
Calvinists was motivated by the conviction that God is primarily and fundamentally good.[43] God, held Taylor,
must always prefer holiness to sinfulness. He permits sin
because "in the nature of things" it is impossible for Him
to do otherwise. God's government is a "moral government." In a moral system there must be freedom. Where
there is freedom, there is sin.[44] It is man's duty not to
sin.[45] Therefore, men should be urged to perform their
duty as moral agents, and control those propensities which
lead them to sin.[46]

However, in a more Calvinistic mood, Taylor conceded
that men are so constituted that they "sin and only sin." [47]
Therefore, answered Harvey, admitting that God is the
maker of man and man invariably sins, "what advantage
has the author of this sermon really gained, or what difficulty has he avoided, respecting the origin of sin?" [48]
Taylor was practically certain that sin is not "necessary
to the greatest good," and that therefore it cannot be God's
will that men should sin. Harvey's genuinely Calvinistic
rejoinder was, "All we pretend to know or assume, concerning God and his ways, is, what he has revealed of himself, and what he actually does." [49] God does permit sin.
He is good and almighty. Therefore, it is His will that
there should be sin in the world. God's will is good,
therefore sin is conducive to the "greatest good." Just

what this good is it is sometimes possible to ascertain, and sometimes not. Taylor's contention assumes an untruth, namely, that reason and common sense always have a just conception of the goodness and the badness of a given event.[50] He had gone so far as to assert that "the doctrines of religion are not good because they originate in God, but they originate in God because they are good." [51] Harvey accused Taylor of dogmatism, a dogmatism concerning the validity of particular judgments of value, which was far more dangerous than the dogmatism of the Calvinist concerning the truth of his "dogmas." The latter had a far greater appreciation of the relativity of moral values than those who protested against his absolutism and dogmatism.

In the course of his humane attempt to free infants from the charge of sinfulness, Taylor went one step further. He asserted that the sufferings of infants are irrelevant to the moral government of God, who is concerned with only moral facts. All other facts are merely "natural phenomena." Thus, really, much in the world of nature and in human experience has no religious significance. Taylor was striking at the roots of the religious concept of divine providence. It was, as yet, plausible to consider miracles and moral experience as evidences of divine agency. But consistent and thoroughgoing naturalism had become a matter of time. If infants suffer and die "by nature," then grown-ups may suffer and die for the same reason and in the same way. If what is "by nature" is not by God, the more men understood concerning the ways of nature, the less reason they had to attribute the facts of life to divine providence and agency. The problem of evil was eliminated by the extension of the naturalistic treatment of infant existence to the rest of the world, human and non-human. If infants are natural beings, there is no reason why grown-ups should not be the same. Moral agency is as irrelevant to divine agency as is natural agency, unless moral agency is the same thing as divine agency.

Taylor did not go this far, but he had made a good beginning. His views were spreading far and wide.[52] His disciples, "by preaching, and conversation, and pamphlets, and specially by a popular periodical," were "zealously laboring to propagate his tenets."[53] Leonard Woods of Andover, the great opponent of Henry Ware, was alarmed by the errors of this would-be Calvinist professor of theology. His attack on Taylor was disconcerting.

"Your theory, which asserts continually and in terms so emphatical, the doctrine of human power, even, as it would seem, at the expense of the doctrine of divine power, is likely, if I mistake not, to produce a very different effect. In the representations which you and others make on this subject, and which are, in language at least, at variance with the Scriptures, I cannot but apprehend a tendency to cherish in the heart a feeling of independence and self-sufficiency."[54]

To Woods' mind, Taylor has done away with divine power and influence altogether.[55] If man has a "self-determining power of the will," so that God cannot influence him except through his word, or by "moral suasion," then God has no power wherewith to enforce His moral government. The use of the term "moral power," to describe divine power, is merely an evasion of the issue.[56] The "self-determination of the will" and divine "influence" are contradictory notions, and in holding fast to the former, Taylor has denied the latter. He has repudiated the idea of divine government, except as a system of rewards and punishments. A government is set up for a certain purpose. It is the end of a governing power to accomplish this purpose. The activity of the governed must also be directed to the same end. When there is a harmony between the ends of moral agents and the moral government of God, then the conduct of the former conforms to the purposes of God, so that it is voluntary but not free. When there is no such harmony, God must employ His power to bring it about, or relinquish his purposes, in which case there will be no divine government. This exercise of divine power need not be such as to eliminate voluntary behavior or moral agency, but it must be such that because of it the divine purposes are accomplished.

Holding such a view of divine government, Woods claimed that God permits sin because His wisdom demands it, and not because His power is circumscribed by that of the human will.[57] Since the fact is that there is sin in the world, it must be conceived as somehow serving the eternal purposes of God. In many instances, we see good coming out of evil. Where we do not discover such results, it is presumption to assert that no good does come out of sin. Therefore, the analogy between God and a human father, which was very pleasing to Taylor and the even more enlightened Unitarians, is not perfect.[58] The conception of the "good," entertained by a father and by his intelligent offspring, are often very much alike, though never identical. The conceptions of the "good," entertained by God and man, are very much less alike because the wisdom of God exceeds greatly the wisdom of a human father.

Therefore, we may not assume that, in every instance, "God our Father" would, if He could, do that which we think He should do. The paternal care of God transcends the "good" of any man, of any race, of the whole of creation at any given instant, and extends to the whole of Being in eternity. Since the depth and the breadth of human vision is, as a matter of fact, limited, it is proper for men to forbear from judging any event as absolute evil and irreconcilable with the eternal purposes of God. It is in this sense that Woods regarded the "problem of evil" as a "grand" and insoluble mystery.[59] He repudiated Taylor's notion that there is a realm of "nature" in which events occur independently of, and contrary to, the will of God. Taylor's way seemed to him as a poor solution of the "problem of evil," accomplished through an ultimate metaphysical dualism, a denial of divine providence and control of the universe. It was a dismissal of the religious interpretation of life, without which there can be no Christianity, much less Calvinism.

The *Christian Spectator,* the mouth-piece of "Taylorism," was strongly apologetic. Taylor merely *questioned* the orthodox *theory* as to why God permitted sin to enter the world.[60] Is not Woods also limiting God's power by maintaining that He cannot accomplish good without evil? Why does not God make His creation happy if He can? To produce good by counteracting the evil which He has decreed, is a strange procedure for a deity![61] But, surely, these are matters which concern only the "philosophy of religion," wherefore they are of very little consequence.[62]

"The question between them and us, is not whether there is some impossibility in the nature of things, which limits omnipotence . . . But the question is simply, where this impossibility may be supposed to lie? *They* maintain, that it lies in the nature of sin as a better means of happiness, than holiness in its stead. We maintain that it *may* lie in the nature of free agency. This is the only point in the present controversy; and we have looked with amazement on the multiplicity of extraneous topics, which Dr. Woods has intermingled with his discussion." [63]

It seems great injustice to the author of this article that Taylor and his "poor students" should have been accused of heterodoxy. He is inclined to think that the opponents of Taylor are motivated by jealousy, rather than by a regard for theological truth.[64] But, whatever the merits of such reflections may have been, orthodox Calvinists refused to take them as a solution to the controversy. The Rev. Joel Hawes, in a friendly letter to Taylor, requested him to "relieve the minds of many who are suspicious of your orthodoxy." [65] Taylor was much alarmed. He presented his creed in eleven brief articles, which have every appearance of sound Calvinism, and then proceeded to give a list of some "philosophical" differences of "minor importance" between him and his opponents. He offered the strange apology that his "philosophical" views were due to purely practical considerations.

"I believe, that both the doctrines of dependence and moral accountability must be *admitted by the public mind*, to secure upon that mind the full power of the Gospel. I also believe, that greater or less *prominence* should be given to the one, or the other of these doctrines, according to the prevailing state of public opinion." [66]

Bennet Tyler was unmoved by this exhibition of practical wisdom and prudence.[67] He attacked Taylor's letter, and reasserted the orthodox position on the "philosophical" questions in dispute in no uncertain terms. He pointed out that the presumably insignificant philosophical opinions of Taylor were in reality vital divergences from orthodox theology, and vitiated the whole of the Calvinistic scheme of salvation.

"If it be true, that God, *all things considered*, prefers holiness to sin in all instances in which the latter takes place, then it must be his choice, *all things considered*, that all men should become holy and saved; and his infinite benevolence will prompt him to do *all in his power* to bring all men to repentance. What then becomes of the doctrine of election?" [68]

For if God wills that all men be saved, then He has not elected some for salvation, and forsaken others to their sins. If there be no election, the doctrine of regeneration by the Holy Spirit is also to be abandoned. For, if this doctrine be true, it follows that there are some upon whom God does not bestow His grace.[69] If regeneration by the Spirit be untrue, then God is not the author of the salvation of men. Thus all the basic doctrines of Calvinism are vitiated, and Taylor's "philosophy" turns out to be an important perversity.[70]

The total effect of Tyler's charge was impressive. Taylor defended himself by questioning the contention of Tyler which appeared to be most obnoxious, namely, that it is the will of God that men should be sinners.

"I have said, that sin, in respect to divine prevention, *may be* incidental to the best possible system;—or, that it *may be* true, that if God created those beings and adopted that system of measures and of influence, which were necessary to secure the greatest amount of holiness and happiness which he could secure, sin would exist . . .

But, while I have said, that such *may be* the reason why sin exists, I have never said, that it *is* the reason, nor that, some other, is not the reason. Contrary to Dr. Tyler's repeated representations, I have advanced *no theory*, which professes to assign the *actual* reason of the fact, that sin exists." [71]

Taylor could not admit that *may be* it is not the will of God that *all* men should be holy and happy. Therefore, he came forth with a profound distinction between the will of God and the decrees of God. God never wills that men should be anything but holy and happy. But, He has decreed sin, *may be,* because "the adoption of the best system of influence will result in disobedience." [72] God has decreed sin because, in the "nature of things," it is necessary for "perfect moral government." Taylor's subtle distinctions between divine foreknowledge, election, will, wisdom, etc., are all intended to preserve his one cherished and inviolable conviction, that any sinful act is in no sense according to the will of God.

Where neither profundity nor apology is of any avail, he must needs compromise. The influence of the Spirit, although not irresistible, is uniformly unresisted. [73] The non-resistance of the sinner is contemporaneous with, and not prior to, divine influence. [74] Selfishness is distinct from discrete acts of sinfulness; thus it may be constitutional, but it is not propagated. [75] Sometimes it looks as though Taylor were about to give up the whole case, but a new "possibility" comes to his rescue. The pamphlet ends with a repeated assertion that *theories* are always vague and variable, and with the complaint that Tyler has done him great injustice and injury by presenting some few minor theoretical details as though they were matters of great consequence.[76] The truth is, of course, that so far as Taylor was concerned, the doctrines of orthodoxy were little more than "philosophical theories," tenable only in so far as they did not contradict the truths that God is good and that man is a free moral agent.

It is now Tyler's turn to apologize. He has been "represented as maintaining, that 'sin is a good thing'—'good in itself'—'the only real good to man.' "

"I have maintained directly the contrary—that sin is evil, infinitely evil—that it tends to evil, and evil only; and if I have maintained that it is the means and occasion of good, I have maintained that it is only by being overruled and counteracted in its tendencies." [77]

Unfortunately, this is what he could not prove to the satisfaction of his enlightened opponents. So far as they could see, the fact is that there is some sin which God does not overrule and make "the means and occasion of good." He does not produce the kind of good which men had come to consider as essential to His self-respect. Assuming that the good God would make all men always holy and happy, it is empirically true that He cannot do it, because He does not do it. It is just this assumption that Tyler failed to question in a convincing way. According to the Calvinism of Edwards and Bellamy, it is the last end of God in creating the world that is the mystery, and not the manner in which He will, somehow and somewhere, produce a well-defined species of good. Given the certainty that God's conception of the "good" is always identical with that of man, the only alternative to making God "a malevolent being" was to limit Him by the "nature of things," as Taylor did. Tyler's contention was at least an apparent concession to the anthropocentric theology of the liberals. And they naturally took him to mean that God overrules sin so as to bring about some good as perceived by man, which is contrary to the facts. Hence his apology for the Omnipotent God was a failure. Anthropocentric Calvinism is a contradiction in terms. Having "unawares" appropriated the humanistic foundations of Taylor's thought, Tyler became similarly profound and inconsistent.

Nevertheless, Tyler was invariably effective when he insisted that Taylor had denied divine agency and providence. In his last and animated reply to Taylor, he made it clear that if the moral agency of man is that which must account for all sin, then altogether too much happens independent of and contrary to divine will and operation.

On the other hand, Taylor also had his effective retorts. In his *Further Reply* to Tyler, he pointed out repeatedly that the latter's interpretation of the Calvinistic doctrines had reduced them to *mechanical phenomena*; that his view of "propagated propensity to sin" made sin "natural" or "constitutional," and not a "moral" act; [78] that his view of "irresistible grace" made divine grace a "physical compulsion," "crushing and destroying moral agency in the very act of securing moral action"; [79] that his view of divine government was a denial of the "moral system," or the reality of free moral agency.[80]

The controversy had reached an impasse. However, Taylor continued to resent Tyler's charges of heresy, and insisted that too much noise had been made about very little.

"He has publicly charged me, 'as a teacher in theology,' with being engaged 'in a gradual undermining process,' 'leading my pupils to renounce some of the *fundamental*

doctrines of the Gospel,' and 'introducing the GREAT ER-
RORS which have *infested* the Christián Church, and which
have usually *crept in unawares*'; with having 'disturbed the
peace of the New England Churches'—'impugned THE
FAITH of the Pilgrims,'—and of departing from the Orthodox of New England, by agreement with Pelagius, with
a distinguished Unitarian writer, and with 'the great champion of Arminianism.'—These things Dr. Tyler has done,
while he has been obliged to confess without qualification,
my soundness in the faith, and to confine all his objections and all his terrors to my *theories,* i.e., to *mere sup-
positions,* made to obviate objections to our common
FAITH." [81]

Nevertheless, Taylor may have known that what made
his "system" attractive to the liberals and obnoxious to the
orthodox, were his "theories," and not his "faith." Men
were adopting his "theories," while they joined with him
in the profession of "our common faith." Thus the
churches were *peacefully* drifting away from Calvinism.
Tyler's kind were merely arousing suspicion and unrest,
and making it harder for the liberals like Taylor to bury
the Calvinistic faith under a thick coating of enlightened
theories.

Tyler had charged Taylor with disturbing the "peace
of the churches." To this Taylor replied:

"We have indeed again and again attempted to arrest
the progress of this controversy; and to allay the agitation
and alarm so causelessly excited by others. We have
scrupulously avoided all personality and invective. We
have called no man heretic, Unitarian, Pelagian, or Arminian. If then the peace of the churches has been disturbed, the responsibility does not rest with us. It is the

apprehension of HERESY *creeping in unawares,* which, by sounding its note of alarm and denunciation, has disturbed the peace of the churches." [82]

The public was getting tired of the whole thing, and the editor of *The Spirit of the Pilgrims* announced that "after the conclusion in the next number of what is now in progress, this species of matter, so far as strictly controversial, will be excluded." The controversy was dropped; the issues were soon dead and buried, and on the tombstone was written "strictly controversial."

EPITAPH

RELIGIONS often die a hard death, and when they are dead, it is hard to bury them. There must be periods of "transition" and confusion. Vague loyalties to habits of thought must struggle with new interests, and there must be reconciliations and restatements. Such processes are highly fluid. They involve currents and counter-currents. They never are the same, therefore to describe them is to falsify them. Such was the enlightened Calvinism of New England after the Unitarian movement. Its advocates were respectable moderns, whose task was to reconcile the doctrines of Calvinism with the new dogmas relevant to human dignity and "free moral agency," which were no less dear to them than to their opponents. Really bad ideas, such as original sin and divine complicity in evil, were quietly set aside; others underwent drastic operations, and became no less harmless. Divine grace became moral, resistible, insufficient. Predestination became a harmless species of foreknowledge on the part of God. Damnation was postponed to the next world. Human depravity and regeneration by the Spirit of God were reconciled with "free moral agency," and moralized and confused beyond recognition. Such Calvinism was really not very objectionable, but it also was not Calvinism. It was the faith of the fathers ruined by the faith of their children. The machinery of Calvinistic theology was useless as a vehicle for the insights of the new Christianity, and it was forgotten.

But Calvinism continued to live without reason. It per-

sisted as a religion of unenlightened folk and their ex-
horters, a religion of "enthusiasm" and fanaticism. Its
incongruity with normal life led to an unhealthy sense of
sin among its adherents, to exaggerated introspection for
signs of a "state of grace," and to a deplorable fear of the
absence of the Holy Spirit in the recesses of their souls,
the evidence of impending doom in hell-fire. The popular
Calvinism of the time had to choose between "enthusiasm" and elimination. It had truly become a dialectical
superstition, kept alive by the artificial respiration of revivalism. The practical fruits of such religion were rigid
legalism and animosity to "free-thinking."

Good and intelligent Christians discarded such Calvinism with little remorse. They were busy men, proclaim-
ing the fatherhood of God, the brotherhood of men, and
the moral ideal set up by the "gentle Jesus"; telling men
of the dignity and the value of the human soul, its poten-
tial likeness to the perfectly good God, and its ultimate
destiny in heaven. They were urging men to believe in
"God, freedom, and immortality"; to be good, to do good,
and to live in peace with their fellowmen. They preached
these things, and expected men to believe and practice
them. They were great optimists.

NOTES

Fuller descriptions of the works mentioned in these notes are given in the Bibliography.

CHAPTER I

1. John Barnard, *Two Sermons*, p. 62.
2. 1700. See below, pp. 97-98.
3. *Doctrine of Instituted Churches*, p. 18.
4. *Ibid.*, p. 12.
5. *Ibid.*, pp. 3, 19.
6. 1709. Increase Mather's book against Stoddard was *The Order of the Gospel*, Boston and London, 1700.
7. *Appeal to the Learned*, p. 2.
8. Williston Walker, *The Creeds and Platforms of Congregationalism*, p. 282.
9. *Serious Exhortations address'd to young Men*, 1732.
10. *New England's Lamentations*, p. 1.
11. *Ibid.*, pp. 1-2.
12. *Ibid.*, p. 11.
13. *Ibid.*, p. 15.
14. *Ibid.*, p. 16.
15. H. W. Schneider, *The Puritan Mind*, p. 95; S. H. Cobb, *The Rise of Religious Liberty in America*, pp. 235-238; W. Walker, *A History of the Congregational Churches*, p. 187; *Creeds and Platforms*, pp. 433 ff.
16. Joseph Tracy, *The Great Awakening*, p. 12.
17. Jonathan Edwards, *Thoughts concerning the present Revival of Religion, Works*, vol. 4, pp. 105 ff.
18. *A plain Narrative*, p. 5.
19. Charles Chauncy, *Seasonable Thoughts*, Preface.
20. *Ibid.*, pp. 345 ff. *The Testimony of the President . . . of Harvard College.*
21. Alice Baldwin, *The New England Clergy and the American Revolution*, p. 68; H. L. Osgood, *The Puritan Colonies in the eighteenth Century*, vol. 3, pp. 85-86, 119, 408-409; H. W. Schneider, *The Puritan Mind*, p. 193.
22. *A Narrative* (see bibliography), pp. 51, 54.
23. *Ibid.*, p. 54.

24. *Ibid.*, pp. 59, 62.
25. *Ibid.*, p. 70.
26. *Ibid.*, pp. 55-58.
27. *An Examination and some Answer to a Pamphlet* (see bibliography), 1736.
28. *Letters from the First Church in Glocester to the Second in Bradford*, p. 11.
29. Samuel Wigglesworth and John Chipman, *Remarks*, p. 7.
30. *Ibid.*, p. 34.
31. *Ibid.*, p. 40.
32. *Ibid.*, p. 42.
33. *Ibid.*
34. *Ibid.*, p. 43.
35. Alden Bradford, *Memoir* of Mayhew, pp. 118 n., 138 n.
36. *Ibid.*, pp. 8, 85 ff., 179, 186, 193, 202.
37. *Ibid.*, pp. 18-20, 36, 46, 179 ff.
38. *Ibid.*, p. 93.
39. *Ibid.*, pp. 43, 46, 75.
40. *Ibid.*, pp. 187, 8.
41. *Ibid.*, pp. 140-141; Schneider, *The Puritan Mind*, p. 194.
42. *Unlimited Submission*, p. 36 n.
43. *Ibid.*, p. 29.
44. Election Sermon for 1754, pp. 14-15, 19, 23, 39, 47. In his Election Sermon for 1747, Charles Chauncy declared that "Civil magistrates must be just, ruling in the fear of God." Government is an instrument for social peace and order, and must be used for that end. On the other hand, in his Election Sermon for 1750, Samuel Phillips preached that "Political rulers [are] authorized and influenced by God our Saviour, to decree and execute justice."
45. *Ibid.*, p. 8, *passim*.
46. Alden Bradford, *Memoir* of Mayhew, pp. 32, 42, 118 n., 119.
47. *Seven Sermons*, pp. 39-40.
48. *Ibid.*, pp. 24 ff.
49. *Ibid.*, p. 131.
50. *Ibid.*, pp. 103 ff. *On the Nature, Extent and Perfection of the Divine Goodness*, pp. 12 ff.
51. *On the Nature, Extent and Perfection of the Divine Goodness*, p. 50.
52. Andrew Croswell. 1747.
53. Clap had previously been active in the opposition against the revivalism of Edwards and Whitefield. He was a solid Calvinist, against both liberalism and "enthusiasm." H. M. Dexter, *The Congregationalism of the last three hundred years*, pp. 140-141.

CHAPTER II

1. *The great Doctrine of Original Sin defended, Works,* vol. 2, pp. 338-339.
2. *Ibid.,* pp. 324-325.
3. *Ibid.,* p. 540.
4. *Ibid.,* p. 556.
5. *Ibid.,* p. 543.
6. *Ibid.,* pp. 399 ff.
7. *Ibid.,* p. 399.
8. *Ibid.,* p. 556.
9. *Ibid.,* p. 547.
10. *Ibid.,* p. 547.
11. *Ibid.,* pp. 534-536.
12. *Ibid.,* p. 537.
13. *Ibid.,* p. 410.
14. *Ibid.,* p. 543.
15. *Ibid.,* p. 513.
16. *Ibid.,* p. 519.
17. *Ibid.,* p. 521.
18. *Ibid.,* p. 309.
19. *Winter-Evening's Conversation,* p. 5.
20. *Ibid.,* pp. 5-6.
21. *Ibid.,* p 8.
22. *Ibid.,* p. 7.
23. *Ibid.,* p. 17.
24. *Ibid.,* p. 24.
25. *Ibid.,* p. 25.
26. *Ibid.,* pp. 3-4.
27. *Ibid.,* p. 5.
28. *Ibid.,* Supplement, pp. ii-iv.
29. See bibliography.
30. *Summer-Morning's Conversation,* Preface.
31. *Ibid.,* p. 2.
32. *Ibid.,* p. 3.
33. *Ibid.,* p. 6.
34. *Ibid.,* p. 42.
35. *Ibid.,* Appendix, p. 22.
36. *Ibid.,* pp. 7-8.
37. *Ibid.,* p. 8.
38. *Ibid.,* p. 12.
39. Published anonymously. Chauncy, as a liberal, was second only to Jonathan Mayhew.
40. *The Opinion of One,* etc., pp. 13-14.
41. *Ibid.,* p. 16.

42. *Ibid.*, p. 19.
43. See ch. 1, note 44.
44. *Works*, vol. 2.
45. *Ibid.*, p. 35.
46. *Ibid.*, p. 22.
47. *Ibid.*, pp. 9 ff.
48. *Ibid.*, pp. 14-15
49. *Ibid.*, pp. 43-44.
50. *Ibid.*, p. 45.
51, 52. *Ibid.*, p. 46.
53. *Ibid.*, pp. 49-50.
54. *Ibid.*, pp. 27-28.
55. *Ibid.*, p. 90.
56. *Ibid.*, p. 91.
57. *Ibid.*, p. 87.
58. *Ibid.*, pp. 51-52.
59. *Ibid.*, p. 45.
60. *Ibid.*, p. 83.
61. *Ibid.*, p. 75.
62. *Ibid.*, p. 47.
63. *An Attempt*, etc. (see bibliography), 1759.
64. *Ibid.*, p. 8.
65. *Ibid.*, p. 24.
66. *Ibid.*, p. 7.
67. *Ibid.*, pp. 20-21.
68. *Ibid.*, p. 20.
69. *Ibid.*, pp. 9, 12-13.
70. *Ibid.*, p. 21.
71. *Ibid.*, pp. 16 ff.
72. *Ibid.*, pp. 18-19.
73. *Ibid.*, p. 19.
74. *The Wisdom of God in the Permission of Sin, vindicated*, *Works*, vol. 2.
75. *Ibid.*, p. 103.
76. Samuel Hopkins, *Works*, vol. 2, p. 494.
77. Compare with the title of Bellamy's sermons on the same subject.
78. *Works*, vol. 2, p. 497.
79. *Ibid.*, p. 508.
80. *Ibid.*, p. 503.
81. Jonathan Edwards, *The great Doctrine of Original Sin defended*, *Works*, vol. 2, p. 547.
82. Samuel Hopkins, *Works*, vol. 2, p. 530.
83. *Ibid.*
84. *Ibid.*, p. 519.

CHAPTER III

1. *Works*, vol. 2, p. 556.
2. *Works*, vol. 1, pp. 60, 65, 93.
3. *Religious Affections, Works*, vol. 5, p. 179.
4. *Ibid.*, p. 181.
5. *Ibid.*, p. 102.
6. *Ibid.*, p. 106.
7. S. H. Cobb, *The Rise of religious Liberty in America*, p. 235; W. Walker, *A History of the Congregational Churches*, pp. 261-263.
8. The following controversy was anticipated in more than one discussion between the champions of "enthusiasm" and their opponents; e.g., between Solomon Williams, a powerful "old light," and Andrew Croswell.
9. *Striving to enter in at the strait Gate*, p. 6.
10. *Ibid.*, p. 11.
11. *Ibid.*, p. 12.
12. *Ibid.*, p. 17.
13. *Ibid.*, p. 16.
14. *Ibid.*, p. 17.
15. *Ibid.*, p. 69.
16. *Ibid.*, pp. 22-23.
17. *Ibid.*, pp. 21, 42.
18. *Ibid.*
19-20. *Ibid.*, p. 21.
21. *Ibid.*, p. 32.
22. See above, p. 11.
23. *An Inquiry concerning the Promises of the Gospel, Works*, vol. 3, p. 200.
24. *Ibid.*, p. 201.
25. *Ibid.*, p. 202.
26. *Ibid.*, pp. 191, 192.
27. *Ibid.*, p. 205.
28. *Ibid.*, pp. 204-205.
29. *Ibid.*, p. 205.
30. *Ibid.*, p. 236.
31. See above, pp. 12-13.
32. *The Promises of the Gospel*, p. 217.
33. *Ibid.*, p. 235.
34. *Ibid.*, pp. 235-236.
35. *Ibid.*, pp. 223-224.
36. *Ibid.*, pp. 259-260.
37. *Ibid.*, p. 262, *passim.*
38. "Minister of the Gospel in Ripton, Stratford."

39. *Works*, vol. 3, pp. 264-265.
40. *An Inquiry concerning the State of the Unregenerate under the Gospel*, pp. 18-19.
41. *Ibid.*, p. 26.
42-43. *Ibid.*, p. 68.
44. *Ibid.*, p. 17.
45. *Ibid.*, p. 121.
46. *Ibid.*, p. 102-103.
47. *Works*, vol. 3.
48. *Ibid.*, p. 303.
49. *Ibid.*, pp. 304 ff., *passim*.
50. *Ibid.*, p. 300.
51. *Ibid.*, p. 296.
52. See above, p. 58.
53. See below, p. 59.
54. "Pastor of a Church in Farmington"; a student of Joseph Bellamy, and a foremost exponent of Edwardeanism.
55. *The Consistency of the Sinner's Inability*, etc., p. 38.
56. *Ibid.*, p. 6.
57. *Ibid.*, p. 10.
58. *Ibid.*, p. 10.
59. See above, pp. 15-16; and below, p. 132.
60. 1769. During the Awakening Hart wrote *A Discourse concerning the Nature of Regeneration*, 1742, against the methods of the revivalists.
61. "Minister of the Gospel in Salem."
62. *Brief Remarks*, p. 43.
63. *Ibid.*, p. 32.
64. *Ibid.*, p. 33.
65. *Ibid.*, p. 45.
66. *Ibid.*, p. 46.
67. *Ibid.*, p. 47.
68, 69. *Ibid.*, p. 52.
70. *Ibid.*, pp. 59-60.
71. *Ibid.*, p. 58.
72. *Ibid.*, p. 57.
73. *Ibid.*, p. 65.
74. *Ibid.*, p. 69.
75. *Ibid.*, p. 49.
76. *Ibid.*, pp. 49-50.
77. See below, pp. 76-77. Nathaniel Whitaker, ordained a Congregationalist, became a Presbyterian, and formed a church at Salem, Mass.
78. *Two Sermons on the Doctrine of Reconciliation*, pp. 136 ff.
79. *Ibid.*, p. 113.

80. *Animadversions on Mr. Hart's late Dialogue,* 1770.
81. *Ibid.,* pp. 22-23.
82. *A Letter to the Rev. Samuel Hopkins,* 1770, p. 4.
83. *Ibid.,* pp. 4-5.
84. *Ibid.,* p. 7.
85. *Ibid.*
86. See below, pp. 76 ff. In 1767, Moses Hemmenway wrote *Seven Sermons on the Obligation and Encouragement of the Unregenerate, to labour for the Meat which endureth to everlasting Life.* Hopkins answered him in an appendix to his *The Nature of true Holiness (Works,* vol. 3). Hemmenway answered back with a *Vindication.* Hemmenway's great concern was the vindication of "self-love" as a "principle of action." In 1778, Isaac Foster preached a sermon entitled, *Fallen Sinners of Men able to do Well;* in which D. S. Rowland and Theodore Hinsdale "detected" heresy, and "exposed" it.
87. *A letter to the Rev. Samuel Hopkins,* p. 12.

CHAPTER IV

1. *The Nature of true Virtue, Works,* vol. 3, p. 94.
2. *Ibid.,* p. 136.
3. *Ibid.,* pp. 114-117.
4. *Ibid.,* p. 109.
5. *Ibid.*
6. *Ibid.,* p. 108.
7. *Two Sermons,* pp. 113, 136 ff.
8. *A Letter to the Rev. Nathanael Whitaker,* p. 10.
9. *A Letter to the Rev. Samuel Hopkins,* p. 13.
10. *Works,* vol. 1, p. 94.
11. *Remarks on President Edwards's Dissertations,* p. 9.
12. *Ibid.,* p. 40.
13. *Ibid.,* pp. 40-41.
14. *Ibid.,* p. 43.
15. *Ibid.,* p. 21.
16. *Ibid.,* pp. 48-49.
17. *Ibid.,* p. 49.
18. *Ibid.,* pp. 49-50.
19. *Ibid.,* p. 50.
20. *Ibid.,* p. 47.
21. Alice Baldwin, *The New England Clergy,* etc., chaps. VII-VIII.
22. Appendix I to *Inquiry into the Nature of true Holiness, Works,* vol. 3.
23. *Ibid.,* p. 69.
24. *Ibid.,* p. 75.

25. *Ibid.*, p. 78.
26. *Ibid.*, p. 16.
27. *Ibid.*, p. 37.
28. *True Religion delineated, Works,* vol. 1, pp. 20-21.
29. *Ibid.*, p. 50.
30. See below, p. 207.
31. *The Nature of true Holiness, Works,* vol. 3, p. 38.
32. *Ibid.*, pp. 38-39, 42, 43-44.
33. H. W. Schneider, *The Puritan Mind,* chap. 1.
34. Jonathan Edwards, *A History of the Work of Redemption, passim.*
35. See above, pp. 5-7.
36. See above, pp. 3 ff.
37. See above, pp. 15 ff.
38. *Works,* vol. 1.
39. *Ibid.*, pp. 26, 29.
40. *Ibid.*, pp. 405-406.
41. *Ibid.*, p. 409.
42. *Ibid.*, p. 410.
43. *The great Evil of Sin, Works,* vol. 2, pp. 482-483.
44. *Works,* vol. 3.
45. *Ibid.*, p. 522.
46. *Ibid.*, p. 523.
47. *Ibid.*, p. 537.
48. *Ibid.*
49. *Ibid.*, p. 540.
50. See below, p. 151.
51. *Works,* vol. 2, p. 528.
52. "Pastor of a Church in Marblehead." He was esteemed highly by Chauncy, and considered a capable person. He did much for the prosperity of Marblehead.
53. *The Imperfection of the Creature,* p. 133.
54. *Ibid.*, pp. 90 ff.
55. *Ibid.*, p. 111.
56. *Ibid.*, p. 137.

CHAPTER V

1. Jonathan Edwards, *Works,* vol. 1, p. 626.
2. See above, pp. 3 ff.; W. Walker, *The Congregational Churches,* pp. 180-181. Herbert W. Schneider, *The Puritan Mind,* pp. 131-133.
3. See above, p. 4.
4. *Qualifications for Communion, Works,* vol. 4, p. 418 n.
5. *Ibid.*, p. 328.
6. *Ibid.*, p. 369.
7. *Ibid.*, p. 370.

8. *Ibid.*, p. 371.
9, 10. *Ibid.*, p. 432.
11. *The true State of the Question concerning the Qualifications, necessary to lawful Communion in the Christian Sacraments,* 1751.
12. *Ibid.*, p. 128.
13. *Ibid.*, p. 18.
14. W. Walker, *Creeds and Platforms*, pp. 88 ff., 116, 121.
15. The Salem Covenant of 1629, *ibid.*, p. 116.
16. *Ibid.*, p. 131.
17. *Ibid.*, pp. 119, 143.
18. See above, chap. 3.
19. Joseph Bellamy, *The Half-Way Covenant, Works*, vol. 2, p. 689.
20. *Ibid.*, p. 678.
21. W. Walker, *Creeds and Platforms*, p. 282. An accurate estimate of this fact is necessarily difficult, and so far as the present writer is aware, it has not been made. However, the controversy throughout the second half of the century is sufficient indication that the Edwardeans were opposing a prevalent tendency to "liberalism."
22. *The visible Church in Covenant with God*, p. 11.
23. *Ibid.*, p. 7.
24. *Ibid.*, p. 14.
25. *Ibid.*, p. 6.
26. *Ibid.*, p. 16.
27. *Ibid.*, p. 36.
28. *Ibid.*, p. 37.
29. *Ibid.*, p. 34.
30. *Ibid.*, p. 40.
31. *Ibid.*, p. 43.
32. *That there is but one Covenant, Works*, vol. 2.
33. *Ibid.*, p. 499.
34. *Ibid.*
35. *Ibid.*, p. 465.
36. *Ibid.*, p. 479.
37. *Ibid.*, p. 482.
38. *Ibid.*, p. 501.
39. *Ibid.*, p. 486.
40. *Ibid.*, p. 501.
41. *Ibid.*, p. 506.
42. *Ibid.*, p. 489.
43. *Ibid.*, p. 494.
44. *Ibid.*, p. 493.
45. *Ibid.*
46. *Ibid.*, p. 574.

47. *The visible Church, in Covenant with God; further illustrated,* p. 58.
48. *Ibid.,* Preface.
49. *Ibid.,* p. 31.
50. *Ibid.,* p. 28.
51. *Ibid.,* p. 34.
52. *Ibid.,* p. 20.
53. *Ibid.,* p. 6.
54. See above, pp. 87 ff.
55. *The visible Church . . . further illustrated,* p. 80.
    So far as I know this reference to the doctrine of assurance stands alone in the present controversy. This doctrine was not a point at issue. Mather's opponents insisted upon "saving grace," and not upon assurance. They knew that the former is a matter of certain experience, while the latter is ultimately uncertain. Any assurance that one was an elect of God could not be absolute. No intelligent Calvinist claimed the contrary. Therefore, Mather's contention was irrelevant and ill-conceived. His failure to arouse a controversy on the subject of assurance was well-deserved.
56. *A careful and strict Examination of the external Covenant, Works,* vol. 2.
57. *Ibid.,* p. 541.
58. *Ibid.,* p. 538.
59. *Ibid.,* p. 658.
60. *Ibid.,* p. 658.
61. *Ibid.,* p. 524.
62. *Works,* vol. 2, p. 667.
63. *Ibid.,* p. 675.
64. *Ibid.,* pp. 674-675.
65. *Ibid.,* p. 675.
66, 67, *Ibid.,* p. 678.
68. *Ibid.,* p. 682.
69. *Ibid.,* p. 686.
70. *Ibid.,* p. 687.
71. *Ibid.,* p. 689.
72. Ebenezer Devotion, *A Letter to the Reverend Joseph Bellamy, D.D.*
73. *Ibid.,* p. 9.
74, 75. *Ibid.,* p. 8.
76. *Ibid.,* p. 21.
77. *Ibid.,* p. 22.
78. *Works,* vol. 2, p. 702.
79. *Ibid.,* pp. 537-538.

80. *Ibid.*, p. 705.
81. *Ibid.*, p. 710.
82. *A second Letter*, p. 17.
83. W. Walker's contention (*Congregational Churches*, p. 182) that the Half-way Covenant was discarded because of the work of the Edwardeans must be supplemented by the view expressed here. There is no necessity for half-way covenanting when full-way covenanting is open to the "morally sincere." In fact, it is clear that the apparent victory of the Edwardeans was achieved only through a surrender.
84. Isaac Backus, *Baptists in New England*, vol. 2, pp. 306, 391. A. H. Newman, *Baptist Churches in the United States* (*The American Church History Series*, vol. 2), p. 271.
85. Amzi Lewis, *The Covenant-Interest, of the Children of Believers*, etc., p. 26.
86. See above, note 83.
87. "Pastor of a Congregational Church in Wells."
88. *A Discourse concerning the Church*, p. 108.
89. *Ibid.*, p. 109.
90. *Ibid.*, pp. 29-30.
91. *Ibid.*, p. 79.
92. *Ibid.*, p. 74.
93. *Ibid.*, p. 85.
94. *Ibid.*, p. 103.
95. *A Dissertation on the scriptural Qualifications for Admission and Access to the Christian Sacraments*, 1793.
96. *Ibid.*, p. 132.
97. *Ibid.*, p. 128.
98. See chaps. 2 and 3.
99. *Scriptural Qualifications*, p. 85.
100. *Ibid.*, pp. 22, 45.
101. *Ibid.*, p. 45.
102. *Remarks on the Reverend Mr. Emmons's Dissertation*, etc.
103. *Ibid.*, p. 23.
104. *Ibid.*, pp. 46, 54.
105. *Ibid.*, pp. 52-53.
106. *Ibid.*, pp. 59, 66.
107. *Ibid.*, pp. 49, 51.
108. *A candid Reply*, p. 51.
109. *Ibid.*
110. *Ibid.*, p. 65.
111. *Ibid.*, p. 66.
112. *Ibid.*, p. 56. Quoting Richard Baxter.
113. *Ibid.*, pp. 87-88.

CHAPTER VI

1. *Five Discourses, Works,* vol. 5, p. 501.
2. *The Eternity of Hell Torments, Works,* vol. 6, pp. 107-108.
3. *Ibid.,* pp. 106-107.
4. *Works,* vol. 5, p. 503; vol. 6, p. 110.
5. *Ibid.,* vol. 6, pp. 106-107.
6. *Miscellaneous Observations, Works,* vol. 7, p. 237.
7. *History of the Work of Redemption, Works,* vol. 3, p. 417.
8-9. See above, pp. 25 ff.
10. See above, pp. 65 ff.
11. *Universalism vindicated,* p. 9, *passim.*
12. Richard Eddy, *History of Universalism,* p. 398.
13. See below, pp. 166 ff.
14. *Salvation for all Men illustrated and vindicated as a Scripture Doctrine,* 1782.
15. W. Walker, *Congregational Churches,* p. 295.
16. 1783. "By one who wishes well to all mankind."
17. *Divine Glory brought to View,* etc., p. 3.
18. *Ibid.,* p. 4.
19. "By one who wishes well to the whole human race."
20. *The Mystery hid from Ages and Generations,* etc., p. 1.
21. *Ibid.,* pp. 167-168.
22. *Ibid.,* p. 168.
23. *Ibid.,* p. 9.
24. *Ibid.,* pp. 11, 168, 328.
25. *Ibid.,* p. 319.
26. *Ibid.,* p. 9.
27. *Ibid.,* pp. 319-320.
28. See chaps. 3 and 5.
29-30. *The Mystery hid,* etc., pp. 320-321.
31. *Ibid.,* pp. 323-324.
32. *Ibid.,* pp. 8 ff.
33. *Ibid.,* pp. 167-168.
34. *Ibid.,* p. 210.
35. *Ibid.,* p. 219.
36. *Ibid.,* p. 225.
37. *Ibid.,* p. 217.
38. *The future State of those who die in their Sins, Works,* vol. 2.
39. *Ibid.,* p. 466.
40. *Ibid.*
41. *Ibid.,* p. 454.
42. *Ibid.*
43. *Ibid.,* p. 453.
44. *Ibid.,* pp. 441-442. Of course, in a legal sense, the degree of

evil involved in a crime varies with its nature and consequences, rather than with the dignity of the legislator who
declares it criminal. In this respect the argument is fallacious.
However, it is a genuine expression of Calvinistic piety. When
one considers Him against Whom one has sinned, the shame of
his ingratitude overwhelms him in the presence of God, and
he recognizes the infinite evil of his sin. It is when the exalted view of divine glory vanished that the argument appeared fallacious.

45. *Works*, vol. 2.
46. *Ibid.*, p. 343.
47. *Ibid.*
48. *Institutes of the Christian Religion*, Bk. 3, chap. 7.
49. *Works*, vol. 3, pp. 100 ff.
50. *Ibid.*, vol. 2, p. 476.
51. See above, pp. 83-84.
52. *Works*, vol. 2, p. 407.
53. *Ibid.*, p. 471.
54. *Works*, vol. 3, p. 780.
55. *Ibid.*, p. 767.
56. "Pastor of the Third Church in Roxbury."
57. *The Salvation of all Men examined, Works*, vol. 1.
58. *Ibid.*, p. 39.
59. *Ibid.*, p. 45.
60. *Ibid.*, p. 49.
61. See above, pp. 170-171.
62. *Works*, vol. 1, p. 115.
63. See above, pp. 132, 142.
64. *Works*, vol. 1, p. 259.
65. *Ibid.*, p. 43.
66. *Ibid.*, p. 68.
67. Compare with Bellamy. See below, p. 162.
68. *The Doctrine of Eternal Misery*, p. v.
69. *Ibid.*, p. xi.
70. *Ibid.*, p. vii.
71. *Ibid.*, p. 181.
72. *Ibid.*, p. 188.
73. *Ibid.*, p. 189.
74. *Ibid.*, p. 191.
75. *Ibid.*, p. 189.
76. A pamphlet containing extracts from the writings of a Scottish
    divine, Thomas Boston (d. 1732), was printed in Exeter
    (1796). It was entitled *A Key to Heaven; or, A Call to flee
    from the Wrath to come.* Presumably it was intended to re-

new acquaintance with a lively view of damnation and hell-fire.

"The damned shall have the society of devils in their miserable state in hell; for they shall depart into fire prepared for the devil and his angels. O horrible company! O frightful association; who would chuse to dwell in a palace haunted by devils? To be confined to the most pleasant spot of earth, with the devil and his infernal furies, would be a most terrible confinement. How would men's hearts fail them, and their hair stand up, finding themselves environed with the hellish crew, in that case! but ah! how much more terrible must it be, to be cast with the devils into one fire, locked up with them in one dungeon, shut up with them in one pit! to be closed up in a den of roaring lions, girded about with serpents, surrounded with venomous asps, and to have the bowels eaten out by vipers, all together and at once, is a comparisn too low, to shew the misery of the damned, shut up in hell with the devil and his angels. . . . How will these lions roar and tear! How will these serpents hiss! these dragons vomit out fire! what horrible anguish will seize the damned, finding themselves in the lake of fire, with the devil who deceived them; drawn hither with the silken cords of temptation, by these wicked spirits, and bound with them in everlasting chains under darkness! Rev. xx. 10." (p. 23.)

"Observe the continual succession of hours, days, months and years, how one still follows upon another; and think of eternity, wherein there is a continual succession without end. . . . Let us take a view of what is eternal, in the state of the damned in hell. Whatsoever is included in the fearful sentence, determining their eternal state, is everlasting; therefore all the doleful ingredients of their miserable state, will be everlasting; they will never end. . . . The damned themselves shall be eternal; they will have a being forever, and will never be substantially destroyed, or annihilated." (pp. 24-25.)

77. *The Question "Is Sin an infinite Evil" tested by Reason and Scripture.*
78. *Ibid.*, p. i.
79. *Ibid.*, p. 4.
80. *Ibid.*, p. 5.
81. *Ibid.*, p. 7.
82. *Ibid.*, p. 8.
83. *Ibid.*
84. *Ibid.*, p. 10.
85. *Ibid.*, p. 11.

86. *Ibid.*, p. 12.
87. *Duration of future Punishment*, pp. 7-9.

CHAPTER VII

1. *Miscellaneous Remarks, Works*, vol. 7, p. 505.
2. *Ibid.*, p. 507.
3. *Ibid.*, p. 527.
4. *Ibid.*, p. 528.
5. *Ibid.*, p. 535.
6. *Five Discourses, Works*, vol. 5, p. 354.
7. *History of the Work of Redemption, Works*, vol. 3, p. 294.
8. *Ibid.*, p. 295.
9. *Ibid.*, pp. 294-295.
10. *Ibid.*, p. 296, *passim.*
11. *Ibid.*, pp. 299, 295-297.
12. Translated by Frank Hugh Foster.
13. *The Satisfaction of Christ*, p. xv.
14. *Ibid.*, pp. 53, 60, *passim.*
15. *Ibid.*, p. 51.
16. *Ibid.*, p. 72.
17. *Ibid.*, pp. 106-107.
18. *Ibid.*, p. 129.
19. *Ibid.*, pp. 116 ff.
20. F. H. Foster, *History of the New England Theology*, p. 114.
21. See above, pp. 90-91.
22. *An Essay on the Nature and Glory of the Gospel of Jesus Christ, Works*, vol. 2, p. 313.
23. *Ibid.*, p. 315, *passim.*
24. *Ibid.*, pp. 323, 331.
25. *Ibid.*, p. 319.
26. *Ibid.*, p. 315.
27. *The Mystery hid from Ages and Generations*, p. 84.
28. *Ibid.*, p. 85.
29. Jonathan Edwards, *Works*, vol. 2, pp. 564-566.
30. 1812. New York edition, pp. 144-145.
31. *Universalism vindicated*, p. 88.
32. *Works*, vol. 2, p. 417.
33. *Ibid.*, p. 419 n.
34. *The Process of General Judgment, Works*, vol. 3.
35. *Ibid.*, p. 773.
36. *Ibid.*, pp. 777-778.
37. P. 9.
38. *A Second Sermon, preached at Wallingford*, p. 11.
39. First sermon, p. 19.

40. *Works*, vol. 2, p. 26.
41. *Ibid.*, p. 27.
42. *Ibid.*, p. 40.
43. *Ibid.*, p. 26.
44. First sermon, p. 9.
45. *Ibid.*, p. 17.
46. *The Scripture Doctrine of Atonement*, pp. 57-58.
47. *Ibid.*, p. 62.
48. *Ibid.*, p. 66.
49. *Ibid.*, p. 105.
50. *Ibid.*, p. 121.
51. *Ibid.*, p. 146.
52. Compare with Emmons, *Works*, vol. 3, pp. 758-761.
53. See below, pp. 198-199.
54. F. H. Foster, *History of the New England Theology*, p. 117.
55. Samuel Hopkins, *A Discourse on Christian Friendship*, *Works*, vol. 2, p. 665.

CHAPTER VIII

1. James Dana, *Two Discourses . . . on the Completion of the eighteenth Century*, p. 49.
2. *Ibid.*
3. *A Discourse on some Events of the last Century*, p. 12.
4. *Ibid.*, p. 13.
5. *Ibid.*, pp. 14 ff.
6. *Ibid.*, p. 16.
7. J. H. Allen, *The Unitarian Movement since the Reformation*, p. 181.
8. *Ibid.*, pp. 180-181.
9. W. Walker, *The Congregational Churches*, pp. 277-278; E. H. Gillett, "History and Literature of the Unitarian Controversy," pp. 225-227.
10. *American Unitarianism*, p. 3.
11. *Ibid.*, p. 22.
12. *Ibid.*, p. 31.
13. *Ibid.*, p. 45.
14, 15. *Ibid.*, p. 6.
16. *Ibid.*, p. 7.
17. *Ibid.*, p. 9.
18. In 1774, Theophilus Lindsey founded the first Unitarian chapel in London.
19. *American Unitarianism*, p. 10.
20. *Ibid.*, p. 9.
21. *Review of American Unitarianism*, p. 1.
22. *Ibid.*

23. *Ibid.*, pp. 6-7.
24. *Ibid.*, p. 9.
25. *Ibid.*, p. 10.
26. *Ibid.*, p. 24.
27. *Ibid.*, p. 21.
28. *Ibid.*, pp. 21-22.
29, 30. *Ibid.*, p. 25.
31. *Ibid.*, p. 19.
32. *A Letter to the Rev. Samuel Thacher*, p. 16.
33. *Ibid.*
34. *Ibid.*, p. 12.
35. *Ibid.*, p. 13.
36. *Ibid.*, p. 20.
37. *Ibid.*, p. 28.
38. *Ibid.*, p. 29.
39. *Ibid.*, p. 23.
40. Samuel Worcester, *A Letter to the Rev. William E. Channing*, p. 27.
41. Pastor of the Tabernacle Church, Salem, *ibid.*, p. 26.
42. *Ibid.*, pp. 27-28.
43. *Remarks on the Rev. Dr. Worcester's Letter*, pp. 7-8.
44. *Ibid.*, pp. 17-18.
45. *Ibid.*, pp. 25-26.
46. *A third Letter*, pp. 29-30.
47. *Ibid.*, pp. 21-22.
48. *Ibid.*
49. *Remarks on the Rev. Dr. Worcester's second Letter*, p. 23.
50. *Ibid.*, p. 22.
51. *A third Letter*, p. 34. The crudity of such a view of the Trinity becomes apparent when one compares it with the cautious metaphysical statements of Edwards in his essay on the Trinity, edited G. P. Fisher.
52. *A second Letter*, p. 39.
53. *A third Letter*, p. 37.
54. *A second Letter*, pp. 38-39; *third Letter*, pp. 41-43.
55. *Remarks on the . . . second Letter*, p. 17.
56. *A second Letter*, p. 30.
57. *Letters to the Rev. Wm. E. Channing*, pp. 51-52.
58. *Ibid.*, p. 37.
59. *A Statement of Reasons*, p. 144, *passim.*
60. *Ibid.*
61. *Ibid.*, p. 141.
62. *Ibid.*, p. 142.
63. *Ibid.*, p. 191.
64. *Ibid.*, p. 203.

65. *Ibid.*, p. 138.
66. *Ibid.*, pp. 176-177.
67, 68. *Ibid.*, p. 164.
69. *Ibid.*, pp. 165-166.
70. *Ibid.*, pp. 169-170.
71. *Are you a Christian*, etc., pp. 15-16.
72. *Ibid.*, p. 15.
73. *Works*, 1875 edition, pp. 367 ff.
74. *Ibid.*, p. 381.
75. *Ibid.*, p. 377.
76. *Ibid.*, p. 369.
77. *Ibid.*, p. 379.
78. *Ibid.*, p. 377.
79. *Ibid.*, p. 371.
80. *Letters to Unitarians, Works*, vol. 4, p. 20.
81. *Ibid.*, pp. 20-21.
82. *Ibid.*, p. 38.
83. *Ibid.*, p. 88.
84. *Ibid.*, p. 82.
85. *Ibid.*, pp. 87-89.
86. *Ibid.*, p. 91.
87. *Ibid.*, p. 54.
88. *Ibid.*, p. 61.
89. *Ibid.*, p. 15.
90. *Ibid.*, pp. 70-71.
91. *Ibid.*, p. 65.
92. *Ibid.*, p. 14.
93. The appointment of Ware to this chair is usually taken as the starting point of the Unitarian controversy.
94. *Letters addressed to Trinitarians and Calvinists*, pp. 54, 55-58.
95. *Ibid.*, p. 55.
96. *Ibid.*, pp. 79-80.
97. *Ibid.*, p. 26.
98. *Ibid.*, pp. 24-25.
99. *Ibid.*, p. 22.
100. *Ibid.*
101. *Reply to Dr. Ware's Letters, Works*, vol. 4, pp. 126-127.
102. *Ibid.*, p. 189.
103. *Ibid.*, p. 193.
104. *Answer to Dr. Woods' Reply*, pp. 82-84.
105. *Ibid.*, p. 15.
106. *Ibid.*, pp. 23-25.
107. *Remarks on Dr. Ware's Answer, Works*, vol. 4, p. 337.
108. *Ibid.*, pp. 314-315.
109. *Ibid.*, pp. 297-299.

110. *Ibid.*, pp. 328, 330.
111. *Ibid.*, pp. 338-339.
112. *A Postscript*, p. 47.
113. *Works*, 1875 edition.
114. *Ibid.*, p. 295.
115. *Ibid.*, p. 293.
116, 117. *Ibid.*
118. *A Review of the Rev. Dr. Channing's Discourse*, pp. 19, 63.
119. *Ibid.*, p. 37.
120. *Answer to a Discourse, etc.*, p. 28.
121. *Ibid.*, pp. 27-28.
122. *Ibid.*, p. 5.
123. *Ibid.*, p. 33.
124. *Ibid.*, pp. 28-29.

Chapter IX

1. *Works*, vol. 2.
2. *Ibid.*, p. 19.
3. *Ibid.*, p. 19.
4. *Ibid.*, p. 15.
5. *Ibid.*, p. 20.
6. *Ibid.*, p. 22.
7. *Ibid.*, p. 37.
8. *Ibid.*, p. 38.
9. *Ibid.*, p. 86.
10. *Ibid.*, p. 34.
11. *Ibid.*, p. 34.
12. *Ibid.*, p. 29.
13. *Ibid.*, p. 34.
14. *Ibid.*, p. 186.
15. *Ibid.*, p. 190.
16. *Ibid.*, p. 150.
17. *Ibid.*, p. 147.
18. See above, pp. 48 ff.
19. The ordination of James Dana at Wallingford became the subject
    of a heated controversy, in which took part Jonathan Todd,
    William Hart, Noah Hobart, Charles Chauncy, and others.
20. *An Examination*, p. 91.
21. *Ibid.*, p. v.
22. *Ibid.*, p. 109.
23. *Ibid.*, p. 1.
24. *Ibid.*, p. 2.
25. *Ibid.*, p. 2 n.
26. *Ibid.*, p. 34.
27. *Ibid.*, p. 61.

28. *Ibid.*, p. 44.
29. *Ibid.*, pp. 44-45.
30. *Ibid.*, p. 19.
31. *Ibid.*, pp. 1, 62.
32. *Ibid.*, pp. 51-52.
33. *Ibid.*, p. 14.
34. Beach Newtoun, 1770.
35. *A Preservative*, p. 3.
36. *Ibid.*, p. 8.
37. *Ibid.*, p. 30.
38. "Pastor of the First Church in Coventry, Conn." *The Vanity*, etc., p. 26.
39. *Ibid.*, p. 8.
40. *Ibid.*, p. 27.
41. *An Essay on Moral Agency.*
42. *Ibid.*, pp. 38-39.
43. *Ibid.*, p. 37.
44. *Ibid.*, p. 22.
45. *Ibid.*, p. 64.
46. *Ibid.*, p. 61.
47. *Ibid.*
48. *Ibid.*, p. 24, *passim.*
49. *Ibid.*, p. 123.
50. *Ibid.*, p. 63.
51. *Ibid.*, p. 64.
52. *Ibid.*, p. 69.
53. *Ibid.*, pp. 99-100.
54. "Pastor of the Church of Christ in New-Bedford." *Essays on Liberty and Necessity*, p. 11.
55. *Ibid.*, p. 22.
56. *Ibid.*, pp. 17-18.
57. *Ibid.*, pp. 23, 28, 43.
58. *Ibid.*, p. 48.
59. *Ibid.*, p. 13.
60. *Ibid.*
61. *Essays on Liberty and Necessity. Second Part*, 1795, p. 82.
62. *Essays*, first part, p. 26.
63. *Liberty and Necessity, Works*, vol. 1, p. 421.
64. *Ibid.*, pp. 334-335.
65. *Ibid.*, p. 381.
66. *Ibid.*, pp. 382-383.
67. *Ibid.*, p. 444.
68. *Works*, vol. 2, p. 435.
69. *Ibid.*, p. 417.

70. *Ibid.*, p. 418.
71. *Ibid.*, pp. 422 ff.
72. *Ibid.*, p. 424.
73. *Ibid.*, p. 425.
74. *Theology*, vol. 1, p. 407.
75. *Ibid.*, p. 371.
76. *Ibid.*, p. 527.
77. *Ibid.*, p. 526.
78. *Ibid.*, p. 265.
79. See above, p. 242; also Elias Smith, *Essay on the Fall*, p. 20.
80. *Essays on some of the first Principles of Metaphysicks, Ethicks, and Theology,* 1824.
81. *Ibid.*, p. 50.
82. *Ibid.*
83. *Ibid.*, p. 19.
84. *Ibid.*, p. 91.
85. *Ibid.*, pp. 97-98.
86. *Ibid.*, p. 117.
87. See above, pp. 237-238.
88. *Revealed Theology*, p. 136.
89. *Ibid.*, pp. 195 ff.
90. *Ibid.*, p. 136.
91. *The moral Government of God*, vol. 1, p. 307.
92. *Ibid.*, p. 2.
93. *Ibid.*, p. 8.
94. *Revealed Theology*, p. 207.
95. *The moral Government of God*, vol. 1, p. 9.
96. *Ibid.*, p. 37.
97. *Ibid.*, pp. 55-56.
98. See p. 64.

CHAPTER X

1. "Pastor of the Brick Presbyterian Church in the City of New-York." *The Means of Regeneration,* 1827, p. 25.
2. *Ibid.*, pp. 26-33.
3. *Ibid.*, p. 41.
4. *Essays on the Means of Regeneration.*
5. *Ibid.*, p. 386.
6. *Ibid.*, pp. 702-703.
7. *Ibid.*, p. 231.
8. *Ibid.*, p. 223.
9. *Ibid.*, pp. 224-225.
10. *Ibid.*, p. 223.
11. *Ibid.*, p. 209.

12. "Pastor of the Second Congregational Church in Portland, Me."
    Strictures on the Review of Dr. Spring's Dissertation, etc.,
    1829.
13. *Ibid.*, p. 11.
14. *Ibid.*, p. 13.
15. *Ibid.*
16. *Ibid.*, p. 15.
17. *Ibid.*, p. 16.
18. See above, pp. 221 ff.
19. *Strictures*, pp. 17 ff.
20. *An Evangelical View*, etc., p. 28.
21. *Ibid.*, p. 20.
22. *An Examination of Dr. Tyler's Vindication*, p. 4.
23. *Ibid.*, p. 4.
24. *Ibid.*, p. 25.
25. See below, pp. 271 ff.
26. *Concio ad Clerum*, p. 5.
27. *Ibid.*, p. 6.
28. *Ibid.*, p. 7.
29. *Ibid.*, pp. 15-16.
30. *Ibid.*, p. 14.
31. *Ibid.*, p. 13.
32. *Ibid.*, p. 38.
33. "Pastor of a Church in West-chester, Conn."
34. A *Review of Dr. Taylor's Concio ad Clerum*, p. 27.
35. *Ibid.*, p. 16.
36. A *Review . . . of Dr. Taylor's Sermon . . . and Mr. Harvey's Strictures on that Sermon*, p. 21, *passim*.
37. *Ibid.*, p. 22.
38. *An Examination of a Review of Dr. Taylor's Sermon on human Depravity*, p. 10.
39. *Ibid.*, pp. 6, 8.
40. *Ibid.*, p. 11.
41-42. *Concio ad Clerum*, p. 33 n.
43. *Ibid.*, p. 28.
44. *Ibid.*, p. 32 n.
45. *Ibid.*, p. 37.
46. *Ibid.*, p. 38.
47. *Ibid.*, p. 13.
48. *Review*, p. 34.
49. *Ibid.*, p. 34.
50. *Ibid.*, p. 35.
51. *Review* of Tyler's *Strictures*, p. 38.
52. Leonard Woods, *Letters to the Rev. Nathaniel W. Taylor, D.D.*,
    Works, vol. 4, p. 359.

53. *Ibid.*, pp. 446-447.
54. *Ibid.*, p. 443.
55. *Ibid.*, p. 386.
56. *Ibid.*, p. 376.
57. *Ibid.*, p. 367.
58. *Ibid.*, p. 374.
59. *Ibid.*, p. 412.
60. A Review of Dr. Woods' Letters, p. 5.
61. *Ibid.*, p. 11.
62. *Ibid.*, p. 39.
63. *Ibid.*, p. 33.
64. *Ibid.*, p. 35.
65. Correspondence between Rev. Dr. Taylor and Rev. Dr. Hawes, p. 2.
66. *Ibid.*, pp. 6-7.
67. Remarks on Rev. Dr. Taylor's Letter to Dr. Hawes.
68. *Ibid.*, p. 10.
69. *Ibid.*, p. 9.
70. *Ibid.*, pp. 11-12.
71. Reply to Dr. Tyler's Examination, p. 2.
72. *Ibid.*, p. 13.
73. *Ibid.*, p. 5.
74. *Ibid.*, p. 16.
75. *Ibid.*, pp. 15, 17.
76. *Ibid.*, pp. 22-23.
77. A Letter to the Editor of the Spirit of the Pilgrims, p. 4.
78. Further Reply, p. 35.
79. *Ibid.*, p. 43.
80. A further Reply . . . on the Doctrine of Decrees, p. 12.
81. Further Reply, p. 58.
82. *Ibid.*, p. 59. New England had lost interest in such controversial Calvinism. Edwards A. Park, the next and last great exponent of the New England Theology, was a liberal Calvinist and a disciple of N. W. Taylor. The champions of real, now literal, orthodoxy, became the Presbyterians; and in due time the New England Congregationalists achieved their now famous theological liberalism. Therefore, at present many people identify Calvinism with "fundamentalist" Presbyterianism—which is an unfortunate error.

BIBLIOGRAPHY

ADAMS, RANDOLPH GREENFIELD, *Political Ideas of the American Revolution*, Durham, N. C., 1922.

ALLEN, JOSEPH HENRY, *Historical Sketch of the Unitarian Movement since the Reformation*, New York, 1894 (*The American Church History Series*, ed. by Philip Schaff, etc., vol. 10).

AMANA, *The Catholick Question at Boston; or an Attempt to prove that a Calvinist is a Christian*, Boston, 1815.

ANDERSON, JAMES S. M., *The History of the Church of England in the Colonies and foreign Dependencies of the British Empire*, London, 1845, 1856. 3 vols.

ANDROS, THOMAS, *An Essay in which the Doctrine of a positive Divine Efficiency exciting the Will of Men to sin, as held by some modern Writers, is candidly discussed*, Boston, 1820.

ARCHAIOS, MATHETEES, *A serious Letter to the young People of Boston . . . to establish them in the present Truth and excite them to the Prosecusion of their Duty and best Interest*, Boston, 1783.

BACKUS, ISAAC, *A History of New England with particular Reference to the Denomination of Christians called Baptists*, Newton, 1871. 2 vols.

BACON, LEONARD W., *A History of American Christianity*, New York, 1897 (*American Church History Series*, ed. by Philip Schaff, etc., vol. 13).

—— *The Congregationalists*, New York, 1904 (*The Story of the Churches*).

BALCH, WILLIAM, *A Vindication of some Points of Doctrine . . . being an Answer to the Remarks of the Rev. Messieurs Wigglesworth and Chipman*, Boston, 1746.

BALDWIN, ALICE M., *The New England Clergy and the American Revolution*, Durham, N. C., 1928.

BARNARD, JOHN, *Two Sermons: The Christians Behaviour under severe and repeated Bereavements, and the fatal Consequence of a Peoples persisting in Sin*, Boston, 1714.

—— *The Imperfection of the Creature, and the Excellency of the Divine Commandment*, Boston, 1747.

BELLAMY, JOSEPH, *The Works of Joseph Bellamy, D.D., first Pastor of the Church in Bethlem, Conn. With a Memoir of his Life and Character*, ed. by Tryon Edwards, Boston, 1850. 2 vols.

BELLAMY, JOSEPH, *True Religion delineated; or experimental Religion, as distinguished from Formality on the one hand, and Enthusiasm on the other, set in a scriptural and rational Light*, 1750 (*Works*, vol. 1).

—— *The great Evil of Sin, as committed against God*, 1753 (*Works*, vol. 1).

—— *The Law our Schoolmaster*, 1756 (*Works*, vol. 1).

—— *The Millenium*, 1758 (*Works*, vol. 1).

—— *A Treatise on the Divinity of Christ*, 1758 (*Works*, vol. 1).

—— *Four Sermons on the Wisdom of God in the Permission of Sin*, 1758 (*Works*, vol. 2).

—— *The Wisdom of God in the Permission of Sin, vindicated*, 1759 (*Works*, vol. 2).

—— *An Essay on the Nature and Glory of the Gospel of Jesus Christ*, 1762 (*Works*, vol. 2).

—— *A Blow at the Root of the refined Antinomianism of the present Age*, 1763 (*Works*, vol. 1).

—— *That there is but one Covenant whereof Baptism and the Lord's Supper are Seals; namely, the Covenant of Grace*, 1769 (*Works*, vol. 2).

—— *A Careful and strict Examination of the external Covenant. . . . A Vindication of the Plan on which the Churches in New England were originally founded*, 1769 (*Works*, vol. 2).

—— *Four Dialogues on the Half-way Covenant*, 1769 (*Works*, vol 2).

BELSHAM, THOMAS, *American Unitarianism; or a brief History of the Progress, and present State of the Unitarian Churches in America*, Boston, 1815.

BOARDMAN, GEORGE NYE, *A History of New England Theology*, New York, 1899.

BOSTON, THOMAS, *A Key to Heaven; or, a Call to flee from the Wrath to come*, Exeter, 1796.

BRADFORD, ALDEN, *Memoir of the Life and Writings of Rev. Jonathan Mayhew, D.D., Pastor of the West Church and Society in Boston*, Boston, 1838.

BRIANT, LEMUEL, *Letter to Mr. Porter*, Boston, 1750.

BROWN, J., *A Letter to the Rev. William E. Channing*, Boston, 1820.

BURTON, ASA, *Essays on some of the first Principles of Metaphysicks, Ethicks, and Theology*, Portland, 1824.

CHANNING, WILLIAM ELLERY, *The Works of William Ellery Channing*, Boston, 1875.

—— *A Letter to the Rev. Samuel C. Thacher, on the Aspersions contained in a late number of the Panoplist, on the Ministers of Boston and the Vicinity*, Boston, 1815.

—— *Remarks on the Rev. Dr. Worcester's Letter to Mr. Channing*, Boston, 1815.

CHANNING, WILLIAM ELLERY, *Remarks on the Rev. Dr. Worcester's second Letter to Mr. Channing*, Boston, 1815.
—— *Unitarian Christianity: Discourse at the Ordination of the Rev. Jared Sparks*, 1819 (*Works*, pp. 367 ff.).
—— *Unitarian Christianity most favorable to Piety: Discourse at the Dedication of the Second Congregational Unitarian Church*, New York, 1826 (*Works*, pp. 384 ff.).
—— *Likeness to God: Discourse at the Ordination of the Rev. F. A. Farley*, 1828 (*Works*, pp. 291 ff.).
CHAUNCY, CHARLES, *The late religious Commotions in New-England considered . . . By a Lover of Truth and Peace*, Boston, 1743.
—— *Seasonable Thoughts on the State of Religion in New-England*, Boston, 1743.
—— *Civil Magistrates must be just, ruling in the Fear of God*, Boston, 1747 (Election Sermon).
—— *The Opinion of one that has perused the Summer Morning's Conversation*, Boston, 1758.
—— *Salvation for all Men illustrated and vindicated as a Scripture Doctrine. By one who wishes well to all Mankind*, Boston, 1782.
—— *Divine Glory brought to view in the final Salvation of all Men. A Letter to the Friend of Truth*, Boston, 1783.
—— *The Benevolence of the Deity, fairly and impartially considered*, Boston, 1784.
—— *Five Dissertations on the Scripture Account of the Fall; and its Consequences*, London, 1784.
—— *The Mystery hid from Ages and Generations, made manifest by the Gospel-Revelation; or, the Salvation of all Men the grand Thing aimed at in the Scheme of God*, London, 1784.
CLAP, THOMAS, *A brief History and Vindication of the Doctrines received and established in the Churches of New England, with a Specimen of the new Scheme of Religion beginning to prevail*, New-Haven, 1755.
CLARK, JOSEPH S., *A historical Sketch of the Congregational Churches in Massachusetts, from 1620 to 1858. With an Appendix*, Boston, 1858.
CLARK, PETER, *The Scripture-Doctrine of Original Sin, stated and defended. In a Summer-Morning's Conversation, between a Minister and a Neighbour*, Boston, 1758.
COBB, SANFORD H., *The Rise of religious Liberty in America. A History*, New York, 1902.
The Confession of Faith, together with the larger Catechism. . . . With a brief Sum of Christian Doctrine, contained in Holy Scripture, and holden forth in the Confession of Faith and Catechism, Boston, 1723.

COOPER, WILLIAM, *Serious Exhortations address'd to Young Men*, Boston, 1732.

Correspondence between Rev. Dr. Taylor and Rev. Dr. Hawes, Hartford, 1832.

CROSWELL, ANDREW, *Heaven shut against Arminians, Antinomians*, etc., Boston, 1747.

DANA, JAMES, *Two Discourses delivered at Cambridge, May 10, 1767*, Boston, 1767.

—— *An Examination of the Late Reverend President Edwards's "Enquiry on Freedom of Will"; . . . With an Appendix containing a Specimen of Coincidence between the Principles of Mr. Edwards's Book, and those of antient and modern Fatalists*, Boston, 1770.

—— *Two Discourses, I. On the Commencement of a new Year; II. On the Completion of the eighteenth Century*, New-Haven, 1801.

DEVOTION, EBENEZER, *A Letter to the Reverend Joseph Bellamy, D.D., Concerning Qualifications for Christian Communion*, etc., New-Haven, 1770.

—— *A Second Letter to the Reverend Joseph Bellamy, D.D.*, New-Haven, 1770.

DEWEY, ISRAEL, *Letters to the Reverend Mr. Samuel Hopkins: Shewing, that Sin can't be agreeable to the Will and Pleasure of God; as he asserts it is; and laying open the monstrous Consequences of this his Doctrine*, Sheffield, 1759.

DEXTER, HENRY MARTYN, *The Congregationalism of the last three hundred Years, as seen in its Literature. . . . With a bibliographical Appendix*, New York, 1880.

DOW, DANIEL, *New Haven Theology, alias Taylorism, alias Neology; in its own Language*, Thompson, 1834.

DUNNING, ALBERT E., *Congregationalists in America*, New York, 1894.

DWIGHT, SERENO E., *Life of President Edwards*, New York, 1829.

DWIGHT, TIMOTHY, *The true Means of establishing public Happiness*, New Haven, 1795.

—— *A Discourse on some Events of the last Century*, New Haven, 1801.

—— *Theology; explained and defended in a Series of Sermons*, Middletown, Conn., 1818. 5 vols.

—— *Duration of future Punishment*, New York (no date).

ECKLEY, JOSEPH, *Divine Glory, brought to View, in the Condemnation of the Ungodly*, Boston, 1782.

EDDY, RICHARD, *History of Universalism,* New York, 1894 (*The American Church History Series,* ed. by Philip Schaff, etc., vol. 10).

EDWARDS, JONATHAN, *The Works of President Edwards: with a Memoir of his Life,* ed. by Sereno E. Dwight, New York, 1829. 10 vols.

—— *God glorified in Man's Dependence,* 1731 (*Works,* vol. 7).

—— *A faithful Narrative of the surprising Work of God, in the Conversion of many hundred Souls, in Northampton,* 1736 (*Works,* vol. 4).

—— *Five Discourses on important Subjects,* 1738 (*Works,* vol. 5).

—— *The Eternity of Hell Torments,* 1739 (*Works,* vol. 6).

—— *A History of the Work of Redemption, containing the Outlines of a Body of Divinity, including a View of Church History, in a Method entirely new,* 1739 (*Works,* vol. 3).

—— *Some Thoughts concerning the present Revival of Religion in New England,* 1740 (*Works,* vol. 4).

—— *Sinners in the Hands of an angry God,* 1741 (*Works,* vol. 7).

—— *The distinguishing Marks of a Work of the Spirit of God,* 1743 (*Works,* vol. 3).

—— *Miscellaneous Observations on important theological Subjects.* (The essays included under this and the following title "were inserted in the author's common-place book prior to the composition of his elaborate publications on the same subjects." *Works,* vol. 7.)

—— *Miscellaneous Remarks on important Doctrines* (*Works,* vol. 7).

—— *A Treatise concerning Religious Affections,* 1746 (*Works,* vol. 5).

—— *An humble Inquiry into the Rules of the Word of God, concerning the Qualifications requisite to a complete Standing and full Communion in the visible Church,* 1749 (*Works,* vol. 4).

—— *Misrepresentations corrected, and Truth vindicated, in a Reply to the Rev. Mr. Solomon Williams's Book . . . concerning the Qualifications necessary to lawful Communion in the Christian Sacraments,* 1751 (*Works,* vol. 4).

—— *A careful and strict Enquiry into the modern prevailing Notions of that Freedom of Will, which is supposed to be essential to moral Agency, Virtue and Vice, Reward and Punishment, Praise and Blame,* 1754 (*Works,* vol. 2).

—— *A Dissertation concerning the End for which God created the World,* 1755 (*Works,* vol. 3).

—— *A Dissertation concerning the Nature of true Virtue,* 1755 *Works,* vol. 3).

—— *The great Christian Doctrine of Original Sin defended,* 1758 (*Works,* vol. 2).

—— *An unpublished Essay on the Trinity. With Remarks on Ed-*

wards and his Theology, ed. by George P. Fisher, New York, 1903.

EDWARDS, JONATHAN, JR., *The Works of Jonathan Edwards, D.D., Late President of Union College. With a Memoir of his Life and Character*, ed. by Tryon Edwards, Boston, 1850. 2 vols.

—— *Three Sermons on the Necessity of the Atonement, and its Consistency with free Grace in Forgiveness*, 1875 (*Works*, vol. 2).

—— *The Salvation of all Men examined; and the endless Punishment of those who die impenitent, argued and defended against the Objections and Reasonings of the late Rev. Doctor Chauncy, of Boston*, 1789 (*Works*, vol. 1).

—— *A Dissertation concerning Liberty and Necessity; containing Remarks on the Essays of Dr. Samuel West*, 1797 (*Works*, vol. 1).

ELIOT, ANDREW, *An inordinate Love of the World inconsistent with the Love of God*, Boston, 1744.

EMLYN, THOMAS, *Extracts from an humble Inquiry into the Scripture Account of Jesus Christ*, Boston, 1790.

EMMONS, NATHANAEL, *The Works of Nathanael Emmons, D.D., third Pastor of the Church in Franklin, Mass. With a Memoir of his Life*, ed. by Jacob Ide, Boston, 1861. 3 vols.

—— *A Discourse concerning the Process of general Judgment*, 1783 (*Works*, vol. 3).

—— *The Gospel Scheme of Grace*, 1789 (*Works*, vol. 1).

—— *A Dissertation on the scriptural Qualifications for Admission and Access to the Christian Sacraments: comprising some Strictures on Dr. Hemmenway's Discourse concerning the Church*, Worcester, Mass., 1793.

—— *A candid Reply to the Reverend Doctor Hemmenway's Remarks on a Dissertation on the scriptural Qualifications for Admission and Access to the Christian Sacraments*, Worcester, Mass., 1795.

—— *A Sermon, delivered Dec. 31, 1820. The last Lord's Day in the second Century since our Forefathers first settled in Plymouth*, Dedham, 1821.

—— *A Discourse delivered October 13, 1813, before the Mendon Association*, New-York, 1826.

EVANS, CHARLES, *American Bibliography . . . with bibliographical and biographical Notes, 1639-1797*, Chicago, 1903-1931. 11 vols. (In progress.)

An Examination of a Review of Dr. Taylor's Sermon on human Depravity and Mr. Harvey's Strictures on that Sermon, Hartford, 1829.

An Examination of and some Answer to A Pamphlet, intitled, A Narrative and Defense of the Proceedings of the Ministers of Hampshire, who disapproved of Mr. Breck's Settlement at Springfield, Boston, 1736.

An Exhibition of Unitarianism with scriptural Extracts, Greenfield, Mass., 1824.

A faithful Narrative of the Proceedings of the ecclesiastical Council convened at Salem in 1734. Occasioned by the scandalous Divisions in the First Church in that Town, Boston, 1735.

FISHER, GEORGE PARK, *History of Christian Doctrine*, New York, 1896.

FOSTER, FRANK HUGH, *A genetic History of New England Theology*, Chicago, 1907.

FOSTER, ISAAC, *Fallen Sinners of Men able to do Well*, Massachusetts-Bay, 1778.

FULLER, ANDREW, *The Calvinistic and Socinian Systems examined and compared, as to their moral Tendency*, 1793 (*Works*, London, 1851, pp. 50-109).

GILLETT, E. H., "History and Literature of the Unitarian Controversy," Morrisania, N. Y., 1871 (*The Historical Magazine*, vol. 9, 2nd series).

GOHDES, CLARENCE, "Aspects of Idealism in early New England," 1930 (*The Philosophical Review*, vol. 39, no. 6).

GORDON, WILLIAM, *The Doctrine of final universal Salvation examined and shown to be unscriptural*, Boston, 1783.

GROTIUS, HUGO, *A Defense of the catholic Faith concerning the Satisfaction of Christ, against Faustus Socinus*, Andover, 1889 (translated by Frank Hugh Foster).

HART, WILLIAM, *A Discourse concerning the Nature of Regeneration and the Way wherein it is wrought*, New-London, 1742.

—— *A Sermon of a new Kind, never preached, nor ever will be; containing a Collection of Doctrines belonging to the Hopkintonian Scheme of Orthodoxy; or the Marrow of the most modern Divinity*, New-Haven, 1769.

—— *Brief Remarks on a number of false Propositions, and dangerous Errors, which are spreading in the Country; collected out of sundry Discourses lately publish'd, wrote by Dr. Whitaker and Mr. Hopkins. Written by Way of Dialogue*, New-Haven, 1769.

—— *A Letter to the Rev. Samuel Hopkins, occasioned by his Animadversions on Mr. Hart's late Dialogue*, New-London, 1770.

—— *A Letter to the Reverend Nathaniel Whitaker, D.D.*, New-London, 1771.

—— *Remarks on President Edwards's Dissertations concerning the Nature of true Virtue. . . . To which is added, an Attempt to shew wherein true Virtue does consist*, New-Haven, 1771.

—— *A scriptural Answer to this Question "What are the necessary*

Qualifications for a lawful and approved Attendance upon the Sacraments of the New Covenant?" New-London, 1772.

HARVEY, JOSEPH, *A Review of Dr. Taylor's Concio ad Clerum*, Hartford, 1829.

HEMMENWAY, MOSES, *Seven Sermons, on the Obligation and Encouragement of the Unregenerate, to labour for the Meat which endureth to everlasting Life*, Boston, 1767.

—— *A Vindication of the Power, Obligation and Encouragement of the Unregenerate to attend the Means of Grace*, Boston, 1772.

—— *A Discourse on the Divine Institution of Water-Baptism, as a standing Ordinance of the Gospel*, Portsmouth, N. H., 1780.

—— *Discourse on the Nature and Subjects of Christian Baptism*, Boston, 1781.

—— *A Discourse concerning the Church, designed to remove the Scruples and reconcile the Differences of Christians*, Boston, 1792.

—— *Remarks on the Reverend Mr. Emmons's Dissertation on the Scriptural Qualifications for Admission and Access to the Christian Sacraments*, Boston, 1794.

HOLLY, ISRAEL, *Old Divinity preferable to modern Novelty*, New-Haven, 1780.

HOOPER, WILLIAM, *The Apostles neither Impostors nor Enthusiasts*, Boston, 1742.

HOPKINS, SAMUEL, *The Works of Samuel Hopkins, D.D.* . . . *With a Memoir of his Life and Character*, ed. by Edwards A. Park, Boston, 1854. 3 vols.

—— *Sin, through Divine Interposition, an Advantage to the Universe, and yet this no Excuse for Sin, or Encouragement to it, illustrated and proved*, 1758 (*Works*, vol. 3).

—— *A Dialogue between a Calvinist and a Semi-Calvinist* (*Works*, vol. 3).

—— *An Inquiry concerning the Promises of the Gospel; whether any of them are made to the Exercises and Doings of Persons in an unregenerate State*. . . . *Also a brief Inquiry into the Use of Means; showing their Necessity in order to Salvation*, 1765 (*Works*, vol. 3).

—— *A Discourse on Christian Friendship, as it subsists between Christ and Believers and between Believers themselves*, 1767 (*Works*, vol. 2).

—— *The Cause, Nature, and Means of Regeneration*, 1768 (*Works*, vol. 3).

—— *The Importance and Necessity of Christians considering Jesus Christ in the Extent of His high and glorious Character*, 1768 (*Works*, vol. 3).

—— *The Knowledge of God's Law necessary to the Knowledge of Sin*, 1768 (*Works*, vol. 3).

HOPKINS, SAMUEL, *The true State and Character of the Unregenerate, stripped of all Misrepresentation and Disguise*, 1769 (*Works*, vol. 3).

—— *Animadversions on Mr. Hart's late Dialogue; in a letter to a Friend*, New-London, 1770.

—— *An Inquiry into the Nature of true Holiness. With an Appendix*, 1773 (*Works*, vol. 3).

—— *An Inquiry concerning the future State of those who die in their Sins; or, endless Punishment consistent with Divine Justice, Wisdom, and Goodness*, 1783 (*Works*, vol. 2).

—— *Three Sermons: the Decrees of God the Foundation of Piety*, 1789 (*Works*, vol. 2).

—— *System of Doctrines*, 1792 (*Works*, vols. 1-2).

—— *The Sins of Men so ordered and controlled by God, as to glorify Him, and subserve the Good of His Kingdom, in every Instance of it which He suffers to take place*, 1800 (*Works*, vol. 3).

—— *Farewell to the World*, 1800 (*Works*, vol. 3).

HUMPHRY, EDWARD FRANK, *Nationalism and Religion in America, 1774-1789*, Boston, 1924.

HUNTINGTON, JOSEPH, *The Vanity and Mischief of presuming on Things beyond our Measure*, Norwich, 1774.

—— *Thoughts on the Atonement of Christ*, Newburyport, 1791.

—— *Calvinism improved; or, the Gospel illustrated as a System of real Grace, issuing in the Salvation of all Men*, New-London, 1796.

JAMESON, J. F., *The American Revolution considered as a social Movement*, Princeton, 1926.

LATHROP, JOSEPH, *Damnable Heresies defined and described, in a Sermon*, Brookfield, 1821.

LAYMAN, A., *A Letter to Rev. Mr. Channing, in favour of the Doctrine of the Trinity, and in Opposition to the Sentiments, contained in his Baltimore Sermon*, 1819.

Letters from the First Church in Glocester to the Second in Bradford, with their Answers. To which is added an Appendix containing . . . Mr. Balch's Reply to the Articles of Error alledg'd against him, Boston, 1744.

LEE, UMPHRY, *Historical Backgrounds of Early Methodist Enthusiasm*, New York, 1931.

LEWIS, AMZI, *The Covenant-Interest, of the Children of Believers, illustrated and proved*, Chatham, 1783.

LORD, BENJAMIN, *Believers in Christ, only, the true Children of God, and born of Him alone*, Boston, 1742.

—— *Religion and Government subsisting together in Society, necessary to their compleat Happiness and Safety*, New-London, 1752.

LOWELL, JOHN, *Are You a Christian or a Calvinist? Or, do you pre-*

fer the Authority of Christ to that of the Genevan Reformer? Boston, 1815.

MATHER, COTTON, *Serious Address to those who unnecessarily frequent the Tavern*, Boston, 1726.

MATHER, MOSES, *The Visible Church, in Covenant with God*, New-Haven, 1769.

—— *The visible Church, in Covenant with God; further illustrated. Containing also, a brief Representation of some other Gospel-Doctrines, which effect the Controversy*, New-Haven, 1770.

—— *A brief View of the manner in which the Controversy about the Terms of Communion in the visible Church has been conducted, in the present Day*, New-Haven, 1772.

MATHER, SAMUEL, *An Apology for the Liberties of the Churches in New England*, Boston, 1738.

MATHEWS, LOIS KIMBAL, *The Expansion of New England*, Boston, 1909.

MAYHEW, JONATHAN, *Seven Sermons*, Boston, 1749.

—— *A Discourse concerning unlimited Submission and non-Resistence to the higher Powers*, 1750, Boston, 1818.

—— *A Sermon preached in the Audience of His Excellency William Shirley, Esq.*, Boston, 1754 (Election Sermon).

—— *Sermons upon the following Subjects, viz. On hearing the Word. . . . On the true Value, Use and End of Life; together with the Conduciveness of Religion to prolong, and make it happy*, Boston, 1755.

—— *Striving to enter in at the strait Gate explained and inculcated; and the Connexion of Salvation therewith proved from the Holy Scriptures*, Boston, 1761.

—— *Two Sermons on the Nature, Extent and Perfection of the Divine Goodness*, Boston, 1763.

—— *Sermons to Young Men*, 1763, London, 1767.

McCARRELL, JOSEPH, *Answer to a Discourse preached by Dr. William E. Channing, at the Dedication of the Second Congregational Unitarian Church, New-York, 1826*, New-York, 1827.

McGIFFERT, ARTHUR CUSHMAN, JR., *Jonathan Edwards*, New York, 1932.

MERRIAM, CHARLES EDWARD, *A History of American Political Theories*, New York, 1903.

MILLS, JEDIDIAH, *An Inquiry concerning the State of the Unregenerate under the Gospel*, New-Haven, 1767.

MODE, PETER G., *Source Book and bibliographical Guide for American Church History*, Menasha, Wis., 1921.

MOODY, SAMUEL, *An Attempt to point out the fatal and pernicious Consequences of the Rev. Mr. Joseph Bellamy's Doctrines, respecting moral Evil*, Boston, 1759.

MORSE, JEDIDIAH, *Review of American Unitarianism*, Boston, 1815.
—— *Review of the Unitarian Controversy*, Boston, 1815.
MURRAY, JOHN, *Universalism vindicated . . . On the Revelation of the unbounded Love of God*, Charlestown, 1790.
—— *The last solemn Scene*, Newburyport, 1793.

A Narrative of the Proceedings of those Ministers of the County of Hampshire, &c. That have disapproved of the . . . Settlement of Mr. Robert Breck, in the pastoral Office in the First Church in Springfield, Boston, 1736.
NEWTOUN, BEACH, *A Preservative against the Doctrine of Fate: Occasioned by reading Mr. Jonathan Edwards against Free Will. . . . Proposed to the Consideration of young Students in Divinity*, Boston, 1770.
NILES, SAMUEL, *The true Scripture-Doctrine of Original Sin stated and Defended*, Boston, 1757.
NORTON, ANDREWS, *Views of Calvinism*, 1822.
—— *A Statement of Reasons for not believing the Doctrines of Trinitarians, concerning the Nature of God and the Person of Christ*, Boston, 1875.
NORTON, JACOB, *The Question "Is Sin an Infinite Evil?" tested by Reason and Scripture*, Boston, 1813.

OSGOOD, HERBERT L., *The American Colonies in the eighteenth Century*, New York, 1924. 4 vols.

PARK, EDWARDS AMASA, *The Atonement. Discourses and Treatises by Edwards, Smalley, Maxcy, Emmons, Griffin, Burge, and Weeks, with an introductory Essay*, Boston, 1859.
PARRINGTON, VERNON LOUIS, *The Colonial Mind 1620-1800 (Main Currents in American Thought*, vol. 1), New York, 1927.
A plain Narrative of the Proceedings which caused the Separation of a Number of aggrieved Brethren from the Second Church in Ipswich, Boston, 1747.
PRINCE, THOMAS, *The People of New-England put in Mind of the righteous Acts of the Lord to them and their Fathers, and reasoned with concerning them*, Boston, 1730 (Election Sermon).
Proofs that the common Theories and Modes of Reasoning respecting the Depravity of Mankind exhibit it as a physical Attribute, with a View of the scriptural Doctrine relative to the Nature and Character of Man as a moral Agent, New-York, 1824.

The Religious History of New England. King's Chapel Lectures, Cambridge, 1917 (A collective work on the various denominations).

RELLY, JAMES, *Union: or a Treatise on the Consanguinity and Affinity between Christ and His Church*, New-York, 1812.

A Review of the Rev. Dr. Channing's Discourse, preached at the Dedication of the Second Congregational Unitarian Church, New York, December 7, 1826, Boston, 1827.

A Review . . . of Dr. Taylor's Sermon on Human Depravity, and Mr. Harvey's Strictures on that Sermon, New-Haven, 1829.

Review of Dr. Tyler's Strictures in the Christian Spectator for March, 1830, New-Haven, 1830.

A Review of Dr. Woods' Letters to Dr. Taylor, on the Permission of Sin, New-Haven, 1830.

RILEY, I. WOODBRIDGE, *American Philosophy. The early Schools*, New York, 1907.

ROWE, H. K., *The History of Religion in the United States*, New York, 1924.

SCHNEIDER, HERBERT WALLACE, *The Puritan Mind*, New York, 1930.

SHEPARD, SAMUEL, *A Sermon, preached in the Audiance of His Excellency Caleb Strong, Esq. . . . . and the House of Representatives of the Commonwealth of Massachusetts*, Boston, 1806 (Election Sermon).

SHERMAN, JOSIAH, *God in no sense the Author of Sin*, Hartford, 1784.

SMALLEY, JOHN, *The Consistency of the Sinner's Inability to comply with the Gospel; with his inexcusable Guilt in not complying with it, illustrated and confirmed. In two Discourses*, Hartford, 1769.

—— *Eternal Salvation on no account a Matter of just Debt; or, full Redemption, not interfering with free Grace. A Sermon, delivered at Wallingford, by particular Agreement, with special Reference to the Murryan Controversy*, Hartford, 1785.

—— *The Law in all respects satisfied by our Saviour, in regard to those only who belong to Him; or, none but the Believers saved, through the all-sufficient Satisfaction of Christ. A second Sermon, preached at Wallingford, with a view to the Universalists*, Hartford, 1786.

—— *The Perfection of the Divine Law; and its Usefulness for the Conversion of Souls*, New-Haven, 1787.

SMITH, ELIAS, *An Essay on the Fall of Angels and Men; with Remarks on Dr. Edwards's Notion of the Freedom of the Will and System of Universality*, Wilmington (Delaware), 1796.

SPRING, GARDINER, *A Dissertation on the Means of Regeneration*, New-York, 1827.

—— *A Dissertation on native Depravity*, New York, 1833.

STODDARD, SOLOMON, *The Doctrine of instituted Churches, explained and proved from the Word of God*, London, 1700.

—— *The Inexcusableness of neglecting the Worship of God, under a Pretence of being in an unconverted Condition*, Boston, 1708.

—— *An Appeal to the Learned. Being a Vindication of the Right of visible Saints to the Lord's Supper, though they be Destitute of a saving Work of God's Spirit on their Hearts: Against the Exceptions of Mr. Increase Mather*, Boston, 1709.

—— *The Duty of Gospel-Ministers to preserve a People from Corruption*, Boston, 1718.

STRONG, CYPRIAN, *A Discourse on Acts ii. 42, in which the Practice of owning the Covenant is examined . . . and Reasons offered for its Abolition*, Hartford, 1791.

STRONG, NATHAN, *The Doctrine of eternal Misery reconcilable with the infinite Benevolence of God, and a Truth plainly asserted in the Christian Scriptures*, Hartford, 1796.

STUART, MOSES, *Letters to the Rev. Wm. E. Channing, containing Remarks on his Sermon recently preached and published at Baltimore*, Andover, 1819.

—— *Two Discourses on the Atonement*, Andover, 1828.

SWEET, WILLIAM WARREN, *The Story of Religions in America*, New York, 1930.

TAYLOR, JOHN, *The Scripture-Doctrine of Original Sin proposed to free and candid Examination*, London, 1750.

TAYLOR, NATHANIEL W., *Essays on the Means of Regeneration*, New-Haven, 1829.

—— *Concio ad Clerum. A Sermon delivered in the Chapel of Yale College*, New-Haven, 1828.

—— *Reply to Dr. Tyler's Examination*, Boston, 1832.

—— *A further Reply to Dr. Tyler, on the Doctrines of propagated Depravity, etc.*, 1833.

—— *A further Reply to Dr. Tyler, on the Doctrine of Decrees*, 1833.

—— *Essays, Lectures, etc., upon select Topics in revealed Theology*, New York, 1859.

—— *Lectures on the moral Government of God*, New York, 1859. 2 vols.

The Testimony of the President, Professors, Tutors and Hebrew Instructor of Harvard College in Cambridge, against the Reverend Mr. George Whitefield, and his Conduct, Boston, 1744.

THACHER, SAMUEL C., *The Unity of God*, Worcester, 1817.

THOMPSON, OTIS, *A Review of the Rev. Thomas Andros's Essay on the Doctrine of Divine Efficiency*, Providence, 1821.

TRACY, JOSEPH, *The Great Awakening. A History of the Revival of Religion in the time of Edwards and Whitefield*, Boston, 1845.

TYLER, BENNET, *Strictures on the Review of Dr. Spring's Dissertation on the Means of Regeneration in the Christian Spectator for 1829*, Portland, 1829.

—— *A Vindication of the Strictures on the Review of Dr. Spring's Dissertation on the Means of Regeneration*, Portland, 1830.

—— *A Letter to Rev. Joel Hawes, D.D., on Dr. Taylor's theological Views*, New-York, 1832.

—— *Remarks on Rev. Dr. Taylor's Letter to Dr. Hawes*, Boston, 1832.

—— *A Letter to the Editor of the Spirit of the Pilgrims*, Portland, 1833.

TYLER, MOSES COIT, *A History of American Literature*, New York, 1879. 2 vols.

WALKER, GEORGE LEON, *Some Aspects of the religious Life of New England*, Boston, 1897.

WALKER, WILLISTON, *The Creeds and Platforms of Congregationalism*, New York, 1893.

—— *A History of the Congregational Churches in the United States*, New York, 1894 (*The American Church History Series*, ed. by Philip Schaff, etc., vol. 3).

—— *Ten New England Leaders*, New York, 1901.

WALTER, NATHANAEL, *The Thoughts of the Heart the best Evidence of a Man's spiritual State*, Boston, 1741.

WARE, HENRY, *Letters addressed to Trinitarians and Calvinists, occasioned by Dr. Woods' Letters to Unitarians*, Cambridge, 1820.

—— *Answer to Dr. Woods' Reply, in a second Series of Letters addressed to Trinitarians and Calvinists*, Cambridge, 1822.

—— *A Postscript to the second Series of Letters . . . in Reply to the Remarks of Dr. Woods on those Letters*, Cambridge, 1823.

—— *Outlines of the Testimony of Scripture against the Trinity*, Boston, 1832.

WEBSTER, SAMUEL, *A Winter-Evening's Conversation upon the Doctrine of Original Sin . . . wherein the Notion of our having sinned in Adam, and being on that account only liable to eternal Damnation, is proved to be unscriptural, irrational, and of dangerous Tendency*, New-Haven, 1757.

—— *Young Children and Infants declared by Christ Members of His Gospel Church or Kingdom: And, therefore, to be visibly marked as such, like other Members, by Baptism. And plunging not Necessary*, Salem, 1773.

WEEDEN, WILLIAM B., *Economic and Social History of New England, 1620-1789*, Boston and New York, 1890, 2 vols.

WEST, SAMUEL, *Essays on Liberty and Necessity*, Boston, 1793.

—— *Essays on Liberty and Necessity. Second Part*, Newbedford, 1795.

WEST, STEPHEN, *An Essay on Moral Agency*, New-Haven, 1772.
—— *The Scripture Doctrine of Atonement, proposed to careful Examination*, New-Haven, 1785.
—— *An Inquiry into the Ground and Import of Infant Baptism*, Stockbridge, 1794.
WHITAKER, NATHANAEL, *Two Sermons: On the Doctrine of Reconciliation*, Salem, 1770.
WHITE, JOHN, *New England's Lamentations . . . The Decay of the Power of Godliness; the Danger of Arminian Principles; the declining State of our Church-Order, Government and Discipline*, Boston, 1734.
WIGGLESWORTH, SAMUEL, and JOHN CHIPMAN, *Remarks on some Points of Doctrine, apprehended by many as unsound, propagated . . . by the Reverend Mr. William Balch*, Boston, 1746.
WILBUR, EARLE MORSE, *Our Unitarian Heritage*, Boston, 1925.
WILLARD, SAMUEL, *A compleat Body of Divinity, in two hundred and fifty, expository Lectures on the Assembly's Shorter Catechism*, Boston, 1726.
WILLIAMS, ELEAZAR, *An Essay to prove, that when God once enters upon a Controversie with His professing People; He will manage and issue it*, New-London, 1722.
WILLIAMS, SOLOMON, *A Vindication of the Gospel-Doctrine of Justifying Faith*, Boston, 1746.
—— *The true State of the Question concerning the Qualifications, necessary to lawful Communion in the Christian Sacraments*, Boston, 1751.
WILSON, MELBA P., *Pre-Revolutionary Liberalism and Post-Revolutionary Unitarianism in America* (M.A. dissertation, Columbia University, 1930, not published).
WINSLOW, H., *An evangelical View of the Nature and Means of Regeneration; comprising a Review of "Dr. Tyler's Strictures," by Evangelicus Pacificus*, Boston, 1830.
—— *An Examination of Dr. Tyler's Vindication of his "Strictures" on the Christian Spectator. By Evangelicus Pacificus*, Boston, 1830.
WISNER, WILLIAM, *A Letter from Rev. William Wisner to a clerical Friend; on the theological Views of Dr. Taylor*, Hartford, 1830.
WOODS, LEONARD, *The Works of Leonard Woods, D.D., lately Professor of Christian Theology in the Theological Seminary, Andover*, Boston, 1851. 5 vols.
—— *Letters to Unitarians*, 1820 (*Works*, vol. 4).
—— *A Reply to Dr. Ware's Letters to Trinitarians and Calvinists*, 1821 (*Works*, vol. 4).
—— *Remarks on Dr. Ware's Answer*, 1821 (*Works*, vol. 4).
—— *Letters to Nathaniel W. Taylor*, 1830 (*Works*, vol. 4).

Woods, Leonard, *An Essay on Native Depravity*, Boston, 1835.

Worcester, Noah, *The atoning Sacrifice, a Display of Love—not of Wrath*, Cambridge, 1829.

Worcester, Samuel, *Two Discourses on the Perpetuity and Provision of God's gracious Covenant with Abraham and his Seed*, Salem, 1805.

—— *A Letter to the Rev. William E. Channing*, Boston, 1815.

—— *A second Letter to the Rev. William E. Channing, on the Subject of Unitarianism*, Boston, 1815.

—— *A third Letter to the Rev. William E. Channing, on the Subject of Unitarianism*, Boston, 1815.

INDEX

323